# THE HUDSON VALLEY
## A CULTURAL GUIDE

# THE HUDSON VALLEY
## A CULTURAL GUIDE

### ALLIANCE FOR THE ARTS

TEXT AND PHOTOGRAPHS BY BENJAMIN SWETT

THE QUANTUCK LANE PRESS | NEW YORK

Publication of this book was partially underwritten by a grant from Furthermore: a program of
the J. M. Kaplan Fund.

Editor: Randall Bourscheidt
Text and Photographs: Benjamin Swett
Design and composition: Laura Lindgren
Maps: Myra Klockenbrink

Page 1: New York Harbor from Staten Island.
Pages 2–3: View south from Olana, Frederic Edwin Church's hilltop house near Hudson.

Manufacturing by South China Printing Co. Ltd.

Library of Congress Cataloging-in-Publication Data
  The Hudson Valley : a cultural guide / Alliance for the Arts ; edited by Benjamin Swett. — 1st ed.
     p. cm.
  Includes bibliographical references and index.
  ISBN 978-1-59372-035-3
  1. Hudson River Valley (N.Y. and N.J.)—Description and travel. 2. Hudson River Valley (N.Y.
and N.J.)—Guidebooks. 3. Historic sites—Hudson River Valley (N.Y. and N.J.)—Guidebooks.
4. Museums—Hudson River Valley (N.Y. and N.J.)—Guidebooks. 5. Art centers—Hudson River
Valley (N.Y. and N.J.)—Guidebooks. I. Swett, Benjamin. II. Alliance for the Arts (New York, N.Y.)
  F127.H8H864 2009
  917.47'30444—dc22
  2008048500

The Quantuck Lane Press
New York
www.quantucklanepress.com

Distributed by W. W. Norton & Company, 500 Fifth Avenue, New York, NY 10110
www.wwnorton.com

1 2 3 4 5 6 7 8 9 0

# CONTENTS

# PREFACE

This book, published on the 400th anniversary of Henry Hudson's voyage up the Hudson Valley, is both a celebration and a new beginning. We hope it will be for the reader a voyage of discovery, an opportunity to see the valley in a new light, from the great bay of New York City to its source in the Adirondack Mountains. Both the grand sweep of the Hudson and many fascinating local features are well captured by the prose and photographs of Benjamin Swett.

The Alliance for the Arts offers this guide as part of the official celebration organized by the Hudson-Fulton-Champlain Quadricentennial Commission of the State of New York. We hope it will contribute to the appreciation of culture, living and past, in the valley, both for those who live in it and for those who will visit it for the first time this year.

We invite the reader to experience the river as Hudson did 400 years ago: as a unity, extending 315 miles north from New York Harbor. In these pages, you can see the grandeur of one of America's great river valleys. The natural beauty that must have impressed Hudson and his Dutch crew is still surprisingly preserved, in large part because of the efforts of early conservationists and parks advocates in the late 19th and early 20th centuries.

Of course, the hand of man is everywhere evident, not just in these same parks and the bridges and roads that give access to them, but in the cities and towns that line the valley. The heart of this river system is the greatest metropolis in the United States, the City of New York, a major source of wealth and ideas and artistic expression for the entire valley.

This is a cultural guide, offering an in-depth look at a great variety of cultural institutions and centers. It has been written with a strong sense of the unique history of the Hudson, but it is not a history of the valley. All the important sites which preserve the heritage of the valley are included, since they are essential to understanding and enjoying this stretch of land and water.

We have focused on one of the most interesting aspects of contemporary life in the Hudson Valley: the entire region has once again become an integral part of modern art and culture in America. Artists in large numbers have chosen in recent years to live in the valley beyond New York City, restoring the give and take between upstate communities and the city that characterized the area's greatest contribution to American culture, the Hudson River School of painting.

Stimulated by the presence of working artists and the establishment of new galleries and cultural organizations, many of the cities and towns along the Hudson have experienced a cultural renaissance. Music and film and painting and photography and the spoken word are abundant in the Hudson Valley of 2009. It is now as normal to enjoy a gallery crawl in Hudson or Beacon as in Manhattan's Chelsea gallery district, or to hear a concert of classical Western or Chinese music or jazz in Troy or New Paltz or Poughkeepsie as at Carnegie Hall or the Brooklyn Academy of Music.

The great painters of the Hudson River School would surely be astonished to see some of the most ambitious sculpture gardens in the world, including Storm King Art Center, the Kendall Sculpture Gardens at Purchase, and the Fields Sculpture Park at Omi International Arts Center. The public art collection assembled by Governor Nelson Rockefeller and on view at the Empire State Plaza in Albany remains as little-known as it is impressive and, like those just mentioned, echoes the magical sculpture garden at the Museum of Modern Art in the heart of New York City.

The performing arts are flourishing in the Hudson Valley, with the addition of Frank Gehry's stunning Fisher Center at Bard College and Nicholas Grimshaw's EMPAC (the Experimental Media and Performing Arts Center) at the Rensselaer Polytechnic Institute in Troy, both worthy of comparison to Lincoln Center. These two new buildings demonstrate the continuing devotion to innovative architecture in the valley, evident in Frederic Church's Persian-style house Olana and Wallace Harrison's ambitious state buildings in Albany such as the New York State Museum and the Egg. They also give form to the creative drive now alive in the Hudson Valley, from Lower Manhattan to the capital and beyond.

Randall Bourscheidt
President
Alliance for the Arts

# ACKNOWLEDGMENTS

A comprehensive guide such as this one is a collaborative effort dependent on the contributions of hundreds of people, most of whom cannot be acknowledged by name. This includes, in our case, the many anonymous authors of the Web sites and brochures of the cultural organizations in the Hudson Valley, who not only provided much of the basic information on which this book is based but entertained and inspired us with their often highly sophisticated graphic and written presentations.

A second major source of material for the book was listings from our own New York State Arts Web site, written previously by various Alliance for the Arts authors including Brennan Gerard, Fern Glazer, Dan Kellum, Zac Pelicano, Blake Radcliffe, and Eric Shiner.

The dedicated staff of many county arts councils and cultural affairs offices very kindly reviewed each of the chapters, and we wish to express our appreciation to them for the time and effort they put in to reading and often rereading our text and offering numerous suggestions and corrections. These include Mark Judelson (Rockland County), Janet Langsam and Catherine Bruno (Westchester County), Joyce Picone and KC Anderson (Putnam County), Rebecca Lust and Susan Linn (Orange County), Benjamin Krevolin (Dutchess and Ulster Counties), Jan Hanvik and Sue Chiafullo (Columbia County), Kay Stamer (Greene County), Amy Williams (Albany and Rensselaer Counties), Joel Reed (Saratoga County), and Anne Smoczynski (Warren County). In New Jersey, the chapters were reviewed by Bill Larosa, Bob Foster, Gerri Fallo (Hudson County), and Carol Messer (Bergen County).

The writer and photographer wishes personally to thank Ruth Adams and Bill Maynes for assistance with photography at the Fields Sculpture Park; Winthrop Aldrich for his support and help; Beth Barker for her tour of the town of Hunter; Karl Beard of the National Park Service for helpful suggestions early in the project; Ann Birckmayer of Furthermore for gracefully shepherding the project; Bim and Evie Chanler for information on Rhinebeck and contacts in the world beyond; David Collens and Mary Ann Carter for their support in photographing at the Storm King Art Center; Joan Davidson for her numerous wise suggestions during informal discussions of the project, and Liz McEnany for hers; Mark di Suvero for his permission to reproduce the photograph of his sculpture at the Storm King Art Center, Dewitt Godfrey for his to reproduce the photograph of his sculpture at the Fields Sculpture Park, Harold Holzer for his to reproduce the photograph of the lobby of the Metropolitan Museum of Art, and Nora Johnson for hers to reproduce the photograph of her mural at the Stewart House; Bill Larosa for an entertaining and instructive day driving the waterfront in Hudson County; Owen Lipstein for permission to photograph at the Stewart House; Stuart Lehman for an inspiring and informative two hours in the State Capitol building and for his historical knowledge of Albany; Jessica Marquez and Seth Erickson of the Paula Cooper Gallery; Shannon McSweeney for arranging photography of Bethel Woods Center of the Arts; Laurie Parsons for her connections in Hoboken; Laura Raicovich and Jeanne Dreskin for their cooperation in photographing at Dia:Beacon; Tad Richards for permission to reproduce the photograph of Opus 40, and David Rockefeller Jr. and Cynthia Altman for permission to reproduce the photograph taken at Kykuit; Elizabeth Strein and Johanna Dekray for helping with the photography of Mohonk Mountain House; and Harry Wilks for his unerring photographic counsel and superior knowledge of the Hudson Valley. Above all, he appreciates the support of his wife, Katherine, and children, Rachel, Nicholas, and William, throughout the project, and is honored that Randall Bourscheidt, the president of the Alliance for the Arts, asked him to help produce the book and showed such confidence in him during the undertaking.

The staff at the Alliance for the Arts contributed in many ways. Erin Butler coordinated every aspect of the manuscript preparation; Lane Harwell completely relieved the editor of any concerns about fund-raising; Anne Coates kept the project on schedule and took care of all legal aspects; Christina Knight and Zac Pelicano speedily fact-checked dense swaths of manuscript; Bob Libbey kept the budget in line; James Walsh undertook a timely proofread; and Blake Radcliffe, Elena Matsui, and Joe Harrell offered numerous helpful suggestions to a writer and photographer whose presence in the office was infrequent yet demanding.

We are grateful to Jim Mairs, publisher of the Quantuck Lane Press, for his enthusiasm for a cultural guide to the Hudson Valley and his support of the project from the beginning; to Austin O'Driscoll, the assistant publisher, for her good-humored management of the publication; to Laura Lindgren for her elegant design; and to Myra Klockenbrink for such great maps.

We acknowledge with pleasure the support of the United States Department of Housing and Urban Development, the New York City Department of Cultural Affairs, the New York State Council on the Arts, Furthermore, Brandon Fradd, and John S. Dyson in the publication of the book.

Randall Bourscheidt
Benjamin Swett

# INTRODUCTION

In 1609, in the service of the Dutch, the English explorer Henry Hudson sailed a small ship called the *Half Moon* into a large bay and up a wide river in North America, looking for a route to India. As we know from the journals of his mate, he and his crew spent four weeks on this river, trading and occasionally even sharing a meal with the Native Americans they met. Running aground just north of present-day Troy, they turned back downstream and sailed for home. Upon their arrival in Europe, English forces prevented Hudson from continuing on to Holland and reporting back to his Dutch employers, and his ship and the Dutch members of his crew, together with his journals and logs, returned to Holland without him. Dutch printers later published a few segments from those logs but the logs themselves were eventually lost. The only firsthand descriptions of the voyage that have come down to us are from the scanty journal of the mate Robert Juet.

Since Hudson's trip, many influences have made their way up the river that the English later named after him, transforming a sparsely populated forested land into a cultivated landscape of towns, industries, and roads. Because of its military and commercial importance, its natural beauty, and its connection to the great port of New York, this 315-mile stretch of land and water collected, over the years, a complex cultural heritage. The greatest American artists came, and stayed, to paint it; architects and gardeners rearranged it; writers settled into its towns; and

*Launched in 1969 by the folk singer Pete Seeger as a traveling environmental education classroom, and now the center of an even larger program, the Hudson River Sloop Clearwater sails up and down the river through most of the year, a much-loved and somehow reassuring presence.*

*Nora Johnson's 2007 mural at the Stewart House Restaurant in Athens represents one of numerous artistic interpretations—through four centuries—of Henry Hudson's welcome by the Native Americans in 1609.*

performing artists spent summers entertaining the often sophisticated audiences who lived along its banks.

Today, at the beginning of the 21st century—400 years after Hudson's visit—a new phase of life has begun in the valley, one that combines the great energy of working artists and their audiences with an urge to preserve the landscape and buildings. Up and down the river, there is a conscious effort to create new art and new kinds of art. Not only have an increasing number of artists of all disciplines moved back along the Hudson and made it their home and workplace, but the number of places presenting contemporary art—museums, galleries, theaters, performing arts centers—has exploded in the past 10 or 15 years. Institutions up and down the valley—the New Museum of Contemporary Art, the Dia Art Foundation, Bard College, and the Rensselaer Polytechnic Institute, for example—have opened astonishing new buildings, as admired for their architecture as for the work they present within, and the smallest villages now boast theaters and art centers, often in former churches and other buildings of architectural merit, many specializing in avant-garde and experimental work. Such a flowering of artistic activity has not been seen in the valley since the founding of the Hudson River School of painting more than 150 years ago.

Along with this movement by living artists, curators, performers, and artistic directors to create new works is a second, equally powerful one to recover the human culture and natural environment that evolved here during the 17th, 18th, 19th, and 20th centuries. In recent years a great many citizens, nonprofits, and government agencies have banded together to protect endangered places along the river, from fragile marshes to Dutch Colonial houses. The National Park Service, the New

11

*At 4,324 feet above sea level, Lake Tear of the Clouds (page 274), on the flank of Mt. Marcy in the Adirondacks, is the highest source of the Hudson.*

York State Department of Parks, Recreation and Historic Preservation, the New York State Department of Environmental Conservation, and the Palisades Parks Commission (to name a few) have forged alliances with organizations such as Hudson River Valley Heritage, the Hudson Valley Greenway, Scenic Hudson, the Hudson River Sloop Clearwater, and many others to conserve these sites and make them available to the public.

This book is a celebration of these two concurrent developments in the Hudson Valley, whose net result has been an increase in places of interest that are open to the public. A trip along the river today—whether by car, train, bus, boat, or bicycle—provides a relatively complete survey of American culture from its wilderness beginnings to its experimental present. It is our hope to inspire both visitors from afar and current residents to become better acquainted with this story and to visit these places that are redefining themselves even as they explore their own pasts.

One of the main reasons to spend time in the Hudson Valley is to become better acquainted with a natural landscape that inspired generations of American artists and writers, a tidal estuary scooped out by glaciers over the course of millions of years, draining an area totaling more than 13,000 square miles and containing four spectacular groups of mountains, the Shawangunks, the Catskills, the Berkshires, and the Adirondacks. From its source at Lake Tear of the Clouds high in the Adirondacks to a point roughly parallel with the contemporary city of Troy 161 miles to the south, the Hudson River is fresh. From Troy to the river's mouth in New York Harbor 154 miles farther south, the river is increasingly salty as tides bring brine from the Atlantic back upstream twice a day. In this southern stretch the river is as much a part of the Atlantic Ocean in which it ends as it is of the Adirondack streams from which it begins. The Lenape people had a word for this double nature of the river, calling it "Muhheakantuck," or "the river that flows both ways." New Yorkers have always had this double identity, confidently agrarian yet—as the Hudson Valley writer Herman Melville might have said—at home in the deeps.

This historic natural landscape is more accessible to the public today than it has been for a hundred years. Whether attempting the summit of Mount Marcy, the highest peak in the state, for a glimpse of the Hudson's source; setting out in New York Harbor in a kayak, much as the Native Americans did who greeted Hudson on his arrival; or passing a quiet afternoon in a black locust grove near Athens, listening to the water lap against the shore, visitors can explore most of the Hudson in parks, natural areas, greenways, bird sanctuaries, and the greens of waterside villages. Rugged mountain scenery described by Washington Irving and James Fenimore Cooper still exists much as it did in "Rip Van Winkle" and *The Last of the Mohicans*, and the celebrated views of the Hudson River School—of Kaaterskill Falls, Storm King, and the expanses leading away from Olana and the Catskill Mountain House—require only a bus ticket and a sturdy pair of legs to experience. Mountains, marshes, fertile plains, and forests exist as they have for thousands of years, and black bear, deer, bobcat, beaver, wild turkey, skunks, and other native animals still roam the land.

A second major reason for visiting the Hudson Valley is to experience its remarkable record as a place of human habitation, industry, and warfare. Near Tivoli, in Dutchess County, archaeologists have found ceramics and arrowheads dating back 9,000 years, and art historians con-

sider a visit to the Hudson Valley a kind of primer of American architectural history. The arch-roofed houses of Lenape villages, Dutch Colonial farmhouses, Federal-style mansions, industrial buildings of all kinds, and public spaces from the Romanesque to the postmodern can be

*One of the best examples of the early Dutch architectural styles in the Hudson Valley is the 1663 Bronck House in Coxsackie (page 208), one of the oldest surviving dwellings in upstate New York.*

13

*The New York State Capitol (page 224) took 32 years and five great architects to complete, and was the grandest and most sumptuous state capitol in the country when it was finished in 1899.*

experienced in museums and in their original settings as nowhere else in the country.

Historic houses, public archives, historic districts, churches, and government buildings retain the record of the human experience along the river, whether of the Native Americans who were the land's first inhabitants; of the Dutch, English, and French who were its second; or of the ethnically diverse populations of today. Forts and battlefields remain little changed from the days of the French and Indian War, the American Revolution, and the War of 1812—in all of which the valley played a central role—and monuments in almost every village attest to the sacrifices of the generations who fought in those wars as well as in the Civil War and the great wars of the 20th century.

Finally, and most important for those choosing this guide, a third reason to investigate the Hudson Valley is to experience the new work that artists of every kind are producing, and that sophisticated institutions are presenting, from Staten Island nearly to Lake Tear of the Clouds—the new plays being brought before the public at the Powerhouse Theater at Vassar, the cross-genre experiments unleashed at the Experimental Media and Performing Arts Center at RPI in Troy, the sculptures at Socrates Sculpture Park in Queens or Storm King Art Center in Orange County, and paintings from the Jersey City Museum to the Albany Institute. The Hudson Valley itself is an evolving work of art, a place that people have adorned, interpreted, depicted, and celebrated for as long as they have lived here, and that artists in every discipline continue to grace with buildings, sculptures, songs, paintings, photographs, and performances.

Much of this new work can be seen in places particularly suited to the Hudson Valley. Outdoor performing arts centers such as Bethel Woods Center for the Arts, the Maverick Concerts in Woodstock, the Saratoga Performing Arts Center, and Caramoor integrate music, dance, and theater with a changing natural backdrop of woods, mountains, light, and weather. Wave Hill in the Bronx, the Hudson River Museum in Yonkers, Boscobel in Putnam County, and the Empire State Plaza in Albany offer combined experiences of architecture, landscape, performance, and visual art. The Hudson River waterfront itself, from Liberty State Park to Albany Riverfront Park, is alive on summer evenings with free jazz, folk, rock, and chamber music concerts.

This book is intended, then, as a resource for visitors and residents who want to learn more about the contemporary artistic life and cultural and natural heritage of this remarkable part of the world. The aim is to provide practical information for artists and the public on the arts centers, artists' associations, sculpture parks, museums, performance spaces, and theaters where new work is being shown and produced,

*Part of Empire State Plaza in Albany, Wallace K. Harrison's unusual performing arts center, The Egg (page 224), comes from a tradition of architectural experimentation in the Hudson Valley.*

and to set this information in the context of a beautiful valley with a rich history and bounteous landscape. In particular, as more artists discover the region as a place to live and work, we hope this book will help them find support, encouragement, and new outlets for their work.

## A Note on Organization

The listings in this book are organized geographically, from south to north, following the route that Hudson sailed and that most visitors take to reach the valley but continuing farther than Hudson to the very source of the river at Lake Tear of the Clouds in the Adirondacks. We have organized the chapters by county or groups of counties, going back and forth across the river to ensure proximity in pages to places that are close together in miles. Within each county, we have listed the places most worth visiting alphabetically by city or town.

Because of the large number of cultural organizations in each county (and with new ones opening all the time) it has been impossible to include every one in this guide. We have tried to include all those in some proximity or with some connection to the Hudson River that are open to the public and can be visited during regularly published hours. If we have inadvertently left any place out that ought to be included, please notify us through our web site at www.nystatearts.org.

## The Hudson River School

The aesthetic movement most closely associated with the Hudson River, later identified as the Hudson River School, sprang from an intellectual excitement at the end of the first quarter of the 19th century among a number of young, talented, energetic American artists over the romantic possibilities of the American landscape—particularly in the Hudson Valley but also over much of New York State as well as New England, in addition to parts of the western United States and Latin America. Setting out on strenuous hikes and camping in remote locations, often in the Catskills, Shawangunks, and Adirondacks, these painters made field sketches during the spring, summer, and fall and then returned to their studios in New York City during the winter to combine their sketches into immense, detailed paintings on large canvases. Many of these canvases, exhibited fresh from the easel in carefully lit rooms, drew huge crowds and sensational reviews when they first appeared, and it was not unusual for them to be shipped off to Europe for further enthusiastic showings.

Primary among these landscape painters was the Englishman Thomas Cole (1801–1848), who immigrated to the United States in 1818 and made his first trip to the Catskills in 1825. Determined to elevate the genre of landscape to the level of history painting, Cole spent his relatively short life perfecting a style involving a realistic clarity of detail, grand compositions, and a feeling of sublimity communicated through striking effects of light and dramatic arrangements of trees, mountains, and water. Tirelessly revisiting and eventually moving to the town of Catskill (where his house, Cedar Grove, now a national monument, can be visited today; see Greene County), Cole became the center of a group of landscape painters, many of them founders of the National Academy of Design, who by the close of the century were considered the grand old men of American painting. Among this group were:

- Asher B. Durand (1796–1886). Cole's close friend and a founder of the National Academy of Design, the New Jersey–born Durand gained early respect as an engraver but switched to painting, in which he earned lasting fame for his landscapes of the Catskills, Adirondacks, and White Mountains. His most famous painting, *Kindred Spirits*, executed as a memorial to Cole, depicts Cole and the poet and journalist William Cullen Bryant (1794–1878) communing with a wild and beautiful Catskills landscape.

- John F. Kensett (1816–72). Born in Connecticut and like Durand trained as an engraver, Kensett is best known for his exquisitely modulated use of light in landscapes drawn from his travels through upstate New York and New England, particularly to Lake George, the Adirondacks, the White Mountains, and Newport.

- Sanford R. Gifford (1823–80). Raised in Hudson, in Columbia County, and traveling all over New England, to the West Coast, and Europe in his quest for scenery and experiences, Gifford was most drawn to the Hudson Valley and the Catskills, where he painted Kaaterskill Clove, near Catskill, over and over throughout his life.

- Jasper F. Cropsey (1823–1900). The Staten Island–born painter and architect reached a pinnacle of fame after impressing Queen Victoria with his brilliant renderings of fall foliage along the Hudson. In the last years of his life he turned mainly to watercolor and continued to paint Hudson River scenes—long after the movement had gone out of fashion—at his conveniently located home in Hastings-on Hudson, where his house and studio can be visited today (see Westchester County, below).

- Frederic Edwin Church (1826–1900). Cole's most famous pupil devoted himself to painting landscapes from an early age. After becoming perhaps even more famous than his teacher, Church brought back from travels in the Middle East ideas for a Persian-style dream house that he began building, with the help of the architect Calvert Vaux, on a hill overlooking the river near Hudson in 1870. Olana, this expressive, colorful house, is the most visible memorial to the Hudson River School and can be seen today from miles away.

It is open and can be visited throughout the year, and its 250 acres of fields, ponds, and woods are now a state park open to the public from dawn to dusk (see Columbia County, below).

- Albert Bierstadt (1830–1902). One of the most successful American painters during his own time and still one of the most famous in ours, the German-born Hudson River School painter was best known for his gigantic, theatrical depictions of the Rocky Mountains and the American West.

Paintings by Hudson River School artists can be seen in museums around the world. Institutions in the Hudson Valley region with major holdings include the Metropolitan Museum of Art, the Brooklyn Museum, and the New-York Historical Society in New York City; the Newark Museum in New Jersey; the Albany Institute of History and Art; Olana, the Frederic Church house in Columbia County; Locust Grove/the Samuel F. B. Morse House and the Frances Lehman Loeb Arts Center at Vassar College, both in Poughkeepsie in Dutchess County; and the Jasper Cropsey Home and Studio in Hastings-on-Hudson, in Westchester County. The Hudson River Valley National Heritage Area (888-576-4784; www.hudsonrivervalley .com) and Cedar Grove, the Thomas Cole House (518-943-7465. www .thomascole.org), have published, in print and on the Web, informative brochures on the Hudson River School and locations where the painters worked and lived.

## Bridges, Tunnels, Lighthouses
Builders have altered the Hudson Valley in many ways, sometimes for the better and sometimes for the worse, but some of the most striking—and most practical—are the structures that engineers have erected over, along, and under the river to improve transportation—the lighthouses to keep boats from shoals and rocks and the bridges and tunnels that allow cars and trains to cross at high speed. The world's greatest designers drew on their talents to plan and build these structures, and some of them have become cultural icons. In our usual south-to-north order, we list the major ones below, together with the chapters in which longer descriptions of them are to be found. For further information on lighthouses of the valley, contact the Hudson River Lighthouse Coalition at www.hudsonlights.com; on bridges and tunnels, www.nycroads.com, the New York State Bridge Authority (www.nysba.state.ny.us), the New York State Thruway Authority (www.nysthruway.gov), the MTA Bridge and Tunnel Authority (www.mta.nyc.ny.us/bandt), or the Port Authority of New York and New Jersey (www.panynj.gov).

*One of eight lighthouses still standing on the Hudson, Sleepy Hollow Lighthouse (page 92) was built in 1883.*

## Bridges and Tunnels

Verrazano Narrows Bridge (Brooklyn—Staten Island, page 28)
Holland Tunnel (New York City—New Jersey, page 41)
Lincoln Tunnel (New York City—New Jersey, page 44)
George Washington Bridge (New York City—New Jersey, page 40)
Tappan Zee Bridge (Tarrytown—Nyack, page 95)
Bear Mountain Bridge (Peekskill—Fort Montgomery, page 105)
Newburgh-Beacon Bridge (Beacon—Newburgh, page 151)
Mid-Hudson Bridge (Poughkeepsie—Highland, page 157)
Walkway Over the Hudson (page 160)
Kingston-Rhinecliff Bridge (near Rhinebeck—Kingston, page 174)
Rip Van Winkle Bridge (near Hudson—Catskill, page 207)

## Lighthouses

Statue of Liberty (New York Harbor, page 24)
Little Red Lighthouse (Manhattan, page 44)
Sleepy Hollow Lighthouse (Westchester County, page 92)
Stony Point Lighthouse (Rockland County, page 111)
Esopus Meadows Lighthouse (Westchester County, page 180)
Rondout Lighthouse (Ulster County, page 174)
Saugerties Lighthouse (Ulster County, page 179)
Hudson-Athens Lighthouse (Columbia and Greene Counties, page 194)

# NEW YORK CITY

Although located at the mouth of the Hudson, New York City and its harbor are very much the beginning of the Hudson Valley, the source of the tides that swell north as far as Troy each day and of the social, commercial, and cultural influences that have been working their way in the same direction for four hundred years. Just as Ellis Island served as the gateway for immigrants entering the United States, so New York City was and remains the entry point for new artistic ideas making their way north along the Hudson.

With its artists, art centers, and schools; its museums, galleries, performance halls, and theaters; its galas, gallery openings, and opening nights, New York City is a kind of cultural engine, generating and promoting new forms of expression that radiate in all directions but especially north into the Hudson Valley. The city expresses its lively presence in the valley in many ways but most often in the form of individual artists who move up the river and continue to work and exhibit in both the city and the country. Galleries in cities from Beacon to Hudson look both to New York and to their own communities for artists and clients. Musicians, dancers, and actors perform in New York but also in Saratoga, Annandale-on-Hudson, Purchase, Woodstock, Cooperstown, Katonah, Beacon, Troy, and Lake Luzerne.

The city's contemporary cultural scene is intense and takes place throughout the five boroughs. At the Snug Harbor Cultural Center, on Staten Island, the Newhouse Center is an energetic center of contemporary art, while a new Chinese Scholar's Garden has been drawing the curious to the Staten Island Botanical Garden. In Brooklyn, avant-garde performances bring vast audiences to St. Ann's Warehouse and the Brooklyn Academy of Music, and a white barge docked under the Brooklyn Bridge features chamber music throughout the year. In Queens, P.S. 1 in Long Island City and Socrates Sculpture Park in Astoria continue to astonish visitors with the latest in contemporary art and sculpture, while in the Bronx the Bronx Museum, Wave Hill, and the Bronx River Art Center have been teaming up to present sweeping cultural statements. In Manhattan the just-opened

*Among its multifarious collections, the Metropolitan Museum of Art contains one of the finest collections of Hudson River art in the world.*

New Museum of Contemporary Art on the Bowery is the symbol of an intensely vital contemporary scene covering all disciplines.

Settled by Dutch merchants in the mid-1620s, but inhabited by Lenape hunters and fishermen for centuries before that, the town known as New Netherland became New York in 1664 when the English assumed power and renamed it for James II, the Duke of York and Albany. From the beginning this busy port and fur trading center was a cosmopolitan place, with people and influences swirling in from around the globe to mix with the local scene and create a vibrancy and creativity that continue to this day.

Originally centered on Manhattan, with a separate but growing city in Brooklyn, the city stretched out over the years and in 1898 consolidated into five boroughs, leading to the sprawling megalopolis we have today. Binding these distinct boroughs is a medium that was often thought to separate them: water. From ferries operated by oar and sail through steam and diesel craft to the roads, tunnels, and bridges of today, over the years New Yorkers have worked to connect the different parts of their far-flung archipelago. In recent years, advocacy and stewardship organizations such as the Metropolitan Waterfront Alliance have helped to bring financially viable high-speed ferries back to the harbor and, more broadly, to replace the perception of New York City as a collection of separate boroughs—and of New York and New Jersey as two very separate states—with a more fluid sense of the city as a network of communities connected by shared waterways.

It is impossible in a guide to the Hudson Valley to include all of the great variety of cultural institutions in a city as large as New

*Built in 1989, a replica of Henry Hudson's* Half Moon *(seen here near Governor's Island) travels up and down the river educating passengers on New York's Dutch heritage (see page 233).*

York, but we have tried to include the places most immediately relevant to the focus of this guide: the Hudson River as a natural phenomenon, as a locus of human habitation, and as an evolving work of art. Complete information for all visitors is available at www.nycgo.com, the Web site of NYC & Company, the city's official tourist agency. As with the rest of the book we have arranged the listings geographically by county, starting with the symbolic and actual entry points for many millions to this country, the Statue of Liberty and Ellis and Governors Islands.

**Ellis Island Immigration Museum**. *Ellis Island. 212-363-3200. www.nps .gov/stli/index.htm. National Register.* The 28-acre island in New York

*It has been estimated that nearly half of all Americans today can trace their ancestry to at least one ancestor who first entered the United States through Ellis Island.*

Harbor where, from 1892 to 1924, some 16 million immigrants were first admitted to the U.S. is now a monument operated by the National Park Service. Its 200,000-square-foot museum—once the main building of the processing center for immigrants—features more than 30 galleries, many of them in the actual rooms where newcomers were processed, and filled with artifacts, historic photographs, posters, maps, oral histories of immigrants, and ethnic music from different nations. *Open every day but Christmas, 9:30 am until 5 pm. Ferries (877-523-9849; www.statuecruises .com) leave from Battery Park in Manhattan and from Liberty State Park in Jersey City throughout the day. Fee.*

**Governors Island**. *www.govisland.com. National Register.* Located half a mile from Battery Park in lower Manhattan and a quarter mile from Brooklyn, this 172-acre island in New York Harbor—the largest in the bay after Staten Island—was a quiet military installation under the jurisdiction of the U.S. Army from 1794 until 1966 and of the Coast Guard until 1996. The federal government conveyed it to New York City and New York state for one dollar in 2003, and, with its great views of the harbor, it is now a popular destination for recreation, music, and art. The historic Fort Jay (dating from 1794) and the distinctive round Castle Williams (dating from 1811) are open to the public under the jurisdiction of the National Park Service, which jointly administers the island with the Governors Island Preservation and Education Corporation. *Open from mid-May until mid-October, Fridays, 10 am until 5 pm, and Saturday and Sunday, 10:30 am until 6:30 p.m. Ferries leave from the Battery Maritime Building, on the corner of South and Whitehall Streets at the east end of Battery Park in lower Manhattan. The ferries are free.*

**Statue of Liberty National Monument**. *Liberty Island. 212-363-3200. www.nps.gov/stli. National Register.* The meaning of this monumental copper-clad statue in New York Harbor to millions of people around the world is so great as to defy representation, yet it continues to stand and welcome visitors from far and wide with its gleaming

*Frederic Auguste Bartholdi's 1884 Statue of Liberty, in New York Harbor, is the largest sculpture—and lighthouse—in the Hudson Valley.*

torch and greenish crown, a beacon of freedom but also of culture and intelligence. Presented as a gift from the French people to the American people on July 4, 1884, and dedicated in 1886, the statue was proposed as early as 1865 to sculptor Frédéric Auguste Bartholdi, who later received the commission. The statue's iron skeleton was engineered by Alexandre Gustave Eiffel (it is five years younger than the Eiffel Tower) and mounted on a base designed by the American architect Richard Morris Hunt. Clad in a skin of verdigris copper, the statue towers more than 151 feet and weighs 225 tons. Visitors take an elevator, then climb 168 steps to the crown with its unforgettable views of the harbor. *Open Monday through Sunday, 9:30 am until 5 pm. Ferries (877-523-9849; www.statuecruises.com) leave from Battery Park in Manhattan and from Liberty State Park in Jersey City throughout the day. Fee.*

## STATEN ISLAND

The first land seen by Henry Hudson on his trip into the bay, this island at the gateway to New York Harbor and the Hudson Valley is the southernmost county in New York City. It was settled by the Dutch in the early 17th century and named for the States General, the governing body in Holland. For information on cultural events and the arts on Staten Island, contact or visit the Council on the Arts and Humanities for Staten Island; for restaurants and transportation, visit NYC & Company (see Visitor Information at the end of the chapter).

**Alice Austen House**. *2 Hylan Boulevard (at Edgewater Street). 718-816-4506. www.aliceausten.org. National Register.* For 77 years, this vine-covered gingerbread cottage was home to the prolific New York photographer Alice Austen (1866–1952). Set amid ample lawns and gardens that slope down to the Verrazano Narrows, the 1715 Dutch Colonial farmhouse commands a sweeping but intimate view of the Statue of Liberty, Manhattan, Brooklyn, and the Verrazano Narrows Bridge. In addition to exhibitions of Austen's photographs (curated in association with the Staten Island Historical Society), there are regular exhibits of the work of other photographers. *Open Thursday through Sunday, 12 pm until 5 pm. Closed January and February. Suggested donation.*

**Art Lab, Snug Harbor**. *1000 Richmond Terrace, 10301. www.artlab.info.* This school of fine and applied art was founded in 1975 by a group of professional artists as a center for art instruction, exhibitions, and events.

**Conference House**. *7455 Hylan Boulevard (at Satterlee Street). 718-984-6046. www.conferencehouse.org. National Register.* Dramatically located on

*One of Staten Island's many contributions to American independence took place in 1776 at the Conference House, now a museum and park.*

the southernmost shore of Staten Island, this two-and-a-half-story fieldstone house was the site of the famous three-hour conference on September 11, 1776, in which the British admiral Lord Howe failed to convince American representatives Benjamin Franklin, John Adams, and Edward Rutledge that the colonies should abandon the revolution and return to the British empire. Built originally as a customs station, and situated in a lovely park with ancient trees overlooking Raritan Bay and the Atlantic Ocean, the house contains fascinating period artifacts and rooms. *Open for guided tours April through mid-December, Friday through Sunday, 1 pm until 4 pm. Fee.*

**Historic Richmond Town/Staten Island Historical Society**. *441 Clarke Avenue (at Arthur Kill Road). 718-351-1611. www.historicrichmondtown .org. National Register.* Located on 100 acres in central Staten Island, this restored village—the only one in New York City—re-creates life in the Hudson Valley in earlier times. Owned by the City of New York but operated by the Staten Island Historical Society, the village consists of 15 restored buildings (some relocated from elsewhere on Staten Island) dating from the late 17th to the early 20th centuries and ranging in style from Gothic and Greek Revival to simpler structures with Dutch and Flemish influences. Costumed staff and volunteers reenact such daily tasks of early Staten Islanders as coopering, blacksmithing, and tinsmithing. A museum exhibits thoughtful, changing displays of objects and documents that the Historical Society has been collecting since its founding in 1856. *Open September through May, Wednesday through Sunday, 1 pm until 5 pm; June through August, Wednesday through Saturday, 10 am until 5 pm, and Sunday, 1 pm until 5 pm. Fee.*

**Jacques Marchais Museum of Tibetan Art**. *338 Lighthouse Avenue (near Richmond Road). 718-987-3500. www.tibetanmuseum.org.* Located among terraced gardens in two former private houses designed to resemble a Himalayan monastery, the museum exhibits works from its unique collection of early Himalayan art and offers regularly changing exhibits, group tours, education programs, tai chi and meditation classes, lectures, and musical performances year-round. A far view of the harbor makes for a serene setting in which to study the small but excellent collection. *Open Wednesday through Sunday, 1 pm until 5 pm. Fee.*

**Newhouse Center for Contemporary Art, Snug Harbor**. *1000 Richmond Terrace, 10301. www.newhousecenter.org*. Founded in 1977, and devoted to the exhibition of modern and contemporary art, this gallery presents two or three major exhibitions each year, plus five Access Gallery and three Artist-in-Residence shows. The Newhouse Center provides 15,000 square feet of gallery space, 30 artist studios, and an international residency program and conducts outdoor and off-site projects and education programs.

**Noble Maritime Collection, Snug Harbor**. *1000 Richmond Terrace, 10301. www.noblemaritime.org*. A museum dedicated to preserving and interpreting art and maritime history symbolized by Sailors' Snug Harbor and captured in the art and writings of John A. Noble (1913–83).

**Snug Harbor Cultural Center**. *1000 Richmond Terrace, 10301. 718-448-2500. www.snug-harbor.org. National Register.* Sailors' Snug Harbor was founded in Manhattan in the 1801 will of Robert Richard Randall as a "haven for aged, decrepit and worn-out sailors" and opened at its current location on Staten Island in 1833. Over the course of more than 100 years the charitable institution grew from three Greek Revival buildings to as many as 50 structures in Beaux Arts, Renaissance Revival, Second Empire, Italianate, and High Victorian styles. Faced with a declining population, the institution moved to North Carolina in the 1970s and the buildings were threatened with destruction. As he did with Carnegie Hall, Mayor John Lindsay intervened at the request of the community and acquired the entire property of 83 acres with the intention of converting it to a cultural facility. Today it is a thriving institution that presents new art and music while preserving its historic tie to the Hudson Valley and providing Staten Island with a bounteous garden.

Snug Harbor is a destination in its own right and also a collection of distinguished cultural institutions. Among them are:

Staten Island Botanical Garden
Staten Island Museum
Noble Maritime Collection
Staten Island Children's Museum
Art Lab
Newhouse Center for Contemporary Art

**Staten Island Botanical Garden, Snug Harbor**. *1000 Richmond Terrace, 10301. 718-448-2500. www.sibg.org*. Staten Island's only public garden includes the New York Chinese Scholar's Garden; the White Garden, inspired by Vita Sackville-West's famous garden at Sissinghurst; and Connie Gretz's

*An authentic classical Chinese garden is among the delightful surprises at the Staten Island Botanical Garden, located at the Snug Harbor Cultural Center.*

Secret Garden, containing a castle, a maze, and a walled secret garden. A subtle juxtaposition of plantings, architecture, and rock gardens, the Chinese Scholar's Garden is one of the most unusual gardens in the Hudson Valley. The gardens also include a Butterfly Garden, an Herb Garden, a Pond Garden, a Rose Garden, and a Sensory Garden, designed to enhance the experience of the physically challenged. In the reception hall are changing exhibitions on horticulture. *Hours and admission fees vary by garden.*

**Staten Island Children's Museum, Snug Harbor**. *1000 Richmond Terrace, 10301. 718-273-2060. www.statenislandkids.org.* Offers hands-on exhibits, family workshops, performances, after-school programs, and parent-child classes involving cooking, crafts, storytelling, and music.

**Staten Island Museum, Snug Harbor**. *75 Stuyvesant Place, 10301. 718-727-1135. www.statenislandmuseum.org.* Founded in 1881, Staten Island's oldest cultural institution explores the art, science, and history of Staten Island through exhibitions from its collections of more than two million artifacts, specimens, and artworks ancient and contemporary. *Open Tuesday through Friday, 12 pm until 5 pm; Saturday, 10 am until 5 pm; and Sunday, 12 pm until 5 pm. Fee.*

**Verrazano Narrows Bridge**. *www.mta.info/bandt.* When it opened in 1964 this double-decker suspension bridge over the Narrows between Staten Island and Brooklyn was the longest bridge of its kind in the world. It is named for Giovanni da Verrazano, the Italian explorer who entered the narrows and is thought to have anchored at the approximate location of the bridge in 1524. He may have gone ashore on Staten Island for water but did not venture deeper into the harbor, leaving that for Henry Hudson 85 years later.

# BROOKLYN

Named for Breukelen in the Netherlands and first settled in the 1630s, New York City's most populous borough, which sits at the western end of Long Island, harbors a rich cultural life emanating from institutions that celebrate and encourage experimentation while holding on to extensive collections of historical materials and legacies of past performances. For complete information on concerts, openings, and other cultural happenings in Brooklyn, visit the Brooklyn Arts Council and BAC Gallery, online or at 111 Front Street, and for maps and guides to restaurants, hotels, and complete transportation information stop by the Brooklyn Tourism and Visitor Center at 209 Joralemon Street downtown or online (see Visitor Information at end of chapter for full listings).

**Barge Music**. *Fulton Ferry Landing just south of the Brooklyn Bridge. 718-624-2083. www.bargemusic.org.* Located on a renovated barge on the East River, with excellent acoustics in its wood-paneled interior, this floating concert hall presents chamber concerts four or five times a week throughout the year.

**Brooklyn Academy of Music (BAM)**. *30 Lafayette Avenue (between Ashland Place and St. Felix Street). 718-636-4100. www.bam.org. National Register.* Founded in 1861, this important New York institution is at once America's oldest and one of its most contemporary performing arts centers, known for its inventive and progressive programming. Through its celebrated Next Wave Festival and other programs, BAM continues to develop and present a unique roster of traditional and contemporary dance, theater, music, opera, and film, placing particular emphasis on artists of international stature who have a cutting-edge artistic vision. Its landmark 1908 Beaux Arts building, designed by Henry Beaumont Herts, was renovated under the direction of Hugh Hardy from 2002 until 2008.

**Brooklyn Arts Council/BAC Gallery**. *55 Washington Street, Suite 218. 718-625-0080. www.brooklynartscouncil.org.* Among its many programs the Brooklyn Arts Council hosts thoughtful, regularly changing exhibits at a gallery known as the BAC Gallery in the midst of the flourishing gallery scene of DUMBO (the landmarked Brooklyn neighborhood that is "Down Under the Manhattan Bridge Overpass"). *The gallery is open Monday through Friday, 10 am until 5 pm. Fee.*

*The collection of American painting and sculpture at the Brooklyn Museum includes great works by Hudson River School artists and others associated with the Hudson Valley.*

**Brooklyn Historical Society**. *128 Pierrepont Street (corner of Clinton and Pierrepont). 718-222-4111. www.brooklynhistory.org. National Register.* Designed by George B. Post and opened in 1881, the landmark headquarters of the Brooklyn Historical Society contains the largest collection of Brooklyn-related research materials in the world, including paintings and photographs of New York Harbor and materials related to transportation and commerce on the Hudson River dating back to the first Dutch settlement of Brooklyn in the 1630s. Permanent exhibits give visitors an overview of Brooklyn history; walking tours illuminate local sites of architectural and historic significance. *Open Wednesday through Sunday, 12 pm until 5 pm. Fee.*

**Brooklyn Museum**. *200 Eastern Parkway (at Washington Avenue). 718-638-5000. www.brooklynmuseum.org. National Register.* Designed by McKim, Mead & White in 1893, with a new entrance designed by Polshek Partnership Architects in 2004, the museum is one of the nation's greatest and has one of the most active exhibition programs in town, ranging from the solidly classical (based on its strong collections) to the provocative art of the present. Of particular relevance for those interested in the Hudson Valley, the museum has one of the country's most comprehensive collections of 19th-century American painting and sculpture, including works by Hudson River School artists and by Winslow Homer, who chronicled the Adirondacks. *Open Wednesday through Friday, 10 am until 5 pm; Saturday and Sunday, 11 am until 6 pm; and the first Saturday of every month, 11 am until 11 pm. Suggested donation.*

**Dumbo Arts Center**. *30 Washington Street (at Plymouth and Water Streets). 718-694-0831. www.dumboartscenter.org.* Administering a range of exhibits and related programs serving local artists, this gallery and arts service organization hosts the annual Art Under the Bridge Festival; five or six shows each year of new work by emerging artists; and studio tours, lectures, and workshops. *The gallery is open Thursday through Monday, 10 am until 6 pm. Free.*

**Harbor Defense Museum at Fort Hamilton**. *230 Sheridan Loop, Fort Hamilton Military Community. 718-630-4349. www.harbordefensemuseum .com. National Register.* Initially constructed in 1825, Fort Hamilton was the earliest fortification built on New York Harbor and today serves as a U.S. Army museum, with displays of generations of guns, mines, airplanes, and missiles. *Open Monday through Friday, 10 am until 4 pm, and Saturday, 10 am until 2 pm. Free.*

**Kentler International Drawing Space**. *353 Van Brunt Street (between Wolcott and Dikeman Streets), Red Hook. 718-875-2098. www.kentler gallery.org.* Founded in 1990 in this burgeoning arts community on New York Harbor the gallery, located in what was once a men's haberdashery, exhibits drawings and works on paper by New York and international artists. *Free.*

**Museum of Contemporary African Diasporan Arts (MoCADA)**. *80 Hanson Place, Brooklyn 11217. 718-230-0492. www.mocada.org.* Through its exhibitions, public programs, community outreach initiatives, and educational tours, this museum founded in 1999 is devoted to using the visual arts to address contemporary issues affecting people of the African diaspora. *Open Wednesday through Sunday, 11 am until 6 pm. Fee.*

**New York Transit Museum**. *Corner of Boerum Place and Schermerhorn Street, Brooklyn Heights 11201. 718-694-1600. www.mta.info/mta/ museum.* Aside from its magnificent collection of vintage subway and elevated trains, this museum devoted to the history of urban public transportation offers exhibits on the construction of New York City's first subway line, the history of surface transportation, methods of fare collection, and changes in fuel technologies. Located in a 1936 IND subway station, the museum is the largest of its kind in the United States and is also known for its collection of model trolleys, its art gallery, and its shop. *Open Tuesday through Friday, 10 am until 4 pm, and Saturday and Sunday, 12 pm until 5 pm. Fee.*

**Rotunda Gallery**. *33 Clinton Street (between Pierrepont Street and Cadman Plaza West), Brooklyn Heights. 718-875-4047. www.briconline.org/rotunda.* The gallery mounts eight to ten exhibitions a year, including group, thematic, and individual artist shows focusing on painting, sculpture, photography, site-specific installations, and video. The gallery also sponsors art in public spaces throughout Brooklyn such as the installation of outdoor sculptures in Cadman Plaza Park and the Artists' Garden Competition. *Open Tuesday through Saturday, 11 am until 6 pm. Free.*

**St. Ann's Warehouse**. *38 Water Street 11201. 718-254-8779. www.stanns warehouse.org.* This innovative performing arts center in an old spice mill on the waterfront in DUMBO has become a respected theater in the city. Known for its multiartist concerts and music and theater collaborations, St. Ann's also presents puppet shows and multidisciplinary theatrical presentations, in addition to commissioning new work.

**Weeksville Heritage Center**. *1698 Bergen Street 11213. 718-756-5250. www.weeksvillesociety.org.* Since 1968 this preservation group— formerly the Society for the Preservation of Weeksville and Bedford Stuyvesant History—has been dedicated to preserving the historic Hunterfly Road Houses, the last surviving intact residential structures of one of the nation's earliest free African American communities, 19th-century Weeksville. Astonishingly intact, these modest houses speak for themselves about who built and lived in them and are rare examples of architectural survival in the changing city. After a major restoration in 2005 and the planned completion of a new visitors' building in 2011,

*From Red Hook to Williamsburg, the transformation of warehouses, piers, and even barges into galleries and performing arts centers has transformed the Brooklyn waterfront into a thriving center for the arts.*

the center has focused on leading tours, conducting research, working with schools, hosting lectures, and conserving the houses. *Open Monday through Friday, 9:30 am until 4:30 pm, and Saturday, 11 am until 3 pm. Tours take place Tuesday through Friday at 1 pm, 2 pm, and 3 pm, and on Saturday from 11 am to 3 pm. Fee.*

# QUEENS

One of the original twelve counties set up under English rule in 1683, Queens is New York City's largest borough in area and ethnically its most diverse. In recent years, the waterfront communities of Astoria and Long Island City in the western part of the county have gained national prominence for their successful transition from manufacturing centers to thriving communities of artists. For information on cultural events and arts organizations throughout the borough, visit or contact the Queens Council on the Arts; for restaurant, hotel, and transportation information, see the Queens Tourism Center (both are listed under Visitor Information at the end of the chapter).

**Museum of the Moving Image**. *35 Avenue at 37 Street. 718-784-0077. www.movingimage.us. National Register.* The museum—the first institution in the United States devoted to the art, history, and technology of motion pictures, television, and video—screens classic films and mounts exhibits on the making of films and on the movie industry itself. *Open Wednesday through Thursday, 11 am until 5 pm; Friday, 11 am until 8 pm; and Saturday and Sunday, 11 am until 6:30 pm. Fee.*

**New York Hall of Science**. *47-01 111th Street, Flushing Meadows–Corona Park (at 48th Avenue). 718-699-0005. www.nyscience.org.* The nation's largest interactive microbiology exhibit, online links to observatories around the world, and live daily science demonstrations are just a few of the 190 exhibits at this cathedral to science and technology on the site of the 1964 New York World's Fair. In 2004 the hall underwent a 55,000-square-foot expansion designed by Polshek Partnership Architects. *Open Tuesday through Thursday, 9:30 am until 2 pm; Friday, 9:30 am until 5 pm; Saturday and Sunday, 12 pm until 5 pm. Summer hours are Monday, 9:30 am until 2:30 pm; Tuesday through Friday, 9:30 am until 5 pm; and Saturday and Sunday, 10:30 am until 6 pm. Fee.*

**Noguchi Museum**. *9-01 33rd Road (at Vernon Boulevard), Long Island City. 718-204-7088. www.noguchi.org.* The former studio of the 20th-century Japanese American sculptor Isamu Noguchi—whose work appears in major Hudson Valley locations including Storm King Art Center and Empire State

Plaza—contains 300 works in stone, metal, wood, and clay reflecting the sculptor's interest in the natural world. The museum has a sculpture garden and is located across the street from the East River and one block from Socrates Sculpture Park. *Open Wednesday through Friday, 10 am until 5 pm, and Saturday and Sunday, 11 am until 6 pm. Fee.*

**P.S.1 Contemporary Art Center**. *22-25 Jackson Avenue (at 46th Avenue), Long Island City. 718-784-2084. www.ps1.org.* Created as a center for emerging visual and performance artists in 1971, and one of the oldest and largest nonprofit contemporary art institutions in the United States, this former public school building in Long Island City became affiliated with the Museum of Modern Art in 2000. The museum is dependably unpredictable, with huge installations, enigmatic performance art, experimental film and video, and works in progress by artists-in-residence known for their intensity and irreverence. *Open Thursday through Monday, 12 pm until 6 pm. Suggested donation.*

**Queens Botanical Garden**. *43-50 Main Street (between Dahlia and Peck Avenues), Flushing. 718-886-3800. www.queensbotanical.org. National Register.* Created to preserve a horticultural exhibit developed for the 1939 New York World's Fair, the garden was moved to its current 38-acre site in 1962. Its beautiful rose gardens and special gardening demonstrations draw crowds during the flowering months. *Open April through October, Tuesday through Friday, 8 am until 6 pm, and Saturday and Sunday, 8 am until 7 pm; November through March, Tuesday through Sunday, 8 am until 4:30 pm. Free.*

**Queens Museum of Art**. *New York City Building, Flushing Meadows–Corona Park. 718-592-9700. www.queensmuseum.org. National Register.* This newly important venue for contemporary art is located in one of the last major structures to survive the 1939 and 1964 New York World's Fairs. Designed by Wallace Harrison and recently reconstructed by Rafael Viñoly, the museum also houses one of the most fascinating and instructive artifacts in the five boroughs, the Panorama of the City of New York, a 9,335-square-foot model of the city originally created for the 1964 World's Fair and recently refurbished. Exhibits span the range of contemporary fine and folk art, and the permanent collection includes examples of 20th-century painting and photography and an archive of world's fair memorabilia. *Open Wednesday through Friday, 10 am until 5 pm, and Saturday and Sunday, 12 pm until 5 pm. Fee.*

**Socrates Sculpture Park**. *32-01 Vernon Boulevard (Broadway at Vernon Boulevard), Astoria. 718-956-1819. www.socratessculpturepark.org.* Created in 1986 by the artists Mark di Suvero and Enrico Martignoni along

*Located on a cove on the East River, Socrates Sculpture Park is one of the most important sites for contemporary sculpture in New York City.*

with local residents, this 4.5-acre city park on a cove on the East River is one of the most important sites for contemporary sculpture in New York City. Rock gardens, specially built walls, walkways, wild grasses, and boulders surround an open space by the water, with the Manhattan skyline seemingly within reach across the East River. The exuberantly eclectic and imaginative outdoor gallery regularly juxtaposes the work of the well-known with that of emerging artists, and offers free drop-in weekend sculpture-making workshops for young people, taught by exhibiting artists. *Free.*

## MANHATTAN

For 400 years, this 13-mile-long island on the eastern shore of the Hudson—named Manna-hata by Robert Juet in his 1609 journal—has been helping to define American culture, absorbing influences from around the world, transforming them, and injecting them back into American society. The result is a wealth of cultural institutions that preserve the past but also encourage the new. For information on upcoming exhibits, openings and performances, visit the Lower Manhattan Cultural Council and the Harlem Arts Alliance; for hotel, restaurant, and transportation information, visit NYC & Company, the official New York City tourist office (see Visitor Information at the end of the chapter).

**American Academy of Arts and Letters, Audubon Terrace**. *633 West 155th Street 10032. 212-368-5900. www.artsandletters.org.* The academy presents two public exhibits annually and other occasional public programs. *During exhibitions the galleries are open Thursday through Sunday, 1 pm to 4 pm, except the Saturday and Sunday of holiday weekends.*

**American Folk Art Museum**. *45 West 53rd Street (between Fifth Avenue and Avenue of the Americas). 212-265-1040. www.folkartmuseum.org.* This respected museum dedicated to the preservation and exhibition of American folk art, founded in 1963, now occupies a startlingly modern building designed by Tod Williams and Billie Tsien, only half a block from the Museum of Modern Art. Its permanent collection of 2,800 objects contains portraits, landscapes, seascapes, trade signs, weather vanes, whirligigs, decorated tin, carousel horses, furniture, pottery, decoys, quilts, and other objects dating from the mid-1700s to the present. *Open Tuesday through Sunday, 10:30 am until 5:30 pm, and Friday 10:30 am until 7:30 pm. Fee.*

**American Museum of Natural History**. *Central Park West at 79th Street (entrances also on 77th Street and at Rose Center/Planetarium on 81st Street). 212-769-5100. www.amnh.org. National Register.* Spanning 4 city blocks, consisting of some 25 interconnected buildings, and displaying only a portion of its 32 million specimens and artifacts in its 40 exhibition halls, this storied 19th-century institution is the largest natural history museum in the world. Its scientists study the diversity of the earth's species, life in the ancient past, and the universe. Among its many stunning dioramas of animals and animal habitats around the world are those depicting a family of peregrine falcons on the Hudson River Palisades and a North American beaver in a Catskills-like glen. The most recent addition, the Rose Center for Earth and Space—a shimmering glass cube created in 2000 according to a design by James Stewart Polshek—updated the museum's planetarium with a more interactive, technologically advanced experience. *Open Monday through Sunday, 10 am until 5:45 pm. Fee.*

**Apollo Theater**. *253 West 125th Street (between Powell and Douglass Boulevards). 212-531-5301. www.apollotheater.com.* One of the landmarks of Harlem, the Apollo Theater is perhaps best known for its amateur night and the syndicated television show that brings African American talent into millions of homes. The theater screens films and hosts rock and gospel concerts, benefits, and theater performances. *Fee.*

**Audubon Terrace**. *Broadway between 155th and 156th Streets. National Register.* This cluster of Beaux Arts buildings by the architects Charles

Pratt Huntington and William M. Kendall was begun in 1908 on the former farm of the naturalist and artist John James Audubon. Among the cultural institutions overlooking the Hudson that currently share the site are:

American Academy of Arts and Letters
Hispanic Society of America

**Battery Park**. *Battery Place, State Street and Whitehall Street. Dial 311 (from inside New York City) or 212-NEW-YORK (from elsewhere). www .nycgovparks.org/parks/batterypark.* One of the city's oldest public spaces, this 25-acre park on landfill at the tip of Manhattan and the confluence of the Hudson and East Rivers is the largest park in lower Manhattan. Its name refers to the battery of cannons once placed here to protect New Amsterdam; Castle Clinton, a round fort constructed to defend the harbor during the War of 1812, is now a visitor center operated by the National Park Service. The park commands a sweeping view of the entire harbor and is the only embarkation point in New York City for ferries for the Statue of Liberty and Ellis Island. Managed by New York City Department of Parks and Recreation with the nonprofit Battery Conservancy (212-344–3491; www.thebattery.org), which hosts regular events throughout the year and has sponsored numerous landscaping and architectural innovations.

**Battery Park City**. *Southwestern shore of Manhattan. 212-417-2000. www .batteryparkcity.org.* With its parks, esplanades, cultural centers, commercial and retail space, and residential towers rising dramatically above the Hudson, this 92-acre development on the southwestern tip of Manhattan was made from the earth excavated during the original construction of the World Trade Center. A public art program has installed sculptures throughout the site.

**Central Park**. *59th to 110th Street, between Central Park West and Fifth Avenue. 212-310-6600. www.centralparknyc.org.* Designed in 1858 by Frederick Law Olmsted and Calvert Vaux, Central Park is New York City's greatest and most enduring work of art. Envisioned as an oasis of green where people of all backgrounds would mingle, the park boasts more than 26,000 trees, 58 miles of scenic pathways, and nearly 9,000 benches on 843 acres. The most frequented urban park in the nation, it attracts more than 15 million visitors yearly. Most of the 200 or so bridges throughout the park, many of them strikingly beautiful, were designed by Vaux. The Central Park Conservancy, a nonprofit organization founded in 1980, administers Central Park in partnership with the New York City Department of Parks and Recreation.

*The six-acre Conservatory Garden, at Fifth Avenue and 104th Street, is the most formal of the many different landscape areas in 843-acre Central Park.*

**Chamber Music Society of Lincoln Center, Lincoln Center**. *Main campus between Broadway and Amsterdam Avenue and 60th and 66th Streets, 10023. 212-875-5788. www.chambermusicsociety.org.* Maintains a permanent roster of nine noted virtuosi who work together in various combinations and collaborate with distinguished guest artists. It has given more than a thousand performances since it was founded in 1969 by Charles Wadsworth. Alice Tully Hall is the home of the Chamber Music Society. *Fee.*

**Chelsea Sculpture Park**. *Between 22nd and 26th Streets along the Hudson. 212-645-2895. www.chelseasculpturepark.org.* Located in Hudson River Park at the edge of the Chelsea arts district, this 9.2-acre park at the water's edge—still unfinished in mid-2009—is planned as the site of rotating exhibits of sculpture that will document the artistic history of New York City and honor New York artists of the post-1945 generation and beyond.

**The Cloisters**. *Fort Tryon Park (between 190th and Dyckman Streets), Washington Heights. 212-923-3700. www.metmuseum.org.* Opened in 1938 and one of New York's most popular museums, this branch of the Metropolitan Museum of Art overlooking the Hudson in northern Manhattan is devoted to the art and architecture of medieval Europe. Its unusual structure incorporates elements of five medieval cloisters dating from the 12th through the 15th centuries, including chapels, monastic abbeys, and a chapter house. It is known particularly for its Romanesque and Gothic architectural sculpture; its stained glass, metalwork, paintings, illuminated manuscripts, and tapestries; its beautiful gardens; and its great views of the river. *Open March through October, Tuesday through Sunday, 9:30 am until 5:15 pm; and November through February, Tuesday through Sunday, 9:30 am until 4:45 pm. Suggested donation.*

**Columbia University/Miller Theatre**. *2960 Broadway (at 116th Street) 10027. 212-854-1633. www.millertheatre.com. National Register.* With its lovely campus designed by Charles McKim, Columbia University contains many interesting attractions including the Miller Theatre, a nationally recognized performing arts center established in 1988 and known for its adventurous programming in music, opera, dance, and film. *Fee.*

**Drawing Center**. *35 Wooster Street (between Broome and Grand Streets), SoHo. 212-219-2166. www.drawingcenter.org.* This downtown gallery presents four group exhibitions a year emphasizing the work of emerging artists and one historical exhibition that highlights the work of acknowledged masters and less celebrated artists whose work merits greater attention. *Open Tuesday through Friday, 10 am until 6 pm, and Saturday, 11 am until 6 pm.*

**Dyckman Farmhouse**. *4881 Broadway (at 204th Street), Inwood. 212-304-9422. www.dyckmanfarmhouse.org. National Register.* Constructed in 1784 in place of an earlier structure burned by the British during

*Overlooking the Hudson River in Fort Tryon Park in northern Manhattan, the unusual building called The Cloisters—a branch of the Metropolitan Museum of Art—is devoted to the art and architecture of medieval Europe.*

the American Revolution, this Dutch-American building with its gambrel roof and double doors is Manhattan's last surviving colonial farmhouse. It contains English and early American furnishings, a Bible and cradle that are Dyckman family heirlooms, relics from the American Revolution (pottery fragments, flintlocks, and kitchen utensils), and a replica of a British military hut near its original site in the garden. *Open Wednesday through Saturday, 11 pm until 4pm, and Sunday, 12 pm until 4 pm. Fee.*

**Empire State Building and Observatory**. *350 Fifth Avenue (between 33rd and 34th Streets). 212-736-3100. www.esbnyc.com. National Register.* Since 1931 the Empire State Building has symbolized New York City as the Statue of Liberty has stood for New York Harbor. On a clear day, the observation deck offers an 80-mile panoramic view of the city and the world beyond, including a tempting peak up the Hudson Valley. *Open Monday through Sunday, 8 am until 2 am. Fee.*

**Film Society of Lincoln Center, Lincoln Center**. *70 Lincoln Center Plaza, 10023. 212-875-5600; www.filmlinc.com.* Sponsors the renowned annual New York Film Festival, one of the world's leading showcases for new American and international films. It also operates the Walter Reade Theater, opened in 1991 as a year-round presenter of films that would not otherwise have a major venue in New York City. The Film Society's programs range from daring new works from around the world to retrospectives of outstanding directors, performers, cinematographers, screenwriters, and other film artists.

**Frick Collection**. *1 East 70th Street (at Fifth Avenue). 212-288-0700. www. frick.org. National Register.* Designed by Thomas Hastings and con- structed in 1913–14 as the residence of steel magnate and art collector Henry Clay Frick (1849–1919), this lavish neoclassical mansion is home to one of the world's most important private collections of painting, sculpture, and decorative art dating from the 14th through the 19th centuries. Bellini, El Greco, Vermeer, Rembrandt, and Watteau are just a tiny portion of the great artists whose work is on permanent display. Free concerts of classical music are presented throughout the year. *Open Tuesday through Saturday, 10 am until 6 pm, and Sunday, 11 am until 5 pm. Closed major holidays. Fee.*

**George Washington Bridge**. *www.panynj.gov/CommutingTravel/bridges/ html.* "When your car moves up the ramp, the two towers rise so high that it brings you happiness; their structure is so pure, so resolute, so regular that here, finally, steel architecture seems to laugh." Thus wrote the architect Le Corbusier in his 1947 memoir *When the Cathedrals*

*Were White: A Journey to the Country of Timid People* about the steel suspension bridge that had been completed 16 years earlier between Washington Heights, in northern Manhattan, and Fort Lee, in New Jersey. Designed by Othmar H. Ammann, chief engineer of the Port Authority, with the help of the architect Cass Gilbert, and today one of the world's busiest bridges, with an estimated 300,000 vehicles crossing it every day, the bridge opened in 1931 with a single level and reopened in 1962 with a second (lower) level. When it opened it had the longest span in the world, 3,500 feet (1,067 meters).

**Grant's Tomb**. *Riverside Drive at 122nd Street. www.nps.gov/gegr. National Register.* Overlooking the Hudson River at the northern end of Riverside Park, this neoclassical monument is the largest mausoleum in North America, reflecting the immense reverence Americans felt for the Civil War general and American president Ulysses S. Grant. Dedicated in 1897, the memorial was designed by John Duncan after Mausolus' Tomb at Halicarnassus of 350 B.C. The structure rises 150 feet from a bluff overlooking the river and was built between 1891 and 1897. *Open daily, 9 am until 5 pm.*

**Solomon R. Guggenheim Museum**. *1071 Fifth Avenue (at 89th Street). 212-423-3500. www.guggenheim.org. National Register.* In its famed spiral building built by Frank Lloyd Wright in 1959, the museum hosts a vast range of exhibits of contemporary art and design and maintains an important collection of 20th-century European modern masters such as Wassily Kandinsky, Paul Klee, Franz Marc, Robert Delaunay, and Marc Chagall. One of the first museums to have international branches, the Guggenheim has sister institutions in Berlin, Bilbao, and Venice. *Open Saturday through Wednesday, 10 am until 5:45 pm, and Friday, 10 am until 7:45 pm. Fee.*

**The Hispanic Society of America, Audubon Terrace**. *613 West 155th Street (entrance on Broadway between 155th and 156th Streets). 212-926-2234. www.hispanicsociety.org.* Founded in 1904, this museum and research library focuses on the culture of Spain and the New World peoples it has influenced. The society's holdings range from prehistoric art to paintings by 18th- and 19th-century Spanish masters. A well-regarded library contains some 200,000 books and rare maps, globes, and prints. *Open Tuesday through Saturday, 10 am until 4:30 pm, and Sunday, 1 pm until 4 pm.*

**Holland Tunnel**. *www.panynj.gov.* Named for Clifford Milburn Holland, its chief engineer, and constructed between 1920 and 1927, this 8,500-foot two-tube toll tunnel under the Hudson River connects Canal Street in lower Manhattan with Jersey City in New Jersey. It carries an average of 100,000 vehicles per day.

**Intrepid Sea-Air-Space Museum**. *Pier 86, Twelfth Avenue at 46th Street. 212-245-0072. www.intrepidmuseum.com. National Register.* This museum of military technology presents permanent and short-term exhibits on undersea exploration, satellite communication, ship and aircraft design, naval equipment, and aircraft aboard a battle-scarred aircraft carrier docked on the Hudson River. On the flight deck are 40 aircraft, including a Soviet MIG and a Lockheed A-12 Blackbird built for CIA surveillance missions at 90,000 feet. *Open Memorial Day through Labor Day, Saturday through Monday, 10 am until 5 pm, and Sunday, 10 am until 6 pm (final admission at 5 pm); the rest of the year, Wednesday through Sunday, 10 am until 5 pm; final admission at 4 pm. Fee.*

**Inwood Hill Park**. *Dyckman Street, Hudson River, and the Harlem River Ship Canal at Spuyten Duyvil, Inwood. Dial 311 (from inside New York City) or 212-NEW-YORK (from elsewhere). www.nycgovparks.org/parks/ inwoodhillpark.* Located along the Hudson at the very northern tip of the island, this 196-acre park contains the last stand of native forest on Manhattan and a stone marker commemorating the spot where Peter Minuit is said to have purchased the island from local Reckgawawancs for various trinkets and beads. A new shoreline bike path provides even closer links to the river.

**Jazz at Lincoln Center, Lincoln Center**. *Located off the main campus on Broadway at 60th Street, Columbus Circle. 212-258-9800. www.jalc.org.* The largest nonprofit jazz organization in the world, Jazz at Lincoln Center produces and presents world-class jazz performances involving the Lincoln Center Jazz Orchestra, other resident orchestras and ensembles, and special groups that it assembles as well as visiting artists, ensembles, and soloists at three performance spaces, Rose Hall, the Allen Room, and Dizzy's Club Coca-Cola, in the Time Warner Center. *Fee.*

**Jewish Museum**. *1109 Fifth Avenue (at 92nd Street). 212-423-3200. www .thejewishmuseum.org. National Register.* This museum in the former Warburg Mansion explores 4,000 years of art and Jewish culture. Its encyclopedic permanent exhibit *Culture and Continuity: The Jewish Journey* covers the unfolding story of Jewish history and identity, and provides a frame of reference for subjects explored in temporary shows of the work of powerful artists of the world. Founded in 1904, the museum also has a 232-seat auditorium, a café, two shops, an education center with classrooms, and a children's gallery. *Open Sunday through Wednesday, 11 am until 5:45 pm, and Thursday, 11 am until 8 pm. Fee.*

*Known throughout the world for its sterling orchestra, its extraordinary singers and performers, and its inventive costumes and sets, the Metropolitan Opera is one of the great cultural institutions of New York.*

**Juilliard School**. 155 W. 65th Street *(between Broadway and Amsterdam Avenue), 10023. 212-799-5000. www.juilliard.edu.* Founded in 1905, it is the leading music conservatory in the country, also training students in dance and drama. Juilliard students perform frequently in the Peter Jay Sharp Theater.

**Lincoln Center**. *Main campus between Broadway and Amsterdam Avenue and 60th and 66th Streets, 10023. 212-875-5456. www.lincolncenter.org.* Undergoing substantial renovations in 2009–10 in honor of its 50th anniversary, this complex of modernist buildings on the Upper West Side comprises the world's largest performing arts center, providing space for 11 of the city's most important performing arts organizations and presenting many major programs of its own. Lincoln Center was conceived in the 1950s and substantially completed during the 1960s. Under the original aegis of Wallace K. Harrison, the buildings were designed by some of the great architects of the period including Philip Johnson (the central plaza and the David H. Koch Theatre, formerly the New York State Theater), Max Abramovitz (Avery Fisher Hall), Eero Saarinen (the Vivian Beaumont Theater), and Harrison himself (the Metropolitan Opera). The New York firm of Diller Scofidio + Renfro is designing the renovation. In

2010, a new visitor center and discount ticket booth will open across the street in the Harmony Atrium, designed by Tod Williams Billie Tsien. Among the famous programs hosted by Lincoln Center itself are Great Performers and the Lincoln Center and Mostly Mozart Festivals (see Festivals, below). The resident organizations include:

Chamber Music Society of Lincoln Center
Film Society of Lincoln Center
Jazz at Lincoln Center
Juilliard School
Lincoln Center Theater
Metropolitan Opera
New York City Ballet
New York City Opera
New York Philharmonic
New York Public Library for the Performing Arts

**Lincoln Center Theater, Lincoln Center**. *150 West 65th Street, 10023. 212-362-7600. www.lct.org.* The 1,050-seat Beaumont and the 280-seat Newhouse theaters are home to the Lincoln Center Theater Company, which presents dozens of productions at Lincoln Center as well as in theaters on and off Broadway. Although nonprofit, the Lincoln Center Theater is considered part of Broadway because of the size of its productions. *The box office is open Monday through Saturday, 10 am until 8 pm, and Sunday, 12 pm until 6 pm. Fee.*

**Lincoln Tunnel**. *www.panynj.gov.* Designed by Ole Singstad and completed in three stages in 1937, 1945, and 1957, this 1.5-mile three-tube toll tunnel under the Hudson River connects West 39th Street in midtown Manhattan with Weehawken in New Jersey. The tunnel carries 120,000 vehicles per day and is considered the busiest vehicular tunnel in the world.

**Little Red Lighthouse**. *Fort Washington Park, 178th Street and the Hudson River under the George Washington Bridge (at the western end of West 181st Street, take the footbridge over the Henry Hudson Parkway and follow the path to the river). 212-304-2365 (tours). www.hudsonlights.com. National Register.* NYC Landmark. Originally—and still officially—known as the Jeffrey's Hook Lighthouse, this 40-foot red steel tower was constructed in 1880 at another location and reconstructed here in 1920 to guide ships through the narrow channel between New York and New Jersey. Although an important part of the New York State Barge Canal shipping route, the lighthouse was rendered obsolete by the more powerful lights of the George Washington Bridge, completed in 1931.

*Rendered obsolete by the construction of the George Washington Bridge in 1931, the Little Red Lighthouse was saved from demolition by the publication of Hildegard Swift's* The Little Red Lighthouse and the Great Grey Bridge *in 1942.*

Hildegard H. Swift's 1942 children's book *The Little Red Lighthouse and the Great Grey Bridge* popularized the structure and saved it from demolition after it was deactivated in 1948. Tours of the lighthouse are available throughout the year at special events such as Open House New York (see Fairs and Festivals, below) and by appointment with the Urban Park Rangers (call the number above).

**Lower East Side Tenement Museum**. *108 Orchard Street. 212-982-8420. www.tenement.org. National Register.* Opened in 1988, this museum located in an 1863 tenement pays tribute to America's 19th- and early-20th-century immigrants through the preservation of one of their dwelling places. Each apartment in the building at 97 Orchard Street has been designed to capture a moment in the life of an immigrant family that actually lived there. A gallery a few steps away at 90 Orchard Street offers a slide show recounting the story of the preserved building, Depression-era photographs, and a scale model of the building depicting changes that occurred during the period 1870 to 1915. *Open Monday, 11 am until 5:30 pm, Tuesday through Friday, 11 am until 6 pm, and Saturday and Sunday, 10:45 am until 6 pm. Fee.*

**Metropolitan Museum of Art**. *1000 Fifth Avenue (at 82nd Street). 212-535-7710. www.metmuseum.org. National Register.* This vast and encyclopedic museum was incorporated in 1870 and moved to its present location in 1880. Any single one of its permanent collections could be considered a museum in itself. With nearly 3 million works that span 5,000 years, the museum can display only a fraction of its holdings at a time. Stunning and often groundbreaking temporary exhibits explore particular artists, art movements, and historical periods more completely. Among the 22 curatorial departments, the departments of American Decorative Arts and American Paintings and Sculpture—both located in the American Wing—contain, among many highlights, a large repository of works by Hudson River School painters and other American artists who depicted the Adirondacks, Catskills, and Hudson Valley, such as Thomas Cole, Frederic Edwin Church, Asher B. Durand, and Winslow Homer; 25 furnished period rooms depicting American domestic architecture and interior design over three centuries; and a specially designed circular room containing the Kingston painter John Vanderlyn's 1818–19 *Panoramic View of the Palace and Gardens of Versailles*. The original building was designed by Calvert Vaux and J. Wrey Mould. The neo-Renaissance Fifth Avenue facade was designed and built in two stages: the central section (1902) by Richard Morris Hunt and the side wings (1906) by McKim, Mead & White. *Open Tuesday through Thursday and Sunday, 9:30 am until 5:30 pm, and Friday and Saturday, 9:30 am until 9 pm. Suggested admission.*

**Metropolitan Opera, Lincoln Center**. *Main campus between Broadway and Amsterdam Avenue and 60th and 66th Streets, 10023. 212-362-6000. www.metopera.org.* One of the great companies of the world, presenting works from the classical and traditional to the newest and most daring, the Met is committed to presenting works from the broadest range of the operatic repertory and making its programs available to a wide audience through national and international broadcasts on radio and television, home video releases, free summer performances in parks in the New York metropolitan area, podcasts and simulcasts, and educational programs for students and aspiring young singers. *The box office is open Monday through Saturday, 10 am until 8 pm, and Sunday, 12 pm until 6 pm. Fee.*

**Morris-Jumel Mansion**. *65 Jumel Terrace at 160th Street (between West 160th and West 162nd Streets, one block east of St. Nicholas Avenue), Washington Heights. 212-923-8008. www.morrisjumel.org. National Register.* This Georgian Federal–style landmark house is one of the city's few remaining pre–Revolutionary War buildings. Constructed by British colonel Roger Morris in 1765 as a summer house for his family, the mansion, with its commanding view of the city then 12 miles to the south, became the headquarters of General Washington during the American Revolution. Madame Jumel's boudoir contains two chairs believed to have belonged to Napoleon. *Open Wednesday through Sunday, 10 am until 4 pm. Fee.*

**El Museo del Barrio**. *1230 Fifth Avenue (at 104th Street) 10029. 212-831-7272. www.elmuseo.org.* Founded in 1969, this museum representing the art and culture of the Caribbean and Latin America evolved from a small museum in a school through a series of storefronts on Third and Lexington Avenues into New York's leading Latino cultural institution, located in a neoclassical building on upper Fifth Avenue. Its collections of pre-Columbian art, secular and religious objects, works on paper, paintings, sculpture, photography, film, and video are among the best in the city. Its name refers to the Spanish-speaking neighborhood that extends from 96th Street to the Harlem River and from Fifth Avenue to the East River on Manhattan's Upper East Side. The galleries and museum shop reopen in 2010 after renovations. *Fee.*

**Museum of Chinese in America**. *211-215 Centre Street between Howard and Grand Streets, Manhattan. 212-619-4785. www.mocanyc.org.* Through exhibits and educational and cultural programs based on its growing collection of art and objects, this museum founded in 1980 works to improve understanding of the Chinese experience in America. The museum opened a new expanded space on Centre Street in March 2009. *Fee.*

**Museum of Jewish Heritage—A Living Memorial to the Holocaust**. *36 Battery Place (at First Place), Battery Park City. 646-437-4200. www .mjhnyc.org.* Opened in 1997, this hexagonal ziggurat on the waterfront memorializes the murder of 6 million Jews at the hands of the Nazis while honoring those who survived the Holocaust to rebuild their lives and create vibrant communities. In addition to some 2,000 photographs and 800 artifacts, 24 video documentaries chronicle the experiences of survivors. Three full-floor exhibitions depict the Holocaust within the context of 20th-century Jewish life. *Open Sunday through Tuesday and Thursday, 10 am until 5:45 pm; Wednesday, 10 am until 8 pm; and Friday, 10 am until 3 pm. Closed Saturday and Jewish holidays. Fee.*

**Museum of Modern Art**. *11 West 53rd Street (between Fifth Avenue and Avenue of the Americas). 212-708-9400. www.moma.org.* Since opening in 1929, MoMA has become perhaps the most important critical force in modern art. Its collections span the major movements in European and American art since 1880. It was the first U.S. museum to recognize film, photography, architecture, and design as legitimate art forms and to collect accordingly. Its current building, designed by Yoshio Taniguchi and completed in 2004, expands and alters a building that has evolved in stages from its original International Style structure by Edward Durrell Stone and Philip L. Goodwin. The 54th Street Sculpture Garden was originally designed by Philip Johnson and built in 1964. The West Wing

*The collection inside Joseph Freedlander's 1932 neo-Georgian Museum of the City of New York details the narrative of New York City from its Dutch beginnings to the present.*

and residential tower was designed by Cesar Pelli and constructed in 1984. *Open Saturday through Monday, Wednesday and Thursday, 10:30 am until 5:30 pm; Friday, 10:30 am until 8 pm; and on Thursdays during July and August, 10:30 am until 9 pm. Fee.*

**Museum of the City of New York**. *1220 Fifth Avenue (at 103rd Street). 212-534-1672. www.mcny.org. National Register.* The narrative of New York City—from its beginning as a small Dutch trading post to its status today as one of the world's most important cities—unfolds through special exhibitions and the diverse collections of this museum founded in 1923. The permanent collection contains more than 3 million items maintained by six curatorial departments: costumes, decorative arts, paintings and sculpture, prints and photographs, theater, and toys. In addition to period rooms, exhibits explore the city's cultural diversity, architecture, and economic significance. The museum moved to its current home, a five-story neo-Georgian building designed by Joseph Freedlander, in 1932; current renovations by James Polshek, to be completed in 2011, include a new glass pavilion housing a curatorial center at the rear of the building. *Open Tuesday through Sunday, 10 am until 5 pm. Fee.*

**National Museum of the American Indian—Smithsonian Institution**. *One Bowling Green (between State and Whitehall Streets), lower Manhattan. 212-514-3700. www.americanindian.si.edu. National Register.* Located on the waterfront in one of the most splendid Beaux Arts buildings in the city, the 1907 Custom House designed by Cass Gilbert, the museum possesses one of the world's most comprehensive collections of Indian artifacts. The collection spans 10,000 years of Native American heritage. Originally an independent institution located in Audubon Terrace in northern Manhattan, the museum became part of the Smithsonian Institution in 1989 and opened at its current location

*Devoted to the work of living artists created during the last 10 years, the New Museum of Contemporary Art was founded in 1977 and moved to its new building on the Bowery in 2007.*

in 1994. Since 2004 the museum has also operated out of its new main building on the Mall in Washington, D.C. *Open 10 am until 5 pm daily; closed Christmas Day. Free.*

**New Museum of Contemporary Art**. *235 Bowery (at Prince Street). 212-219-1222. www.newmuseum.org. National Register.* Designed by the Tokyo-based architects Sejima + Nishizawa/SANAA, this innovative exhibition space focuses primarily on the work of living artists created during the past ten years. Each year the museum mounts up to four major exhibitions and about twelve smaller shows in its galleries. Painting, sculpture, photography, installation, performance, and multimedia works including interactive video and computer projects are shown in group shows. *Open Wednesday through Sunday, 12 pm until 6 pm, and Thursday and Friday, 12 pm until 10 pm. Fee.*

**New York City Ballet, Lincoln Center**. *20 Lincoln Center, 10023. 212-870-5570. www.nycballet.com.* Founded by ballet enthusiast Lincoln Kirstein and choreographer George Balanchine in the 1940s, this extraordinary company remains true to Balanchine's innovative, neoclassical choreography and singular vision. His legacy runs through the teaching methods of the School of American Ballet and through his repertory of more than 125 works. The New York City Ballet also performs works by celebrated choreographers Jerome Robbins, Peter Martins (its current director), and others in the David H. Koch Theatre (formerly the New York State Theatre), at the Saratoga Performing Arts Center (see Saratoga County, below), and on tour around the world. *Fee.*

**New York City Opera, Lincoln Center**. *Main campus between Broadway and Amsterdam Avenue and 60th and 66th Streets, 10023. 212-870-5630. www.nycopera.com.* One of the resident companies of the New York

State Theater, this "opera company for the people" is known for its pioneering productions, unusual repertory, and presentation of new American works. The company was one of the first in the United States to make its operas more accessible through the use of supertitles, and works to build new audiences for the art form through substantial outreach and education programs. *Fee.*

**New-York Historical Society**. *170 Central Park West (at 77th Street), 10024. 212-873-3400. www.nyhistory.org. National Register.* Founded in 1804 and the city's oldest museum, now located in a neoclassical building by York & Sawyer completed in 1908 and expanded in 1938 by Walker & Gillette, the historical society maintains a collection of 1.6 million objects that includes fine examples of painting, furniture, prints, maps, books, and manuscripts covering the history of the United States and of the State of New York. There are numerous paintings by artists of the Hudson River School including Thomas Cole's five-part *Course of Empire.* Works by early New York silversmiths and all but one of the original watercolors printed by John James Audubon for his book *The Birds of America* are also in the collection. The society's famous library possesses some of the country's more important documents: the correspondence between Alexander Hamilton and Aaron Burr leading up to their 1804 duel in Weehawken (see Chapter 2); George Washington's proposed plan for retaking British-occupied New York City; and a copy of *Freedom's Journal*, the first newspaper published by African Americans starting in 1827. *Open Tuesday through Saturday, 10 am until 6 pm, and Sunday, 11 am until 5:45 pm. Fee.*

**New York Philharmonic, Lincoln Center**. *Main campus between Broadway and Amsterdam Avenue and 60th and 66th Streets, 10023.* Founded in 1842, is the oldest orchestra in the United States and a major fixture in the city's cultural life. It presents about 170 concerts a year, primarily at Avery Fisher Hall. It also hosts free concerts in various parks throughout all five boroughs and on Long Island. The Philharmonic is seen regularly by audiences around the country on PBS's *Live from Lincoln Center* telecasts. The orchestra records frequently and has always been at the vanguard of musical promotion and education. Its former conductors and music directors have included Gustav Mahler, Arturo Toscanini, Pierre Boulez, and Leonard Bernstein. *Fee.*

**New York Public Library**. *Fifth Avenue and 42nd Street 10018. 212-930-0800. www.nypl.org. National Register.* The famous Beaux Arts building with the two lions out front, designed by Carrère & Hastings and opened in 1911, is the heart of the great library system serving Staten Island, Manhattan, and the Bronx. It contains 15 million objects including maps, rare manuscripts, special collections, and millions of noncirculating books that make up one of the world's preeminent research resources in the humanities and social sciences. *Open Monday, Thursday, and Friday, 11 am until 6 pm; Tuesday and Wednesday, 11 am until 7:30 pm; Saturday, 11 am until 6 pm; and Sunday, 1 pm until 5 pm.*

**New York Public Library for the Performing Arts, Lincoln Center**. *40 Lincoln Center Plaza 10023. 212-870-1630. www.nypl.org/research/lpa.* This unique branch of the vast New York Public Library system contains one of the world's great collections of reference and research materials on music, dance, theater, recorded sound, and other performing arts. The collections comprise historic recordings, videotapes, manuscripts, correspondence, sheet music, press clippings, programs, posters, photographs, and designs for sets, lighting, stage mechanics, and costumes.

**92nd Street Y**. *1395 Lexington Avenue 10128. 212-415-5500. www.92y.org.* Founded in 1874, and known for its classes in every aspect of the arts, this famous Jewish community and cultural center presents readings and performances by some of today's literary, musical, and performing artists in its two theaters and exhibits of contemporary visual art in its galleries.

**Public Theater**. *425 Lafayette Street 10003. 212-539-8500. www.public theater.org. National Register.* Opened by Joseph Papp in 1967, the Public produces new plays, musicals, productions of Shakespeare, and other classics at its Lafayette Street headquarters and at the open-air Delacorte Theatre in Central Park. At the Delacorte, the Public continues to run the celebrated Shakespeare in the Park festival, as it has each summer since 1959.

**Riverside Church**. *490 Riverside Drive 10027. 212-870-6700. www.the riversidechurchny.org.* Overlooking the Hudson River and the Palisades from one of the highest points in New York City, this Gothic edifice with its striking tower, modeled after the 13th-century Gothic cathedral at Chartres, was dedicated in 1931 for a congregation that dates back to 1841. It was designed by Henry C. Pelton and Allen & Collens. Dr. Martin Luther King Jr., Nelson Mandela, and other socially progressive Christian luminaries have preached here.

**Riverside Park**. *Riverside Drive to the Hudson River, 59th Street to Clair Place. Dial 311 (from inside New York City) or 212-NEW-YORK (from elsewhere). www.nycgovparks.org/parks/riversidepark.* This popular 266-acre park, designed by Frederick Law Olmsted, Gilmore D. Clarke, and Clinton Lloyd, stretches along five miles of the Hudson and provides some of

*The South Street Seaport Museum re-creates New York City's maritime history in six restored buildings and four historic ships docked at city piers.*

the best views of the river in Manhattan, especially from the bike path and the piers at 70th and 125th Streets. A popular summer restaurant overlooks a 110-slip marina at 79th Street.

**Schomburg Center for Research in Black Culture**. *515 Malcolm X Boulevard at 135th Street 10037. 212-491-2200. www.nypl.org/research/ sc. National Register.* Devoted to preserving materials on the global African and African diasporan experiences, and one of the world's leading research libraries in its field, this branch of the New York Public Library makes its extensive archives available to scholars and sponsors programs and events that illuminate black history and culture. *Open Monday through Wednesday, 12 pm until 8 pm; Thursday and Friday, 11 am until 6 pm; and Saturday, 10 am until 5 pm.*

**Skirball Center for the Performing Arts/New York University**. *566 LaGuardia Place (at Washington Square South) 10012. 212-352-3101. www .skirballcenter.nyu.edu.* Designed by Kevin Roche and Artec Consultants and opened in 2003, this 850-seat performance space presents both university productions and performances from around the world in theater, dance, music, opera, video, and film. *The box office is open Tuesday through Saturday, 12 pm until 6 pm. Fee.*

**South Street Seaport Museum**. *12 Fulton Street (at South Street), lower Manhattan. 212-748-8600. www.southstreetseaportmuseum.org. National*

*Register*. The museum preserves vestiges of the time when Lower Manhattan was a thriving seaport ringed by a forest of masts, when its narrow cobbled streets were lined with counting houses, ship chandleries, tobacconists, sailor bars, flophouses, and fishmongers. The museum mounts exhibitions in six restored buildings drawing on a collection of paintings, photographs, models, and tools relating to shipbuilding, maritime history, and the surrounding historic district. Berthed nearby are four historic ships open to the public. *Open April through October, Tuesday through Sunday, 10 am until 6 pm, and November through March, Monday through Friday, 10 am until 5 pm. Fee.*

**Cathedral of St. John the Divine**. *1047 Amsterdam Avenue (at 112th Street) 10025. 212-316-7490 (general); 212-932-7347 (tours). www.stjohndivine .org.* Located on the plateau above the Hudson known as Morningside Heights, and begun in 1892 and still unfinished, this huge cathedral (two football fields long) has a Gothic exterior and Romanesque interior and an active music program. *Open to visitors Monday through Saturday, 7 am until 6 pm, and Sunday, 7 am until 7 pm, except during July and August when the cathedral closes at 6 pm on Sundays. The grounds and gardens are open during daylight hours. Tours take place throughout the week.*

**Studio Museum in Harlem**. *144 West 125th Street (between Lenox Avenue and Adam Clayton Powell Boulevard). 212-864-4500. www.studiomuseum .org.* Founded in 1968, the Studio Museum is the foremost exhibitor of the work of African American artists in the United States. The permanent collection contains works by James Van Der Zee, who photographed uptown scenes and celebrities from the 1920s through the '80s; important African and Caribbean artifacts; and paintings by post–World War II artists. An outdoor sculpture garden displays large-scale works. *Open Wednesday through Friday and Sunday, 12 pm until 6 pm, and Saturday, 10 am until 6 pm. Fee.*

**Whitney Museum of American Art**. *945 Madison Avenue (at 75th Street). 212-570-3600. www.whitney.org. National Register.* Established in 1931 by Gertrude Vanderbilt Whitney, the museum maintains one of the world's foremost collections of 20th-century American art. Although virtually every American artist of significance is represented, among those most associated with the museum is the Nyack-born Edward Hopper. The Whitney Biennial, an invitational showcasing works by living American artists, is a lightning rod for new trends in contemporary art. The current building, designed by Marcel Breuer and completed in 1966, is sheathed in unpolished granite and resembles a massive inverted staircase fronted by a moatlike well. *Open Wednesday, Thursday, Saturday, and Sunday, 11 am until 6 pm, and Friday, 1 pm until 9 pm. Fee.*

# THE BRONX

Jonas Bronck, a Swedish sea captain, settled along a river in the territory northeast of Manhattan in 1639. He prospered and the river came to be known first as Bronck's River and then simply as "Broncks" or "The Broncks." (Some of Bronck's descendants moved north along the Hudson River and established a farm that can be visited today; see Greene County.) In 1817 a poet, Joseph Rodman Drake, wrote a poem called "Bronx," about the land along the river, and soon people were applying the name of the river to the land. The arts continue to be a defining feature in the borough, with many sculptors and painters choosing to live and work here and exhibit in the museums and galleries, large and small, that have sprung up in recent years. For complete arts and culture information on the Bronx, visit or contact the Bronx Council on the Arts; for help with restaurants, hotels, and transportation, and for a general overview of the borough including maps and itineraries, see the Bronx Tourism Council. A full listing for each organization can be found under Visitor Information at the end of the chapter.

**Bronx County Historical Society**. *3309 Bainbridge Avenue (at 208th Street). 718-881-8900. www.bronxhistoricalsociety.org.* The Bronx County Historical Society maintains the Bronx County Archive and hosts educational programs, walking tours, exhibitions, and lectures on the history of New York City's only mainland borough. Besides the Valentine-Varian House, in which it is located, the historical society also operates, nearby, the Edgar Allan Poe Cottage. *The museum is open Monday through Friday by group appointment only; Saturday, 10 am until 4 pm; and Sunday, 1 pm until 5 pm. The library is open Monday through Friday, 9 am until 5 pm by appointment.*

**Bronx Museum**. *1040 Grand Concourse (at 165th Street). 718-681-6000. www.bronxmuseum.org.* Founded in 1971, and located in a 33,000-square-foot converted synagogue with a three-story glass-enclosed atrium, the museum exhibits paintings, photographs, sculpture, and works on paper primarily by emerging and as yet unrecognized artists from Africa, Asia, and Latin America, as well as American descendants from those regions. *Open Thursday through Monday, 11 am until 6 pm, and also until 8 pm on Friday.*

**Bronx River Art Center**. *1087 East Tremont Avenue (between Boston Road and East 177th Street). 718-589-5819. www.bronxriverart.org.* Established in 1987 and located in a former 1920s dress factory on the banks of the Bronx River, this busy gallery presents works by contemporary artists from the Bronx and the metropolitan area in six to eight exhibitions

*Opened in 1987 in a former dress factory in West Farms, the Bronx River Art Center is devoted to the work of contemporary artists.*

yearly. Shows feature individuals and groups in a range of disciplines with culturally diverse themes. *The gallery is open Monday through Friday, 3 pm until 6:30 pm, and Saturday, 12 pm until 5 pm. Free.*

**Bronx Zoo**. *Bronx River Parkway at Fordham Road (second entrance at Southern Boulevard and 182nd Street). 718-367-1010. www.bronxzoo.com. National Register.* The largest urban zoo in the United States and a major attraction, the Bronx Zoo opened in 1899. It opened its first naturalistic habitats, with woods, streams, and parklands covering 265 acres, in 1941. Its more than 4,000 animals represent some 1,000 species. Visitors view animals in spacious habitats planted and arranged to look like the animals' native lands. The Wildlife Conservation Society, which runs the zoo, also operates the New York Aquarium at Coney Island and the zoos at Prospect Park in Brooklyn, Central Park in Manhattan, and Flushing Meadows–Corona Park in Queens, and oversees some 270 projects in 52 nations and has helped establish 110 wildlife parks and reserves globally. *Open October 29 through March 22, 10 am until 4:30 pm, and March 23 through October 28, 10 am until 5 pm. Fee.*

**Henry Hudson Bridge**. *www.mta.info/bandt/html/henry.htm.* Named for the explorer whose statue can be seen from the upper deck of the bridge, standing atop a column in Henry Hudson Park in Riverdale, this double-decker steel arch toll bridge connects northern Manhattan to the

Bronx across Spuyten Duyvil Creek. When it opened in 1936, the bridge was the longest plate girder arch and fixed arch bridge in the world. Hudson is thought to have anchored the *Half Moon* near here.

**Henry Hudson Park**. *Palisade Avenue, Kappock Street, and Independence Avenue. Dial 311 (from inside New York City) or 212-NEW-YORK (from elsewhere). www.nycgovparks.org/parks/henryhudsonpark.* Located on a bluff along the Hudson in the Spuyten Duyvil section of the Bronx, this 9-acre park contains New York City's only statue of Henry Hudson, a 17-foot-tall bronze-clad figure surveying the river, the Palisades, northern Manhattan, and the Bronx from atop a 100-foot Doric column rising up among the apartment buildings of Riverdale. The statue was originally planned, along with the nearby Henry Hudson Bridge (see above), for the 1909 celebration of the 300th anniversary of Hudson's voyage and the 100th of Robert Fulton's steamboat, but lack of funds delayed construction of statue and bridge until the 1930s.

**Lehman College**. *250 Bedford Park Boulevard West (at Goulden Avenue). 718-960-8000. www.lehman.edu.* An important part of the Bronx cultural community since its founding in 1968, the college presents dozens of public concerts, plays, dance performances, and exhibitions every year at its two primary public spaces:

- **Lehman Center for the Performing Arts**. *718-960-8232. www.lehman center.org.* Founded in 1980, the center was the first professional performing arts facility to be built in the Bronx. It presents both popular and classical performances as well as traditional ethnic art forms in its 2,300-seat concert hall and 500-seat theater. *Fee.*

- **Lehman College Art Gallery**. Located in the Marcel Breuer–designed Fine Arts Building, this well-respected gallery emphasizes contemporary art in its large, main exhibition space and smaller graphics gallery. Shows range from one-artist exhibitions by major innovators such as Romare Bearden, Christo and Jeanne-Claude, and Robert Wilson to surveys honoring established and emerging Bronx artists. *Open Tuesday through Saturday, 10 am until 4 pm.*

**Longwood Art Gallery @ Hostos**. *450 Grand Concourse at 149th Street 10451. 718-518-6728. www.longwoodcyber.org.* Established in 1981 as the exhibition arm of the Bronx Council on the Arts, the gallery mounts contemporary art exhibitions throughout the year. Both individual and thematic group shows are featured. It is located in Longwood, one of the Bronx's last surviving historic brownstone districts. Once a public school, the gallery also houses several studios for artists-in-residence. *Open Monday through Saturday, 10 am until 6 pm.*

*Among famous structures at the 250-acre New York Botanical Garden is the 1902 Enid A. Haupt Conservatory, 11 glass pavilions containing tropical plants, palm trees, desert flora, a fern forest, and changing seasonal exhibits.*

**New York Botanical Garden**. *200th Street and Kazimiroff Boulevard (Bronx River Parkway—Exit 7W—and Fordham Road). 718-817-8700. www.nybg .org. National Register.* Encompassing 250 acres from forests to formal gardens, this Bronx landmark includes the magnificently restored 1902 Enid A. Haupt Conservatory, a soaring Victorian crystal palace based on the greenhouses at the Royal Botanic Garden at Kew, with 11 glass pavilions containing tropical plants, palm trees, desert flora, a fern forest, and diverse seasonal exhibits. One of the world's foremost gardens, the NYBG offers not only many specialized cultivated areas but also stretches of untouched natural terrain—such as the city's last remaining 40 acres of virgin forest and a surprisingly sylvan stretch of the Bronx River. *Open Tuesday through Sunday and holidays, 10 am until 5 pm. Fee.*

**Edgar Allan Poe Cottage**. *Kingsbridge Road and the Grand Concourse. 718-881-8900. www.bronxhistoricalsociety.org/poecottage.html. National Register.* Built in 1812, this small house became the home of Edgar Allan Poe and his wife in 1846. Here Poe wrote "Annabel Lee," "Ulalume," "The Bells," and *Eureka* in the last three years of his life. Furnishings include Poe's own rocking chair and bed. A screening room shows films about Poe and a history of the house. *Open Saturday, 10 am until 4 pm, and Sunday, 1 pm until 5 pm. Fee.*

*Wave Hill, on the shore of the Hudson in Riverdale, is at once a magnificent garden and a sophisticated center of the arts, offering concerts, gallery shows, lectures, classes, a café, and a bookstore in various buildings on its sweeping 26 acres.*

**Van Cortlandt House Museum**. *Van Cortlandt Park, Broadway at West 246th Street. 718-543-3344. www.vancortlandthouse.org. National Register.* Built in 1748 by Frederick Van Cortlandt, this Georgian-style mansion of rough-hewn stone and brick is the oldest surviving private residence in the Bronx. During the American Revolution, General Washington bivouacked on its grounds and lit campfires on a nearby hill to fool the British into believing rebels awaited them while he and his troops moved to Yorktown, Virginia, for the war's final battle. *Open Tuesday through Friday, 10 am until 3 pm; Saturday and Sunday, 11 am until 4 pm. Fee.*

**Wave Hill**. *West 249th Street and Independence Avenue, Riverdale. 718-549-3200. www.wavehill.org. National Register.* This popular 28-acre public garden and cultural center features flower, aquatic, herb, and wild gardens, sweeping lawns, shaded woodlands, and spectacular views of the Hudson and the Palisades. It has an active arts program, with jazz, classical, and cabaret performances in Armor Hall, provocative and inspiring exhibitions of photography, painting, sculpture, and other visual arts in a separate gallery building, a popular family art program, and offerings in photography, writing, gardening, and other subjects, all designed to engage the visitor with nature. Built in 1844 for lawyer William Lewis Morris, the estate has been home (if briefly) to Mark Twain, Theodore Roosevelt, Arturo Toscanini, and others. *Open year-round,*

*Tuesday through Sunday and many holidays, from 9 am to 5:30 pm (closes at 4:30 pm October 15–April 14). Fee.*

## Fairs, Festivals, and Celebrations

New York City is an around-the-clock festival; visit the throngs any day in Times Square or on Main Street, Flushing, to experience the liveliness and fun. The city has many more formal festivals as well (too many to include here), from the Thanksgiving and Caribbean Day Parades to the JVC Jazz Festival. For a complete list, including street fairs, visit www. nycgo.com or www.nyc-arts.com.

**Art Under the Bridge**. *Dumbo Arts Center. 718-694-0831. www.dumboarts center.org.* For two days each September the galleries and performance spaces in the DUMBO (Down Under the Manhattan Bridge Overpass) section of Brooklyn come alive for a celebration of the arts in this arts-friendly waterfront district.

**City of Water Day**. *Metropolitan Waterfront Alliance. 212-935-9831. www.waterwire.net.* Taking place in late July each year, this annual celebration of New York's waterways includes a symbolic convergence of kayaks, fishing boats, ferries, and sailboats on Governors Island, a boat parade, a rally, ecotours, fishing clinics, live music, and lectures on the city's interconnected bays, canals, rivers, estuaries, and salt marshes.

**Historic House Festival**. *212-360-8282. www.historichousetrust.org.* Each year in mid-September, New York City's 22 historic houses—including the Little Red Lighthouse and the Dyckman Farmhouse in Manhattan—open their doors with free public programs and tours. Organized by the Historic House Trust.

**Lincoln Center Festival**. *Lincoln Center. 212-875-5456. www.lincolncenter .org).* Every summer since 1996, Lincoln Center has opened all of its many doors to new types of productions of dance, music, opera, and theater from around the world.

**Metroplitan Opera in the Parks**. *212-362-6000. www.metopera.org.* Each summer, the Metropolitan Opera presents free concert versions of its great productions in various city parks, performing works from its repertoire in the open air, without costumes or sets—drawing huge audiences from throughout the region.

**Mostly Mozart Festival**. *Lincoln Center. 212-875-5456. www.lincolncenter .org.* Another great summer series at Lincoln Center focuses on Mozart and those who have followed in his footsteps, with traditional and experimental performances by famous and emerging musicians.

**Museum Mile**. *Museum Mile Festival Consortium. 212-606-2296. www .museummilefestival.org.* For one evening in early June each year, nine of New York City's greatest museums—all located on Fifth Avenue—remain open late for free, and Fifth Avenue is kept open only to pedestrians, who wander up and down sampling music, food, and the treasures of the Cooper Hewitt/National Design Museum, the Goethe Institute/German Cultural Center, the Solomon R. Guggenheim Museum, the Jewish Museum, the Metropolitan Museum, El Museo del Barrio, the Museum of the City of New York, the National Academy Museum and School of Fine Arts, and the Neue Galerie.

**New York Film Festival**. *Film Society of Lincoln Center. 212-721-6500. www.filmlinc.com.* Founded in 1969, the annual fall film festival in Manhattan screens work by established and emerging filmmakers and celebrates the American and international cinema.

**New York Philharmonic Concerts in the Parks**. *212-875-5656. www .nyphil.org.* Since 1965, the New York Philharmonic (see Lincoln Center, above) has been hosting free summer concerts in parks in all five boroughs, drawing audiences from throughout the region for music-filled picnics under the stars.

**Open House New York**. *555 West 25th Street 10001. 212-991-6470. www .ohny.org.* For one weekend in early October, buildings of architectural merit throughout the five boroughs open their doors to the public in a citywide celebration of the built environment of New York. Free.

**SummerStage**. *City Parks Foundation. 212-360-2756. www.summerstage .org.* This free outdoor performing arts festival has been bringing contemporary, traditional, and emerging musicians and other performing artists from around the world and around the block to Central Park each summer since 1985.

## Visitor Information

**Bronx Council on the Arts**. *1738 Hone Avenue (between Van Nest and Morris Park Avenues), Bronx 10461. 718-931-9500. www.bronxarts.org.* Founded in 1962, this local institution has been a major force in the resurgence of the Bronx arts scene, promoting the work of emerging writers and visual and performing artists and establishing a new gallery, the Longwood Arts Project, and a Writers' Center. The council operates a Culture Trolley that visits museums, galleries, and restaurants on Wednesday evenings, serves as a clearinghouse for arts and culture information for the borough, and works with schools.

**Bronx Tourism Council**. *198 East 161st Street, Bronx 10451. 718-590-3518. www.ilovethebronx.com.* This useful organization provides information on cultural events throughout the Bronx as well as restaurants, nightlife, parks, shopping, and transportation.

**Brooklyn Arts Council and BAC Gallery**. *55 Washington Street. 718-625-0080. www.brooklynartscouncil.org.* Now located in DUMBO (the landmarked Brooklyn neighborhood that is "Down Under the Manhattan Bridge Overpass") this arts service organization has been working since 1966 to support and encourage the arts and artists in Brooklyn. The council sponsors grant programs, professional development seminars, arts in the schools, a folk arts program, a printmaker's project, and an international film festival. The council also hosts thoughtful, regularly changing exhibits at a gallery known as the BAC Gallery in the midst of DUMBO's flourishing gallery scene. *The gallery is open Monday through Friday, 10 am until 5 pm.*

**Brooklyn Tourism and Visitor Center**. *209 Joralemon Street (ground floor), Downtown Brooklyn 11201. 718-802-3846. www.visitbrooklyn.org.* Whether online or at its drop-in office, the center is an excellent place to start for a broader tour of Brooklyn, with maps, transportation information, and advice, lists of museums, galleries, and performing arts centers, and guides to restaurants, cafés, and hotels. *Open Monday through Friday, 10 am until 6 pm.*

**Council on the Arts and Humanities for Staten Island**. *Snug Harbor Cultural Center. 1000 Richmond Terrace (at Snug Harbor), Staten Island 10301. 718-447-3329. www.statenislandarts.org.* Aside from running a helpful booth in the Staten Island Ferry terminal, Staten Island's central source for arts-related information provides grants and technical assistance to artists and art organizations and publishes a bimonthly newsletter for artists and writers.

**Harlem Arts Alliance**. *290 Malcolm X Boulevard (at 125th Street), 2nd floor 10027. 212-410-0030. www.harlemaa.org.* By creating marketing and promotional strategies, providing technical assistance, grants, and grant information, and using fundraising strategies to build new audiences and expand cultural presentation and exhibition opportunities, this nonprofit arts service organization works to nurture the artistic growth and organizational development of artists and arts organizations in Harlem and surrounding communities.

**I Love NY**. *1-800-CALL-NYS. www.iloveny.com.* The official New York State tourism office and Web site provides clear information on cultural events, interesting places to visit at different times of the year, and places to eat and stay not only in New York City but up and down the Hudson Valley.

**John J. Harvey.** *www.fireboat.org.* The restored 1931 fireboat offers public trips in New York Harbor and up the Hudson River to raise awareness of the importance of historic vessels to the city and to promote interest in the waterfront for towns in New York State. The boat became world-famous while aiding in rescue operations after the collapse of the World Trade Center on September 11, 2001.

**Lower Manhattan Cultural Council**. *125 Maiden Lane, 2nd Floor 10038. 212-219-9401. www.lmcc.net.* Founded in 1973, this nonprofit arts organization provides programs and information to artists and art audiences in lower Manhattan and throughout the city, and offers grants, financial advice, and studio space to artists.

**NYC & Company**. *810 Seventh Avenue (between 54th and 53rd Streets), Manhattan 10019. 212-484-1200. www.nycgo.com.* The official tourist Web site for New York City offers extensive and clear information on every aspect of visiting the city including upcoming cultural events, maps, suggested itineraries, and ideas for places to eat, shop, and stay.

**NYC Arts**. *www.nyc-arts.org.* A Web site offering in-depth profiles of every cultural organization in the city and long-term information about programs. This and a companion site—NYCKids Arts—are run by the Alliance for the Arts (www.allianceforarts.org).

**Queens Council on the Arts**. *1 Forest Park at Oak Ridge, Woodhaven 11421. 718-647-3377. www.queenscouncilarts.org.* Founded in 1966, and a comprehensive source of local cultural information, this arts service organization publishes guides, brochures, and maps to the arts scene in Queens, mounts exhibits in various Queens locations, promotes the arts throughout the borough, and provides grants to artists.

**Queens Tourism Center**. *120-55 Queens Boulevard (at 80th Road), Kew Gardens 11424. 718-263-0546. www.discoverqueens.info or www .queensbp.org.* Located in a former subway car outside Borough Hall, this local bureau provides useful information on transportation, restaurants, and arts activities throughout the borough. *Open Monday through Friday, 10 am until 2 pm.*

**www.nyc.gov**. The official New York City government Web site provides links to all of the agencies that make the city run, contact information for places of special interest to visitors, and special announcements about major cultural events.

# HUDSON AND BERGEN COUNTIES, NEW JERSEY

One of the most dramatic stretches of shore on the Hudson—rivaling even those sections of Ulster and Greene Counties that front the Catskills—is the unusual series of reddish, columnar cliffs on the New Jersey side of the river known as the Palisades. Passing through Hudson and Bergen Counties and into Rockland County in New York, this 40-mile upthrust of volcanic rock exposed through erosion—a sort of continuous eyebrow of stone—has been ingrained in the imaginations of Hudson Valley dwellers since long before the Dutch founded New Amsterdam in the 1620s.

The Lenape had a name—Weehawken, which translates roughly into "Land of the Big Cliffs"—for the section of the Palisades across from what is now 42nd Street. From the top of those cliffs, American spies kept secret watch on the English fleet during the American Revolution, and on those same cliffs Aaron Burr mortally wounded Alexander Hamilton in the most famous duel in American history. At once a pleasure ground for wealthy New Yorkers, who built magnificent houses atop them looking back at Manhattan, and the source of the raw stone used to build Manhattan itself, the Palisades were the first of mainland America to be seen by immigrants arriving from Ellis Island and the last glimpsed by soldiers shipping off overseas. The cinematic term "cliffhanger" derives from a type of early suspense film, shot on location near Fort Lee, involving dangerous escapes among the rocks of the Palisades. At the end of the 19th century, the alarming levels of exploitation of this natural feature for stone for building and trees for firewood (a destruction that continues in certain places to this day) led conservationists to push for its protection, and in 1900, as a result of these efforts, the Palisades Interstate Park was born.

Today, this same shore, under rapid development but reconnected to New York City and the rest of the Hudson Valley with improved train and ferry service (as well as by the Lincoln and Holland Tunnels and the George Washington Bridge), draws visitors from both sides of the river to its busy cultural scene. Jazz concerts in Liberty State Park, tours of artists' studios in Jersey City

*Still in operation as a major hub for New Jersey commuter trains, the Beaux Arts Hoboken Terminal was built in 1907.*

and Hoboken, a waterside summer film series, avant-garde dance performances at a cultural center in Teaneck, and a "Cliffhanger" film festival in Fort Lee are just some of what is happening.

The Jersey City Museum and the Liberty Science Center, both reopened after recent renovations, attract visitors almost as much for their unusual buildings as for their thought-provoking exhibitions. A few miles away in Newark, the New Jersey Performing Arts Center, opened in 1997, brings huge audiences across the river and from throughout New Jersey for concerts, operas, plays, and dance performances, while the Newark Museum, opened in 1909, continues to add to its impressive collection of American art (including many paintings by Hudson River School artists and new works by contemporary artists).

Liberty State Park in Jersey City, a 1,122-acre green expanse that opened in 1976 on shorefront property that had been used as a dump, provides perhaps the best view available of the long sweep of the Hudson down past Manhattan into the New York bay—and is the only place in New Jersey to catch the ferry to Ellis Island and the Statue of Liberty (call 877-523-9849 for rates and boat schedules). An increasing number of miles of shoreline, in Liberty State Park, Hoboken, and elsewhere on both sides of the river, have been made accessible to walkers and bicyclists. Passing purely along designated paths, a bicyclist can now easily get from the Battery, in Lower Manhattan, across the George Washington Bridge to the Alpine Picnic Area in the New Jersey section of Palisades Interstate Park without venturing onto a city street.

## BAYONNE

Although the city has long been the sister city of Bayonne, France, its name is thought to have derived from a failed pre–Civil War real estate project on the peninsula, in which a "Bayonia Avenue" connected the New York and Newark bays.

**Bayonne Bridge.** *www.panynj.gov.* One of the most dramatic sights of the lower Hudson—visible from Lower Manhattan and the Brooklyn shore—this graceful steel arch toll bridge connecting Bayonne, New Jersey, with Staten Island over the Kill Van Kull was the longest of its kind in the world when it was completed in 1931, and remains the third longest. It rises 150 feet above the water, and is overseen by the Port Authority of New York and New Jersey.

**Bayonne Historical Society.** *www.bayonnenj.org/historical.* Organized in 1991, the society presents regular programs and organizes exhibits on family genealogy, local landmarks preservation, and local, state, and federal history.

**Chief John T. Brennan Fire Museum.** *10 West 47th Street, Bayonne. National Register. www.bayonnenj.org.* Named for New Jersey's longest-tenured fire chief, this museum is located in Bayonne's first (1875) firehouse and contains vintage firefighting equipment but is closed indefinitely for renovations.

*Visible from throughout New York Harbor, the steel arch Bayonne Bridge, completed in 1931, is the third longest of its kind in the world.*

## HOBOKEN

The city was developed as a resort—and named—in the 1820s by the inventor and entrepreneur John Stevens, who had fought in the American Revolution and was a pioneer in developing steamboats and steam-powered locomotives. Periods of steady immigration in the late 19th and early 20th centuries led to rapid growth; until the advent of containerized shipping, which required more space, Hoboken was a port town.

**DeBaun Center for the Performing Arts**. *Stevens Institute of Technology, Castle Point on Hudson (5th Street between Hudson and River Streets), Hoboken 07030. Box office: 201-216-8937. www.debaun.org.* Professionals, amateurs, and students mount a variety of shows in this 480-seat proscenium theater on the campus of the Stevens Institute of Technology. The theater is located in the historic Edwin A. Stevens Hall, the former main building of the institute, built in 1870 and designed by Richard Upjohn. The view of the river from the institute is one of the most dramatic and sweeping on the lower Hudson. *Fee.*

**Hoboken Historical Museum**. *1301 Hudson Street, Hoboken 07030. 201-656-2240. www.hobokenmuseum.org.* Formed in 1986, the museum works to advance the understanding of Hoboken history, culture, and architecture through collecting, preserving, and interpreting artifacts and oral histories. The museum hosts special events, school and teacher programs, walking and drawing tours, and oral history projects and has regularly changing exhibits on matters of historical interest. *Open Tuesday through Thursday, 2 pm until 9 pm; Friday, 1 pm until 5 pm; and Saturday and Sunday, 12 pm until 5 pm.*

**Hoboken Terminal**. *National Register.* This unusual and beautiful Beaux Arts structure on the waterfront, with its ferry slips facing out toward Manhattan and its luxurious waiting room with Tiffany stained glass, was designed by Kenneth Murchison and built in 1907 for the Delaware, Lackawanna and Western Railroad. It is still in operation as a major hub for New Jersey Transit commuter trains.

**Mile Square Theatre**. *Monroe Center, 720 Monroe Street #E202, Hoboken 07030. 201-208-7809. www.milesquaretheatre.org.* Founded in 2003, this theater company produces new and classic plays at the Monroe Center, puts on an annual festival of 10-minute plays about baseball, and mounts free summer productions in Sinatra Park. *Fee.*

*Howard Pyle's mural of Henry Hudson's arrival off the New Jersey shore is just one of many splendid works of public art in the Beaux Arts Brennan Court House in Jersey City.*

## JERSEY CITY

**Brennan Court House Rotunda Art Gallery and Coffee House**. *583 Newark Avenue, Jersey City 07306. 201-459-2070. www.hudsoncountynj .org and www.visithudson.org. National Register.* The magnificent domed Hudson County Justice William Brennan Court House—an active court-house—contains a lively public art gallery and performance space and is a work of art in itself. Designed by Hugh Roberts, the six-story Beaux Arts building, which opened in 1910, contains a multitude of murals (many depicting historical Hudson River scenes) by some of the greatest American muralists of the early 20th century, including Francis Millet, Howard Pyle, Kenyon Cox, C. Y. Turner, and Edwin Blashfield. Reopening in 1985 following extensive renovations after being closed for nearly 20 years, the courthouse created a gallery under the rotunda and inaugurated a series of Coffee House concerts (www.brennancoffeehouse. com) featuring folk and acoustic performers. *Concerts start at 7:30 pm on the third Friday of every month; the gallery is open Monday through Friday, 9 am until 5 pm.*

**Hudson and Manhattan Powerhouse**. *Bounded by Bay, Washington, First, and Greene Streets, Jersey City. www.jclandmarks.org. National Register.* Completed in 1908, this nine-story Romanesque Revival power plant provided power for the Hudson and Manhattan Railroad, the precursor to the PATH train. It became the center of local preservation efforts led by the Jersey City Landmarks Conservancy in the 1990s—efforts that led to the creation of the Powerhouse Arts District in downtown Jersey City.

**Jersey City Museum**. *350 Montgomery Street (corner of Monmouth Street), Jersey City 07302. 201.413.0303. www.jerseycitymuseum.org.* Reopened in 2001 in a 30,000-square-foot restored 1920s industrial

*The Central Railroad of New Jersey Terminal in Liberty State Park, where from 1892 until 1954 immigrants just arrived from Ellis Island boarded trains for new lives throughout the United States, is now the embarkation point for ferries to the Statue of Liberty and Ellis Island.*

building, this important repository of regional art and artifacts has also become one of the leading presenters of contemporary art in the region. Its permanent collection features American art from New Jersey from the colonial period to the present, with works in nearly all media including painting, sculpture, decorative arts, photography, works on paper, furniture, metals, textiles, maps, and industrial objects. The museum places particular emphasis on exhibiting and supporting the work of contemporary artists as well as on continuing to preserve and make accessible significant regional art and historical and industrial objects. *Open Wednesday through Friday, 11 am until 5pm, and Saturday and Sunday, 12 pm until 5 pm. During fall, winter, and spring, open until 8 pm on Thursdays. Fee.*

**Liberty Science Center**. *Liberty State Park, 222 Jersey City Boulevard, Jersey City 07305. 201-200-1000. www.lsc.org.* Reopened in 2007 after extensive renovations, this 295,000-square-foot science center sees itself as "not just a science center, but as a globally minded science resource." With the latest 3D and digital and sound technology in its theaters, six new exhibition areas, live science demonstrations, and numerous events and programs, the center has a goal of "positively influencing communities and society to take action to improve our world." *Open Monday through Friday, 9 am until 5 pm, and Saturday and Sunday, 9 am until 6 pm. Closed Thanksgiving and Christmas. Fee.*

**Liberty State Park**. *1 Audrey Zapp Drive, Jersey City 07305. 201-915-3440. www.state.nj.us/dep/parksandforests/parks*. Opened on Flag Day, June 14, 1976, on former railroad land that had been used as a dump, this 1,122-acre park overlooking Manhattan, the Statue of Liberty, and Ellis Island is Jersey City's flagship park and at the center of its reborn waterfront. The park contains the historic Central Railroad of New Jersey Terminal (National Register) where, from 1892 through 1954, immigrants freshly arrived from Ellis Island boarded trains for new lives throughout the United States. The renovated terminal is now the embarkation point—the only one in New Jersey—for ferry service to Ellis Island and the Statue of Liberty (call 877-523-9849 for rates and boat schedules). Numerous free concerts and events take place in the park during the summer; naturalists and historians conduct interpretive programs in an education center designed by Robert Graves; and numerous species of birds inhabit a 36-acre tidal salt marsh. The park also contains a marina. *Open daily, 6 am until 10 pm.*

**West Side Theater**. *285 West Side Avenue (on the campus of New Jersey City University), Jersey City 07305. 201-200-2390. www.ascnj.org.* Based at this university theater, the professional Actors Shakespeare Company produces Elizabethan and contemporary plays, develops new work, hosts readings, sponsors internships, and visits local schools. Founded in 2000, the company attempts to re-create an authentic Elizabethan performance atmosphere, with special lighting, costumes, and pre-performance festivities including professional Shakespearean insults, swordplay demonstrations, and songs and dances. *Fee.*

## NEWARK

**New Jersey Performing Arts Center**. *1 Center Street, Newark 07102. 888-466-5722. www.njpac.org.* The home of the New Jersey Symphony Orchestra, the center opened in 1997 as one of the most impressive new performing arts centers in the Hudson Valley. The magnificently appointed building boasts a 2,750-seat four-tiered concert hall, a 514-seat theater, and a more intimate cabaret space. Its operating budget makes it the sixth largest performing arts center in the United States. Many famous performers in all disciplines appear here. *Fee.*

**Newark Museum**. *49 Washington Street, Newark 07102. 973-596-6550. www.newarkmuseum.org.* Founded in 1909, and with a great collection of Hudson River School paintings, including major works by Thomas Cole, Frederic Edwin Church, and Albert Bierstadt, this important museum is also home to sizable collections of works of American modernism, geometric abstraction, photography, contemporary art, and new media. It contains significant collections of the art of Africa and Tibet and, in the natural sciences, has among other things a collection of rocks, minerals, and pressed plants, including rare New Jersey species. *Open throughout the year, Wednesday through Friday, 12 pm until 5 pm; October through June, Saturday and Sunday, 10 am until 5 pm; and July through September, Saturday and Sunday, 12 pm until 5 pm. Fee.*

## UNION CITY
**Park Performing Arts Center**. *560 32nd Street, Union City 07087. 201-865-6980. www.parkpac.org.* Built in 1931 by the German congregation of a Catholic parish to house its cultural and educational programs, this 1,400-seat theater was incorporated in 1983 as a private, nonprofit arts center. The theater is home to professional drama, musicals, opera, community theater groups, dance companies, orchestras, jazz and folk musicians, and dancers. *Fee.*

## WEEHAWKEN
**Hamilton Park/Dueling Grounds**. *Hamilton Avenue. 201-319-6061. www.weehawken-nj.us.* Named for Alexander Hamilton, the former Treasury secretary mortally wounded by Vice President Aaron Burr in a duel on July 11, 1804, this park along the ridge of the palisades across from midtown Manhattan provides sweeping views up and down the river and directly onto 42nd Street. At the south end of the park, just above the infamous dueling grounds (now covered by train tracks), are memorials to Hamilton and Burr. At least eighteen previous duels took place on this spot, including one in 1801 in which Hamilton's son Philip was killed.

# BERGEN COUNTY

## ALPINE
**Kearney House**. *Alpine Boat Basin and Picnic Area, Alpine Approach Road (Exit 2 of the Palisades Interstate Parkway), Alpine. www.njpalisades.org. National Register.* Dating from 1761 and acquired by the Palisades Interstate Park in 1907, this former homestead and tavern at the foot of the Palisades is the oldest building in the New Jersey section of the park. Three period rooms illustrate family and tavern life along the river during the 18th and 19th centuries. *Open May through October, weekends, holidays, or by appointment, 12 pm until 5 pm.*

**Palisades Interstate Park**. *Alpine, New Jersey 07620. 201-768-1360. www.njpalisades.org. National Register.* The 12-mile-long, 2,500-acre New Jersey section of the Palisades Interstate Park is the first land that the Palisades Interstate Park Commission acquired after its creation in

*One of several dramatic viewpoints along the Palisades Interstate Parkway, the Rockefeller Lookout provides a panorama of the Hudson River from the Empire State Building to Yonkers.*

1900. Now, more than 100 years after visionary planners set the land aside to protect it from quarrying, the park has begun to resume its historical wildness. Vines flowing from oaks and tulip trees along rocky, inaccessible cliffs provide a glimpse of the scene that must have greeted Henry Hudson when he sailed past with his crew. A woodsy drive at the base of the cliffs (accessible from exits 1 and 2 of the Palisades Interstate Parkway) allows a quick taste of the place, but far better is to park at one of the picnic areas and venture onto one of the 30 miles of trails that pass along the water (Shore Path) or the top of the cliffs (Long Path). The Palisades Interstate Park Commission and the New York–New Jersey Trail Conference (see Resources, below) provide detailed maps and information on the sometimes dangerous routes. Be prepared!

## DEMAREST

**Old Church Cultural Center School of Art**. *561 Piermont Road, Demarest 07627. 201-767-7160. www.tasoc.org*. This nonprofit, nonsectarian gallery and art school was founded in 1974 in an abandoned 19th-century church. Providing a forum for artists and the art school students, the gallery exhibits established and emerging artists annually. The center offers classes and workshops in schools.

## ENGLEWOOD

**Bergen Performing Arts Center**. *30 North Van Brunt Street, Englewood 07631. 201-227-1030. www.bergenpac.org. National Register.* Located in the former John Harms Center, which opened in 1926 as a movie theater and vaudeville house and was for many years one of the leading theaters in northern New Jersey, this multimedia performing arts center, known for its fine acoustics reopened in 2003 and hosts concerts, dance performances, and plays. *Fee.*

## FAIR LAWN

**Garretson Farm**. *4-02 River Road, Fair Lawn, 07410. 201-797-1775. www.garretsonfarm.org. National Register.* Dating from 1720, and operated by the Garretson Forge and Restoration, this historic sandstone farmhouse features a restored colonial kitchen, a museum, and gardens with heirloom herbs and vegetables. *Open Sunday, 1 pm until 4 pm.*

## FORT LEE

**Fort Lee Historic Park**. *Hudson Terrace, Fort Lee 07024. 201-461-1776. www.njpalisades.org.* At this 33-acre historic site at the top of the Palisades, reproduction gun batteries and firing steps and reconstructed 18th-century huts provide a glimpse of life in a Revolutionary War stronghold in the days before the English overwhelmed it and forced a hasty American retreat. At the visitor center, displays tell the story of Washington's evacuation and his "retreat to victory" across New Jersey in 1776. An auditorium is the scene of cultural events throughout the year, such as the Fort Lee "Cliffhanger" film festival.

Few people realize that the American film industry emerged not in Hollywood but in Fort Lee, New Jersey, with the formation of several local studios into Universal Studios in 1912. Films shot before that in Fort Lee—often making use of the Palisades to suggest dramatic landscapes elsewhere—include the Edison film *Rescued from an Eagle's Nest* (1907), *Hiawatha* (1908), and the D. W. Griffith films *The Lonely Villa* (1909) and *The Battle* (1911). With a mission to preserve this legacy of Fort Lee as the birthplace of the American film industry, the Fort Lee Film Commission (201-592-3663; www.fortleefilm.org) occasionally organizes a summer outdoor film festival and a fall "Cliffhanger" festival of films made on the Palisades and in studios in Fort Lee. *The Fort Lee Historic Park is open Wednesday through Sunday, 10 am until 5 pm.*

**Fort Lee Museum/Fort Lee Historical Society**. *1588 Palisade Avenue (adjacent to Monument Park), Fort Lee 07024. 201-592-3580. www.fortleenj .org.* Located in the Judge Moore House, a 1922 mansion of Palisades blue stone on the site of the American army's encampment during the American Revolution, the museum displays photos, objects, documents, and films from the historical society's archives. *Open Saturday and Sunday, 12 pm until 4 pm, and other times by appointment.*

## HACKENSACK

**Bergen County Academies**. *200 Hackensack Avenue, Hackensack 07601. 201-343-6000. http://bcts.bergen.org.* The Academy of Visual and Performing Arts—one of several separate schools at this elite public high school—presents three major productions annually in its 1,192-seat auditorium, one of the more popular performance spaces in northern New Jersey. Many other groups perform here as well.

**Hackensack Cultural Arts Center**. *39 Broadway, Hackensack 07601. 201-646-8042. www.hackensack.org. National Register.* Operated by the Hackensack Recreation and Cultural Department, this former church and library reopened in 2001 with a new lighting and sound system and has produced a range of readings, plays, concerts, dance recitals, historical reenactments, and other performances. The center produces regular comedy nights and an annual children's show and is a regular stopping place for Hudson Shakespeare (see Visitor Information, below). *Fee.*

## LYNDHURST

**New Jersey Meadowlands Environmental Center**. *2 DeKorte Park Plaza, Lyndhurst 07071. 201-460-8300. www.meadowlands.state.nj.us.* At its headquarters here, the New Jersey Meadowlands Commission provides maps and guides to the Hackensack Meadowlands and oversees school programs, family events, trails, and photo blinds.

## MAHWAH

**Ramapo College of New Jersey, Berrie Center for Performing & Visual Arts**. *505 Ramapo Valley Road, Mahwah 07430. 201-684-7844. www.ramapo.edu/berriecenter.* This 1999 postmodern arts center contains a 350-seat proscenium theater, a 100-seat blackbox theater, and art galleries specializing in contemporary art and the art of the Americas and the Caribbean. *The galleries, which mount shows by international, student, faculty, and community artists, are open Tuesday, Thursday, and Friday, 1 pm until 5 pm, and Wednesday, 1 pm until 7 pm; the box office, Monday through Friday, 12 pm until 8 pm; Saturday and Sunday, 12 pm until 5 pm; and two hours before performances. Fee.*

## NEW MILFORD

**Art Center of Northern New Jersey**. *250 Center Street, New Milford 07646. 201-599-2992. www.artcenter-nnj.org.* Opened in 1956, this busy art center provides classes for adults, teens, and children, hosts regular juried exhibitions, and conducts gallery and museum tours in New York and New Jersey.

## RIVER EDGE

**New Bridge Landing/Bergen County Historical Society**. *1201-1209 Main Street, River Edge 07661. www.bergencounty history.org. National Register.* Located at the narrows of the Hackensack River, this important collection of historic Dutch sandstone buildings includes the Steuben House (201-487-1739), a State Historic Site; the Campbell-Christie House (201-343-9492), a County Historic Site; and the Demarest House. Also at the site are a late-19th-century swing bridge, a mid-19th-century barn, and a replica of a 1770 detached kitchen. The New Bridge was strategically significant to both the English and the Americans during the American Revolution, enabling troops to pass quickly across the Hackensack River. General Washington stayed often in the large Dutch Colonial house at the landing near the bridge, which was later given to one of his generals, Friedrich Wilhelm von Steuben, the highly regarded Prussian officer who volunteered for the war and trained the troops at Valley Forge. The Bergen County Historical Society was founded in 1902 and is located in the Campbell-Christie House, which is open the second Sunday of the month.

## RUTHERFORD

**William Carlos Williams Center for the Performing Arts**. *One Williams Plaza, Rutherford 07070. 201-939-2323. www.williamscenter.org. National Register.* Rebuilt, reopened, and renamed in 1978 after a devastating fire, this former vaudeville and silent movie house contains two theaters, two movie theaters, a concert hall, and a fine arts gallery. It is named for the modernist poet who pioneered new forms in free verse and lived in Rutherford. It houses a number of independent theater companies and other groups. *Fee.*

## TEANECK

**Fairleigh Dickinson University**. *1000 River Road, Teaneck 07666.* The College Art Gallery (201-692-2801; www.fdu.edu) hosts regular art exhibits, open Monday through Friday, 9:30 am until 4:30 pm. Operating in the Becton Theatre, the Garage Theatre Group (201-569-7710; www.garage theatre.org) was founded in 1993 and develops and produces new and classic plays.

**Puffin Cultural Forum**. *20 East Oakdene Avenue, Teaneck 07666. 201-836-8923. www.puffinfoundation.org.* This gallery and performance space is located at the site of the administrative offices of the Puffin Foundation, which provides grants to artists and art organizations outside the mainstream. Through art exhibits, music, dance, theater, author interviews, workshops, film series, lectures, and dialogues, the foundation strives to present work that is thoughtful, socially relevant, and provocative.

## TENAFLY

**African Art Museum of the SMA Fathers**. *23 Bliss Avenue, Tenafly 07670. 201-894-8611. www.smafathers.org.* One of only a few in the United States devoted solely to sub-Saharan sculpture and painting, costumes, textiles, decorative arts, religion, and folklore, the museum is run by the Society of African Missions, a community of Catholic missionaries devoted to the people and culture of Africa.

**Jewish Community Center on the Palisades**. *411 East Clinton Avenue, Tenafly 07670. 201-569-7900 x 433. www.jccotp.org.* With schools of music and the performing arts, the JCC on the Palisades also hosts art exhibits by artists from New Jersey as well as around the country and world.

## *Fairs, Festivals, and Celebrations*

**Bergen County Art in the Park Show**. *Van Saun County Park, Paramus. 201-336-7292. http://co.bergen.nj.us.* The annual show and concert takes place during the third weekend in September, 11 am until 4 pm.

**Bergen County Cabbage Night Family Festival**. *Van Saun County Park, Paramus. 201-336-7292. http://co.bergen.nj.us.* The pre-Halloween event takes place from 1 pm until 4 pm on the last weekend in October.

**Bergen Music & Art Festival**. *Paramus Bergen Mall Shopping Center. Route 4 East, Paramus 07652. 201-291-8848. www.thebergenmuseum.com.* Presented by the Bergen Museum of Art & Science in early September each year.

**Hoboken Arts and Music Festival**. *201-420-2207. www.hobokennj.org.* Taking place in early May and late September each year since 1994, this two-season festival on Washington Street provides a showcase for fine artists, craftspeople, entertainers, musicians, and cooks and draws a range of visitors from families to art collectors.

**Hoboken Artists' Studio Tour**. *Hoboken City Hall, 94 Washington Street, Hoboken 07030. 201-420-2207. www.hobokennj.org.* First started in 1981, the tour features working out-of-town as well as local artists. A tour guide and map to the galleries and studios is printed by the *Hudson Reporter* and available a week in advance or can be picked up on the day of the tour at City Hall.

**Jersey City Artist Studio Tour**. *344 Grove St, PMB 190, Jersey City, NJ 07302. 201-736-7057. www.proartsjerseycity.org.* Since 1991 this two-day event produced through a partnership of Pro Arts Jersey City and the Jersey City Division of Cultural Affairs has exhibited the work of nearly 500 Jersey City artists. A tour guide to the many different studios of Jersey City artists is printed by the *Hudson Reporter* and can be purchased a week in advance or picked up for free at the Grove Street PATH station, City Hall, or Journal Square during the tour weekend. Visitors can either walk or use the bus route on the map.

**Movies Under the Stars**. *Pier A Park, First Street and Frank Sinatra Drive, Hoboken. 201-420-2207. www.hobokennj.org.* Produced by the Hoboken Division of Cultural Affairs, this 12-week series of free contemporary animated and documentary films takes place on the edge of the river at dusk, with views of the Hudson River and the Manhattan skyline. Bring a blanket or a lawn chair (with a low back so others can see).

**The R&B and Jazz Festival**. *Liberty State Park.* During a weekend in mid-September, jazz and soul stars perform under the sun and stars, overlooking the harbor and the Manhattan skyline.

**Shakespeare in the Parks**. *Hudson Shakespeare Company. 973-449-7443. www.hudsonshakespeare.org.* Since 1992 Hudson Shakespeare Company has produced free summer performances of Shakespeare in New Jersey parks and has recently expanded to other states and other classical playwrights.

**Summer Concerts on the Hudson**. *Lincoln Harbor Park, Weehawken. 201-716-4540. www.hrpac.org.* Featuring great performers in pop, jazz, blues, and rock, this series of free summer concerts is sponsored by the Hudson Riverfront Performing Arts Center, a nonprofit organization whose mission it is to build a regional performing arts center on the waterfront in Weehawken. All concerts start at 7 pm; bring a blanket or lawn chair.

## Visitor Information

**Bergen County Division of Cultural and Historic Affairs**. *201-336-7274. www.co.bergen.nj.us/Parks.*

**Hackensack Riverkeeper**. *Hackensack 07601. (201) 968-0808. www .hackensackriverkeeper.org.* Founded in 1997, this organization works to protect the Hackensack River and the Meadowlands after centuries of pollution and neglect, to combat further causes of pollution, and to bring this vast, beautiful, and fragile ecosystem to the attention of the public through a popular series of ecoprograms, a newsletter, river cleanups, riparian restorations, and a Watershed Watch Hotline (1-877-CPT-BILL).

**Hoboken Division of Cultural Affairs**. *City Hall, Hoboken 07030. 201-420-2207. www.hobokennj.org.*

**Hudson County Office of Cultural and Heritage Affairs**. *201-459-2070. www.hudsoncountynj.org/dept/tourism.* Located in the landmark Brennan Courthouse, this busy office is the center for all things cultural in Hudson County, providing brochures, maps, and a Web site on cultural organizations and events throughout the county and running a gallery and coffeehouse series in the courthouse rotunda.

**Jersey City Landmarks Conservancy**. *www.jclandmarks.org.* Founded in 1999, this volunteer organization conducts a wide range of activities to preserve, promote, and protect Jersey City's historic resources, including providing walking and bus tours, advocating at the state and local levels for the preservation of landmarks, and working with neighborhood associations, students, artists, churches, and other individuals and organizations. Among its successes have been saving six of Jersey City's historic cobblestone streets and placing the Hudson and Manhattan Powerhouse on the National Register of Historic Places (see Jersey City, above). The conservancy works with the city's planning department to prevent teardowns.

**New York–New Jersey Trail Conference**. *201-512-9348. www.nynjtc. org.* This federation of hiking clubs, environmental organizations, and individuals, with a membership of more than 100,000, is dedicated to building and maintaining marked hiking trails and protecting related open spaces in the two states. Its maps, available online and at many hiking and outdoor stores, are the best available for many of the parks along the lower Hudson River.

**Palisades Interstate Park Commission**. *201-768-1360. www.njpalisades .org.* This bi-state organization was created in 1900 by Theodore Roosevelt, then governor of New York, and Foster M. Voorhees, then governor of New Jersey, to protect the lands along the Palisades from housing development and quarrying. The Commission, whose central headquarters is in Bear Mountain State Park in Rockland County (845-708-7300), currently oversees 110,000 acres and eight historic sites along 20 miles of the Hudson River.

# WESTCHESTER COUNTY

From the long vistas of the Hudson Highlands to the new concrete pier in Yonkers; from the rocky promontory of St. Anthony's Nose at the Bear Mountain Bridge to the sloping lawns of Kykuit near the Tappan Zee, the Hudson passes very different kinds of territory as it flows south through Westchester County. This diversity in the natural landscape seems to correspond to the tremendous cultural variety in this large (433 square miles) county that bridges the gap between New York City and "upstate." It is as if the whole history of the Hudson Valley were contained in miniature along the Westchester shoreline.

Two of the older settlements along the river, Yonkers and Peekskill, dating from the 1640s and 1680s, respectively, have been shedding long industrial pasts and remaking themselves as centers of art and history, Yonkers with, among other things, an extraordinary museum that manages to combine under one roof the architectural, natural, and artistic legacies of the valley yet also a gallery for contemporary and experimental art, and Peekskill with a museum devoted exclusively to contemporary art, not to mention a serious historical museum, an arts district, and a popular theater.

Westchester's county seat is about 10 miles inland from the river at White Plains, where—as for much of the rest of the county—the abiding presence of General George Washington and his army during the American Revolution still lingers in historic houses and the minds of residents. From huge concerts and performances at the Art Deco county center to chamber performances at the Music Conservatory of Westchester, White Plains is a busy place. Stop by the Westchester Arts Council, online or at 31 Mamaroneck Avenue in White Plains, for information on county happenings throughout the year. Created in 1965, it is located in a former bank that now contains exhibition galleries, performance space, and a tourist information center.

One of the best-known and most-visited sites along the river is Philipsburg Manor, a working reconstruction of the 18th-century farming, milling, and trading center originally owned by the Anglo-Dutch merchant family that controlled much of what is

*The whimsical buildings overlooking the Hudson River at Untermyer Park in Yonkers were once part of the estate of the philanthropist Samuel Untermyer.*

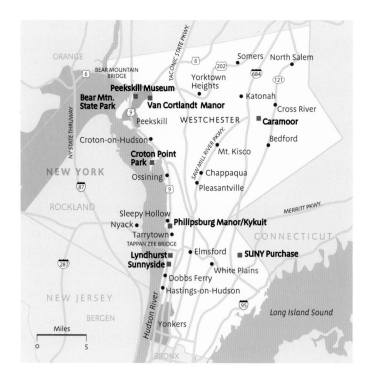

now Westchester. A working gristmill, the 300-year-old manor house, and actors in period costume portraying the daily activities of tenant farmers, slaves, and manorial lords and ladies, provide something of the flavor of life in these parts in much earlier times.

The Westchester shore has its share of grand estates erected in later years as weekend and summer houses for wealthy city dwellers. The Jay Gould house, Lyndhurst, is perhaps the most ornate of these, but the best view—virtually unchanged from what it would have been if Henry Hudson had climbed up to sample it in 1609—is from Kykuit, the Rockefeller house in Pocantico Hills. Both of these houses as well as Van Cortlandt Manor, the Union Church of Pocantico Hills, and Washington Irving's charming cottage Sunnyside are under the jurisdiction of Historic Hudson Valley (see Resource Directory), a nonprofit organization that keeps many of the most important houses along the river in fine condition and open to the public. (Irving, who is buried in Sleepy Hollow Cemetery, is another abiding presence in Westchester County; his memory and that of his characters live on in the names of towns, boat clubs, high schools, and retail establishments.)

Gardens, parks, and natural areas abound in Westchester and include landscapes unchanged since European settlement, historic formal gardens such as those at the John Jay Homestead in Katonah, and sculpture gardens such as the one at PepsiCo headquarters in Purchase, where modern pieces by Alexander Calder, Isamu Noguchi, and others are carefully set among fountains, flower beds, and trees in a landscape designed by Russell Page and others.

## BEDFORD

**Westmoreland Sanctuary**. *260 Chestnut Ridge Road, Bedford Corners. 914-666-8448. www.westmorelandsanctuary.org.* This nature sanctuary was created in 1957. Making use of seven miles of trails and a 200-year-old former church that has been transformed into a nature center, the organization hosts programs for schools and scouting groups during the week and sugarfests, the Amphibian Night Hike, festivals, and other events for the general public throughout the year.

## BUCHANAN

**Indian Point Energy Center**. *Buchanan. www.safesecurevital.org.* Located in the east bank of the Hudson just south of Peekskill, this 2,140-megawatt nuclear power plant has been a source of fear, controversy, and electricity for Hudson Valley residents since it opened in 1974. The plant consists of two nuclear reactors and is one of nine owned and operated by the Entergy Corporation of New Orleans.

## CHAPPAQUA

**Horace Greeley House/New Castle Historical Society**. *100 King Street, Chappaqua 10514. 914-238-4666. www.newcastlehistoricalsociety.org. National Register.* The former country house (1864–72) of the renowned 19th-century newspaper editor is now the headquarters of the New Castle Historical Society, which offers permanent exhibits on the Horace Greeley era and the Quaker heritage and rotating ones from the society's archives of books, photographs, costumes, maps, local diaries, and merchants' records. *Open Tuesday, Wednesday, Thursday, and Saturday, 1 pm until 4 pm, and by appointment. Closed Saturdays in August. Suggested donation.*

**Pruyn Sanctuary Butterfly and Hummingbird Garden**. *275 Millwood Road, Chappaqua. 914-666-6503. www.sawmillriveraudubon.org.* The headquarters of Saw Mill River Audubon, a local chapter of the National Audubon Society, this 92-acre wildlife sanctuary includes a 40-acre wetland and a popular butterfly and hummingbird garden. *Open daily, dawn to dusk. Best butterfly viewing hour is noon on a sunny summer day.*

## CORTLANDT MANOR

**Croton Cortlandt Center for the Arts**. *293B Furnace Dock Road (in Charles J. Cook Memorial Park), Cortlandt Manor 10567. 914-739-4320. www.cccarts.org.* Established in 1989 by a group of local artists and art lovers, the Croton Cortlandt Center for the Arts has grown to become a thriving organization that provides both arts education and exhibition opportunities. The center operates its teaching facilities in a building in Charles Cook Park and organizes art shows at the Manor Gallery in Cortlandt Town Hall, the Hendrick Hudson Library, and in a special installation series called "Art Moves" at the Jefferson Valley Mall. In addition to a public art program that has included a large mural at the Croton-Harmon station served by Amtrak and Metro North, the center is currently working with the town of Cortlandt to establish an art park on Oscawana Island in the Hudson River.

**Oscawana Island Park**. *Furnace Dock Road, off Route 9, Cortlandt Manor. 914-864-7000.* Bird-watchers and botanists have compiled extensive lists of the species in this heavily wooded 161-acre park on the edge of the river, but many just like to come for the classic Hudson Valley views during a stroll at sunset.

## CROSS RIVER

**Ward Pound Ridge Reservation**. *Routes 35 and 121, Cross River. 914-864-7317. www.co.westchester.ny.us/parks.* With its varied inland terrain, Westchester County's largest (4,300 acres) park is home to the Leatherman's Cave, the occasional home of an itinerant peddler, as well as a nature museum and facilities for picnicking, lean-to camping, fishing, and cross-country skiing.

## CROTON-ON-HUDSON

**Croton Point Park**. *Croton Avenue, Croton-on-Hudson. 914-862-5290.* With its popular nature center and protected zones of marshland and woods, this large (508 acres) riverfront park is known for its bird-watching and nature programs but also has a swimming beach and is set up for RV, cabin, and tent camping. *Fee.*

**Van Cortlandt Manor**. *South Riverside Avenue off Route 9, Croton-on-Hudson. 914-271-8981. www.hudsonvalley.org. National Register.* This restored 18th-century working farm, now under the jurisdiction of Historic Hudson Valley (see Resource Directory), demonstrates the domestic life of a prominent patriot family in the years just after the American Revolution. The property includes an 18th-century stone house with period furnishings and traditional gardens, as well as barns and other buildings from various historical periods. An 18th-century tavern located on the property on the Albany Post Road illuminates the history of transportation in the area before the arrival of the railroad. (The Georgian-style Van Cortlandt Mansion, which stands in Van Cortlandt Park in the Bronx, was built in 1748 by Frederick Van Cortlandt.)

## DOBBS FERRY

**Old Croton Aqueduct Trailway**. *15 Walnut Street, Dobbs Ferry 10522. 914-693-4117. www.aqueduct.org. National Register.* One of the most exciting projects in recent years, involving multiple counties and nonprofit organizations as well as New York State and New York City, has been the transformation of the 1842 aqueduct carrying water from the Croton Reservoir in northern Westchester to New York City into a recreational greenway. The northernmost 26 miles, from the Croton Reservoir to Van Cortlandt Park at the Bronx border, has been open since 1968 as New York State's longest and thinnest park (average width is 60 feet). The remaining 15 miles, from Van Cortlandt Park to 42nd Street, passes along city streets and through about 5 miles of city parks. For complete information, maps, and access routes, visit the Friends of the Old Croton Aqueduct at the Web site above or the New York City Parks Department at www.nycgovparks.org.

## ELMSFORD

**Westchester Broadway Theatre**. *1 Broadway Plaza, Elmsford. 914-592-2222. www.broadwaytheatre.com.* This busy Equity theater produces Broadway musicals and presents a popular concert series. *Fee.*

**Westchester County Historical Society**. *2199 Saw Mill River Road, Elmsford 10523. 914-592-4323. www.westchesterhistory.com.* A center for genealogical as well as historical research on Westchester County and New York State since 1874, the society and its extensive library are located in the Westchester County Records and Archives Center. Exhibits, slide shows, seminars, and lectures as well as tours to nearby sites of historical interest help bring topics of historical interest to the people of Westchester.

## HASTINGS-ON-HUDSON

**Jasper F. Cropsey Homestead**. *49 Washington Avenue, Hastings-on-Hudson. 914-478-7990. www.newingtoncropsey.com. National Register.* Ever Rest, the last home of the Hudson River School painter admired by Queen Victoria for the rich reds of his autumn scenes, is maintained by the Newington-Cropsey Foundation much as it might have appeared when Cropsey and his wife lived there. *Open Monday through Friday, 10 am until 1 pm; closed December, January, and August.*

## IRVINGTON-ON-HUDSON

Washington Irving was alive in 1854 when the people of this Hudson River village voted to adopt his name as their own. Among the landmarks on its residential streets are the Armour-Stiner House; an octagon house on West Clinton Avenue that dates from the 1860s and is said to be the only existing eight-sided house in America with colonnades and a dome; and the Villa Lewaro, an Italianate villa on North Broadway that Vertner Tandy, America's first African American registered architect, designed for Madam C. J. Walker, believed to be the first African American millionaire in the United States.

**Scenic Hudson Park at Irvington**. *Bridge Street on the Hudson River, Irvington. 914-591-7736. www.irvingtonny.gov.* The nonprofit landscape preservation organization Scenic Hudson (see Resource Directory) transformed an area of landfill along the Hudson shoreline into a 12-acre riverfront green space of playgrounds, ball fields, and a boat launch. The park, which opened in 2001, has views of the Manhattan skyline, the Palisades, and the Tappan Zee Bridge.

**Town Hall Theater**. *85 Main Street, Irvington 10533. 914-591-6602. www.irvingtontheater.com. National Register.* The restored 1902 community theater, located on the third floor if the Irvington Town Hall, presents concerts and musicals throughout the year.

## KATONAH

With its art museum, its lively galleries and shops, its well-known outdoor music center, and its peaceful houses and horse farms, Katonah and the surrounding areas of Bedford, Chappaqua, Goldens Bridge, and North Salem have long typified the elegant semirural character of northern Westchester.

The Beatrice Coleman Hall

**Caramoor Center for Music and the Arts**. *149 Girdle Ridge Road, Katonah. 914-232-5035. www .caramoor.com.* Since 1946 many of the world's leading chamber music ensembles, orchestras, and solo musicians have performed at this Mediterranean villa in Katonah. The annual International

*In its sculpture garden and in its 1990 building by the modernist architect Edward Larrabee Barnes, the non-collecting Katonah Museum of Art installs (and occasionally commissions) six exhibits a year.*

Music Festival is one of the highlights of the summer music scene in New York State. Once the home of music patrons Walter and Lucie Rosen, Caramoor features formal gardens and a sizable collection of art—from Urbino maiolica to Eastern tapestries to an extensive collection of jade. *Fee.*

**John Jay Homestead**. *400 Jay Street, Katonah 10536. 914-232-5651. www.johnjayhomestead.org. National Register.* With its historic furniture, paintings, and outbuildings, the former home and farm of the founding father and first chief justice of the Supreme Court has been preserved to look much as it did when Jay lived there from 1801 until his death in 1829. The house and its 62 acres are managed by the New York State Office of Parks, Recreation and Historic Preservation with the help of the nonprofit Friends of John Jay Homestead. *Open for hourly tours April through November. Fee.*

**Katonah Museum of Art**. *134 Jay Street—Route 22, Katonah. 914-232-9555. www.katonahmuseum.org.* Located in a 1990 building designed by the modernist architect Edward Larrabee Barnes, this noncollecting institution sponsors six exhibitions a year in its galleries and commissions and installs work in its sculpture garden. With a mission to present the "best of art" from the past to the present, spanning the spectrum of cultures, media, historical periods, and social issues, the museum also offers a range of education and art-appreciation programs. *Fee.*

## NORTH SALEM
**Hammond Museum and Japanese Stroll Garden**. *28 Deveau Road, North Salem. 914-669-5033. www.hammondmuseum.org.* Founded in 1957, this hilltop museum and garden hosts art exhibits and programs that foster intercultural understanding through art and nature. The 3.5-acre garden is based on traditional Japanese design and includes Buddhist sculptures, artful bridges, and a goldfish pond and sand garden. The museum offers art classes, musical performances, and an annual Moon Viewing Festival in August. *Open April through November. Fee.*

## OSSINING
Yes, the Metro North station faces the 1828 prison once spoken of with awe and fear as "Sing Sing," but the town has a gentle elegance, with tree-lined streets and handsome architecture.

**Blueberry Pond Arts Center**. *235 Cedar Lane, Ossining 10562. 914-923-3530. www.blueberrypond.org.* This professional company with its own theater is devoted solely to producing original works written and developed through an ensemble process involving a collaboration of writers, actors, and directors.

**Sing Sing Prison Museum**. *Caputo Community Center, 95 Broadway, Ossining. 914-941-3189. Open Monday through Friday, 9 am until 9 pm, and Saturday, 8:30 am until 9 pm.*

**Teatown Lake Reservation**. *1600 Spring Valley Road, Ossining 10562. 914-762-2912. www.teatown.org.* The 834-acre nature preserve and education center was created in 1963 on property that had belonged to Gerard Swope Jr., a former chairman of General Electric. Its 15 miles of trails through diverse Hudson Highland habitats are open year-round; there is also a Wildflower Island (visited by tour) on the lake and a nature center (Tues–Sun, 9–5). The name "Teatown" derives from a Revolutionary-era skirmish between local ladies and a would-be tea profiteer.

## PEEKSKILL

With one of the best city views on the Hudson, looking north across a great bay to the narrows where the Bear Mountain Bridge crosses the river at Anthony's Nose, Peekskill has been an important stop for travelers since Jan Peeck established a trading post there in the late 1600s. Caught up in the American Revolution during the 18th century and the industrial one during the 19th, the city suffered declines in the second half of the 20th century but has worked to reinvent itself as a center of the arts and new technologies. A downtown arts district mixes artists' studios with galleries, antiques stores, a bookstore, and restaurants, and a walking trail connects parks along Peekskill Bay including China Pier, Riverfront Green, and the new Peekskill Landing. The annual Peekskill Celebration brings music and fun to the city and riverfront each August.

**Blue Mountain Reservation**. *Welcher Avenue, off Route 9A. 914-862-5275, 914-737-2194. http://co.westchester.ny.us/parks/.* The 1,538-acre heavily wooded park has 15 miles of hiking trails, playgrounds, picnic tables, and a lodge that groups can rent during the off-season. The hikes up Mount Spitzenberg and Blue Mountain are favorite local challenges.

**China Pier, Charles Point**. Originally used by Fleischmann's to unload raw materials for its yeast and gin factory here, this dock, with its romantic view across Peekskill Bay to Bear Mountain and the Bear Mountain Bridge, is a favorite local picnic spot. It is the epicenter for the annual Peekskill Celebration (see Fairs and Festivals, below).

**Hudson Valley Center for Contemporary Art**. *1701 Main Street, Peekskill 10566. 914-788-0100. www.hvcca.com.* Founded in 2004, the center operates a 12,000-square-foot gallery devoted to contemporary art and sponsors an annual citywide exhibition of site-specific art around Peekskill.

*The downtown arts district in Peekskill mixes artists' studios with galleries, antiques stores, a theater, a historical museum, a bookstore and restaurants, and a local arts council hosts open studio events and arts festivals.*

*Open on Saturdays and Sundays, 12 pm until 6 pm, and by appointment. Tours available by request. Fee.*

**Paramount Center for the Arts**. *1008 Brown Street, Peekskill. 914-739-2333. www.paramountcenter.org.* Housed in a former movie theater built in 1930, this year-round multidisciplinary center for the arts shows classic and independent films and presents live musicals, plays, arts-in-education programs, and visual art exhibitions. *Fee.*

**Peekskill Landing**. *www.ci.peekskill.ny.us.* This four-acre park reclaiming an industrial site along the river is currently in the planning stages.

**Peekskill Museum**. *124 Union Avenue, Peekskill. 914-736-0473. www .peekskillmuseum.org.* American Revolution and Civil War furnishings and artifacts—including a cannon used to fire out into the Hudson in an attempt to stop the British spy Major John André from escaping down the river with the plans to West Point—are on display in the Victorian Herrick House, completed in 1877 according to a design by William R. Mead of McKim, Mead & Bigelow. *Open Saturdays, 1 pm until 4 pm from June through December, and by appointment. Fee.*

**Riverfront Green**. *Just off Route 9, adjacent to the Metro North Railroad Station. 914-734-PARK. www.ci.peekskill.ny.us.* This popular park near the train station offers excellent views of the river and up to the Hudson Highlands.

## PLEASANTVILLE

**Jacob Burns Film Center**. *364 Manville Road, Pleasantville. 914-747-5555. www.burnsfilmcenter.org.* Housed in a historic Spanish-style cinema built in 1925, the center shows rare, classic, and educational films and offers classes for children and occasional talks by directors, critics, and actors. *Fee.*

**Newman Theatre**. *600 Bear Ridge Road (near Route 120), Pleasantville 10570. 914-741-0333. www.rosenthaljcc.org.* Part of the Richard G. Rosenthal Jewish Community Center of northern Westchester, the theater produces three or four productions a year of classic and contemporary American plays. *Fee.*

## POCANTICO HILLS

Long associated with the Rockefeller family, this hamlet northeast of Sleepy Hollow takes its name from the stream that flows through it to the Hudson, called in the native Wecquaesgeek "pocantico" or "running between two hills."

**Kykuit**. *Tarrytown. 914-631-3992. www.hudsonvalley.org. National Register.* This grand yet subdued house on top of a hill with sweeping views of the Hudson River was the country house of the Rockefeller family for three generations. Now under the jurisdiction of Historic Hudson Valley (see Resource Directory), the house was built in 1913 by John D. Rockefeller Sr. and renovated over the years by his son and grandson John D. Rockefeller Jr. and Governor Nelson Rockefeller, who made it a veritable museum of modernist paintings and sculpture by Isamu Noguchi, Alexander Calder, and others. The view northwest across the river is virtually unchanged from what it would have been when Henry Hudson first sailed past in 1609. *Open May through October. Tours depart from the visitor center at Philipsburg Manor. For schedules call 914-631-8200, Monday through Friday, or 914-631-3992 on weekends. Fee.*

**Rockefeller Preserve**. *Route 117, Pocantico Hills. 914-631-1470. www.nysparks.state.ny.us.* The Rockefeller family started donating the land for this 1,233-acre park to New York

*Marino Marini's Horse, 1951, is part of the great collection of modernist works at Kykuit, the Rockefeller house in Pocantico Hills.*

State in 1983. Especially geared for horses but also enjoyed by runners, bicyclists, fishermen, and nature photographers, the park is intersected by miles of carriage roads with dramatic river views. Among visitors' favorite destinations are a triple-arch bridge, said to be the first of its kind in the United States, and the foundations of Rockwood, a former Rockefeller family house whose grounds were landscaped by Frederick Law Olmsted. *Fee.*

**Union Church of Pocantico Hills**. *555 Bedford Road, Pocantico Hills. 914-332-6659. www.hudsonvalley.org. National Register.* Completed in 1922 on land donated by John D. Rockefeller Sr., this simple, nonde-nominational stone church near Kykuit is both a working church and a tribute to two great 20th-century artists. Henri Matisse's rose window was installed in 1956 in honor of Abby Aldrich Rockefeller, a founder of the Museum of Modern Art. At the instigation of David Rockefeller, the family commissioned nine other stained-glass windows depicting bibli-cal scenes by Marc Chagall, which were dedicated between 1964 and 1966. *Part of Historic Hudson Valley (see Resource Directory), the church is open when church services or activities are not in progress from April to December, 11am until 5 pm weekdays except Tuesday; 10 am until 5 pm Saturdays and 2 pm until 5 pm Sundays. Fee.*

## PURCHASE

**Kendall Sculpture Gardens at PepsiCo**. *700 Anderson Hill Road, Purchase. 914-253-2001. www.hudsonrivervalley.com.* Edward Durrell Stone designed the PepsiCo world headquarters here, completed in 1970. Russell Page, along with François Goffinet and E. D. Stone Jr. (the architect's son), designed the company's world-famous 168-acre sculpture garden. Set among courtyards, trees, ponds, fountains, and flower beds, the collection ranges from monumental pieces by Alexander Calder, Isamu Noguchi, George Segal, and David Smith to smaller works by Henri Lauren, Seymour Lipton, and Henry Moore. *Open to the public without charge 7 am until 7 pm from April through October and 7 am until 4:30 pm November through March.*

**SUNY Purchase**. *735 Anderson Hill Road, Purchase 10577. www.purchase .edu.* Founded by Governor Nelson Rockefeller in 1967 as the cultural centerpiece of the State University of New York, this relatively young teaching institution is recognized around the world for its conserva-tory programs in dance, music, theater, and film and its School of Art+Design.

**Neuberger Museum of Art**. *914-251-6100; www.neuberger.org.* This well-regarded teaching museum at SUNY Purchase offers a wide range of works from ancient to contemporary. The permanent collection contains more than 7,000 paintings, drawings, prints, photographs, sculptures, installations, and videos and embraces 20th-century American and European art, traditional and contemporary African art, and a growing collection of contemporary art from throughout the world. *Fee.*

**Performing Arts Center**. *914-251-6200; www.artscenter.org.* With its four theaters—the Concert Hall, Recital Hall, PepsiCo Theatre, and Abbot Kaplan Theatre—the performing art center at SUNY Purchase presents more than 600 events a year, including chamber and orchestral music performances, dance recitals, and theater engagements by performers from New York City and around the world. Extended residencies with artists such as Philip Glass and the Paul Taylor Dance Company expose audiences to the very best while encouraging the creation of new work. *Fee.*

## SLEEPY HOLLOW

The name "Sleepy Hollow" is thought to derive from a Dutch word, *slapershaven*, or "sleeper's haven," that one of the first settlers of New Amsterdam, Adrian Van der Donck, applied to the narrow depression in the hills along the Pocantico River. Washington Irving, who visited the same river in the 1790s, later brought his own version of the name to much wider recognition when he applied it to the village in his 1820 story "The Legend of Sleepy Hollow." Called North Tarrytown through most of the 20th century, the village formally changed its name in 1996 to honor Irving's legacy.

**Hudson Valley Writers' Center**. *300 Riverside Drive (between Palmer and Kelbourne Avenues), Sleepy Hollow 10591. 914-332-5953. www.writers center.org. National Register.* Housed in the former Philipse Manor train depot since 1996, the nonprofit Hudson Valley Writers' Center hosts readings, classes, and workshops. The center is also the parent of the Slapering Hol Press (the name is a corruption of the Dutch—see Sleepy Hollow above), a small independent publishing imprint. *Fee.*

**Lighthouse at Sleepy Hollow and Kingsland Point Park**. *Palmer Avenue, Sleepy Hollow. 914-366-5109. National Register.* From its completion in 1883 until its deactivation in 1961, this sturdy lighthouse warned ships away from shoals along the eastern shore of the river around Kingsland Point. It is the only lighthouse on the Hudson River built on top of a caisson, or cast-iron cylinder sunk into the mud at the river's bottom. The completion of the Tappan Zee Bridge in 1955 rendered it obsolete but a public outcry saved it from demolition and in 1983 Westchester County reopened it as a public monument. Tours are given on selected weekends and by appointment; access is through Kingsland Point park, an 18-acre riverfront recreation area with ball fields, picnic areas, and a kayak launch.

**Old Dutch Church of Sleepy Hollow**. *42 North Broadway, Tarrytown. 914-631-1123. www.olddutchburyingground.org. National Register.* The original bell, cast in the Netherlands, still hangs in the belfry of this small Dutch Reformed house of worship constructed around 1685 and largely unchanged since then. One of the oldest operating churches in New York State, it is now used mainly at Easter and Christmas and for weddings; the congregation has moved regular services to the "new" church, built in 1837 at Central Avenue and North Broadway in Tarrytown. It is the old church, however, and its three-acre burying ground that figure in Washington Irving's "The Legend of Sleepy Hollow."

**Philipsburg Manor**. *381 North Broadway, Sleepy Hollow. 914-631-3992. www.hudsonvalley.org. National Register.* Part of the Historic Hudson Valley network, this milling, farming, and trading complex with well-preserved commercial buildings was originally settled with a land grant from William and Mary in 1693. Today, interpreters in period costume guide the visitor through a large stone house with 17th-century furnishings; a series of historical gardens; a working, water-powered gristmill; and fields and pens of historic breeds of cattle, sheep, and chickens. *Open March weekends, 10 am until 4 pm, last tour at 3 pm; April through October, daily (closed Tuesday), 10 am until 5 pm, last tour at 4 pm; November through December, daily 10 am until 4 pm, last tour at 3 pm. Fee.*

**Sleepy Hollow Cemetery**. *540 North Broadway, Sleepy Hollow 10591. 914-631-0081. www.sleepyhollowcemetery.org.* Looking out over the Old Dutch Church (see above) but administered by its own separate organiza-

*The partially restored and partially re-created farm, mill, and trading complex at Philipsburg Manor dramatize 17th-century Hudson Valley life for visitors of all ages.*

tion, this 90-acre burying ground with its ancient headstones and large old trees is the final resting place of many a Hudson Valley resident of yore, including, appropriately enough, Washington Irving. *Open year-round, Monday to Friday, 8 am to 4:30 pm, Saturday and Sunday 8:30 am to 4:30 pm.*

## SOMERS

**Lasdon Park**. *Route 35, Somers 10589. 914-864-7263. www.westchestergov .com/parks.* This 234-acre county park, with its woods, meadows, and formal gardens and its three-story colonial house modeled after Mount Vernon, George Washington's house in Virginia, was once the property of William and Mildred Lasdon. The park contains a Chinese Friendship Pavilion, a gift from the People's Republic of China to the citizens of Westchester.

**Museum of the Early American Circus**. *Routes 100 and 202, Somers 10589. 914-277-4977. www.somershistoricalsoc.org. National Register.* The Federal-style three-story brick Elephant Hotel, completed in 1825 by Hachaliah Bailey, an early promotor of traveling menageries, became the town hall of Somers in 1927 and has been the home of the Somers Historical Society and the Museum of the Early American Circus and since 1956. With a statue of Old Bet, Bailey's famous elephant, in front, the museum exhibits items from its extraordinary collection of circus ephemera as well as local artifacts. *Open Thursdays, 2 pm until 4 pm, or by appointment. Fee.*

## TARRYTOWN

**Lyndhurst**. *635 South Broadway, Tarrytown. 914-631-4481. www.lyndhurst .org. National Register.* Situated on a promontory overlooking the Hudson River, Lyndhurst is the finest extant Gothic Revival mansion in the United States. Maintained by the National Trust for Historic Preservation, this estate is only 24 miles north of New York City. Designed in 1838 by architect Alexander Jackson Davis for former New York City mayor William Paulding, the mansion was doubled in size for merchant George Merritt in 1865. The subsequent owner railroad magnate Jay Gould purchased the home in 1880, and the property was passed down through the Gould family until it was bequeathed to the National Trust in 1961 by Gould's daughter Anna, the duchess of Talleyrand-Périgord. The mansion features its original furnishings and decorative arts collection and acres of landscaped grounds that include the country's first steel-framed conservatory. *Open mid-April through October, Tuesday through Sunday and holiday Mondays, 10 am until 5 pm; November through mid-April, Saturday and Sunday and holiday Mondays, 10 am until 4 pm. Fee.*

**Sunnyside**. *West Sunnyside Lane, Tarrytown. 914-591-8763. www.hudson valley.org. National Register.* Washington Irving (1783–1859), America's

*Considered the finest extant Gothic Revival mansion in the United States, Lyndhurst overlooks the Hudson from a promontory in Tarrytown.*

first literary celebrity and the author of "The Legend of Sleepy Hollow" and "Rip Van Winkle," renovated this Dutch farmhouse beginning in 1835. A veritable assemblage of styles and design elements, Sunnyside has a Spanish tower based on Irving's visit to the Alhambra, weathervanes, which Irving associated with Dutch architecture, and a stepped roof. Draped in wisteria, much the way the author left it, the house opened to the public in 1947 and became a National Historical Landmark in 1966. Sunnyside is maintained and operated by Historic Hudson Valley. *Open in March, weekends only, 10 am until 4 pm, last tour at 3 pm; April through October, daily (closed Tuesday), 10 am until 5 pm, last tour at 4 pm; November through December, daily (closed Tuesday), 10 am until 4 pm, last tour at 3 pm. Fee.*

**Tappan Zee Bridge**. Carrying the New York State Thruway (I-87) across the river between Tarrytown and Nyack, in Rockland County, this 16,000-foot, seven-lane cantilever span bridge was completed in 1955. It was originally designed to carry 100,000 cars a day but in 2007 was averaging 135,000. Predicting that it will have to carry 175,000 by 2025, in late 2008 New York State announced a plan to replace the bridge with a new, $16 billion structure that could accommodate commuter trains and high-speed bus lanes. The new bridge is to be completed in 2017.

**Tarrytown Music Hall**. *13 Main Street, Tarrytown 10591. 914-631-3390. www.tarrytownmusichall.org. National Register.* The oldest operating theater in Westchester County opened in 1885. In 1901 it became one of the first theaters to show silent movies. Used exclusively as a movie house from the 1930s to the '70s, it was purchased by a nonprofit

*Beginning in 1835, the author Washington Irving (1783-1859) began transforming a Dutch farmhouse into one of the loveliest and most eclectic houses along the Hudson. He called it Sunnyside.*

organization in 1980 and continues to host films, live performances, and classes and workshops for children. *Fee.*

## VALHALLA

According to legend, the name of this hamlet eight miles east of the Hudson River reflects an obsession with the operas of Richard Wagner by the wife of a 19th-century postal official.

**The Native Plant Center at Westchester Community College**. *75 Grasslands Road, Valhalla. 914-606-7870. www.nativeplantcenter.org.* Dedicated to educating people about the importance of the wildflowers and native plants of the Northeast, this project of the Westchester Community College Foundation operates the Lady Bird Johnson Demonstration Garden at the East Grasslands entrance to the college, named after the former first lady. *Open dawn to dusk. Free.*

## WHITE PLAINS

**Battle-Whitney Park**. *Battle Avenue and Lincoln Avenue, White Plains 10606. 914-422-1336.* The park and National Heritage Area atop Chatterton Hill commemorates the historic Battle of White Plains on October 28, 1776. Although British troops forced the Americans to retreat from this eminence, the strong American resistance stopped the further advance of the British into Westchester and allowed General Washington to escape to New Jersey and save his strength for another day.

**Music Conservatory of Westchester**. *216 Central Avenue (between Tarrytown Road and Harding Avenue), White Plains 10606. 914-761-3900. www.musicconservatory.org.* Based in White Plains since 1929, the oldest professional performing arts organization in Westchester County was formed by a group of influential musicians, including famed cellist Pablo

Casals, to offer music education to the area's youth. In addition to a full degree-granting education program, the conservatory holds concerts throughout the year, including the Jazz on Central series each fall and the Stars on Central series that features members of the conservatory's faculty. *Fee.*

**Washington's Headquarters Museum/Miller House**. *140 Virginia Road, North White Plains. 914-864-7000. www.westchestergov.com. National Register.* George Washington's command post during the Battle of White Plains in 1776 was the home of Ann and Elijah Miller. Westchester County purchased the house in 1917; on display are a table said to have been used by the future president during the battle as well as other period items. *Open third Sunday each month through October, 12 pm until 3 pm. Free.*

**Westchester Arts Council**. *Westchester County Center. 198 Central Avenue, White Plains. 914-995-4050. www.countycenter.biz.* Opened in 1930 and extensively renovated in 1988, the Art Deco performance and convention center, designed by Walker & Gillette, has presented thousands of performances by many famous entertainers and musicians. *Fee.*

**Westco Productions**. *9 Romar Avenue, White Plains 10605. 914-761-7463. www.westcoproductions.org.* Founded in 1979 as a theater for family audiences, Westco presents a number of plays throughout the year based on children's fairy tales, folktales, and legends at locations throughout Westchester County. *Fee.*

## YONKERS

**Beczak Environmental Education Center**. *35 Alexander Street (near the train station), Yonkers. 914-377-1900. www.beczak.org.* Founded in 1989, this nonprofit educational institution in Habirshaw Park provides classes and interactive workshops on the ecology, culture, and history of the Hudson River Valley. Bald eagles are often sighted here. *Open 9 am until 5 pm daily.*

**Ella Fitzgerald Statue**. In the plaza by the Yonkers train station, a bronze memorial honors the popular and beloved 20th-century jazz singer, who was one of the many famous residents of this very old town.

**Lenoir Preserve**. *Dudley Street, Yonkers. 914-968-5851.* A butterfly and hummingbird garden, a dragonfly pond, and views of the Hudson River and Palisades distinguish this 40-acre park known for its nature programs.

*Renovated piers along the Yonkers waterfront have encouraged commuting by water taxi while providing spaces for summer concerts and performances.*

**Hudson River Museum**. *511 Warburton Avenue, Yonkers. 914-963-4550. www.hrm.org.* Founded in 1919 and located partly in a restored 19th-century mansion and partly in a detached modern building, this extraordinary multifaceted institution is a museum of both art and science, holding under its two roofs an extensive collection of 19th- and 20th-century American and European art (including many paintings by members of the Hudson River School), a modern gallery devoted to eclectic and thoughtful exhibitions of contemporary art, an ecology center focused on the natural history of the Hudson River, a dollhouse museum, and the only planetarium in Westchester County. The center-piece of the ecology center is a scale model of the Hudson River and its watershed from Lake Tear of the Clouds to New York Harbor. *Fee.*

**Philipse Manor Hall**. *Warburton Avenue and Dock Street, Yonkers 10702. 914-965-4027. www.philipsemanorfriends.org. National Register.* Westchester County's oldest standing building, this Georgian-style house with its carved woodwork and elaborate plaster ceilings was the home of the loyalist Frederick Philipse III, lord of the manor of Philipsburg. The American Revolution forced Philipse to flee to England, and his houses and lands were taken over by New York State. Although not furnished, the house is of interest not only architecturally but artistically, for its collection of presidential portraits dating from George Washington to Franklin D. Roosevelt and painted by such masters as Thomas Sully, Thomas Eakins, and Charles Willson Peale. *Open April through October, Tuesday to Friday 12 pm until 5 pm and Saturday and Sunday 11 am until 5 pm; November through March, Saturday and Sunday 12 pm to 4 pm. Fee.*

**Untermyer Park and Gardens**. *945 North Broadway (Route 9), Yonkers. 914-377-6450.* When the philanthropist Samual Untermyer died in 1940, he left his house and grounds, including his Beaux Arts walled garden with its reflecting pools, its classical temple, its Greek amphitheater, and its sculptures by Paul Manship, to the City of Yonkers to be used as a park. *It is open daily for strolling and contemplation, and on summer evenings for concerts and special events. Free.*

## YORKTOWN HEIGHTS

**Yorktown Stage**. *1974 Commerce Street, Yorktown Heights. 914-962-0606. www.yorktownstage.com.* This professional musical theater puts on family-oriented productions throughout the year, provides summer theater workshops for children, and is the performing home of the Taconic Opera (914-245-3415; www.taconicopera.org). *Fee.*

## *Festivals, Fairs, and Celebrations*

**Concerts in the Parks**. Each summer, the Westchester County Department of Parks, Recreation and Conservation hosts free concerts in parks throughout the county. Features of past summers have included the New York Philharmonic at Westchester Community College and chamber concerts by the Music Conservatory of Westchester at Governor Malcolm Wilson Park in Yonkers. For complete information call 914-864-7275 or visit www.westchestergov.com/PARKS.

**Hudson River EagleFest**. *Croton Point Park, Croton-on-Hudson. 914-762-2912. www.teatown.org.* During January and February each year, bald eagles congregate in large numbers in trees along the lower Hudson, filling up on fish before flying north to breed. To celebrate the return of this once-endangered species to the Hudson Valley and to teach people how to spot, understand, and respect this extraordinary bird, Teatown Lake Reservation organizes naturalist programs, children's activities, exhibits, and raptor shows on a Saturday each February at viewing sites from Croton to Peekskill. Free.

**Our Great Hudson River Revival/Clearwater Festival**. *Croton Point Park, Croton-on-Hudson. 845-454-7673. www.clearwater.org.* A joint project of the Hudson River Sloop Clearwater (see Dutchess County, below) and Westchester County, this two-day river jamboree started by the environmentalist singer/songwriter Pete Seeger has been taking place in Croton Point Park each June since 1978. The festival features music, food, a juried craft tent, and an artisan village of 50 regional crafters and artisans, exhibits, nature demonstrations, and sails on the famous Hudson River sloop *Clearwater*. *Fee.*

**Peekskill Celebration**. *www.peekskillcelebration.com*. Music, food, carnivals, arts and crafts, special exhibits, and fireworks are among the attractions at this three-day festival during the first weekend in August.

## Also Nearby

The Scarsdale Historical Society, at 937 Post Road in Scarsdale (914-723-1744; www.scarsdalehistory.org), operates the 18th-century Cudner-Hyatt House (National Register) and a Quaker Meeting House built in 1828. Both exhibit materials from the society's collection of photographs, papers, maps, and artifacts relating to the history of Scarsdale. *Fee.*

Rye Playland (914-813-7010; www.ryeplayland.org) bears the distinction of being America's first municipally planned—and the only Art Deco—amusement park in the United States. Still run by Westchester County, this National Historic Landmark offers 50 rides and attractions, 7 of which date to the opening of the park in 1928. Also in Rye, the Rye Historical Society, at 1 Purchase Street (914-967-0098; www.ryehistorical society.org), exhibits photography, artwork, and ephemera relating to Rye in a 1730 tavern called the Square House Museum and operates the 1670 Timothy Knapp House, an historic house that contains the society's library and archives.

Just down the shore in Mamaroneck, the Emelin Theatre for the Performing Arts, at 153 Library Lane (914-698-0098; www.emelin.org), offers classical recitals, cabaret shows, and theater for children. *Fee.*

At Iona College in New Rochelle, the innovative Westchester Chamber Orchestra (914-654-4926; www.westchesterchamberorchestra.org) performs four concerts a year of newly commissioned work or alternative interpretations of classical pieces. The New Rochelle Public Library, at 1 Library Plaza between Huguenot and Main Streets (914-632-7878; www.nrpl.org), presents exhibits in its Lumen Winter Gallery featuring local history, literary traditions, and work by local artists.

In Mount Vernon, the 18th-century stone St. Paul's Church (National Register), at 897 South Columbus Avenue (914-667-4116; www.nps.gov/sapa), was used as a hospital after the Battle of Pell's Point during the American Revolution and remained an active Episcopal church until its transfer to the National Park Service in 1980. It is now a headquarters for the National Park Service in the Bronx. The Mount Vernon Public Library houses a Rotunda Gallery curated by the Westchester Arts Council.

The Pelham Art Center, at 155 Fifth Avenue, between Second and Third Streets in Pelham (914-738-2525; www.pelhamartcenter.org), presents public exhibits, lectures, and performances in addition to classes and outreach programs for the community. The Picture House in Pelham is an old movie theater turned into a film center. *Fee.*

## Visitor Information

**Historic Hudson Valley**. *150 White Plains Road, Tarrytown 10591. 914-631-8200. www.hudsonvalley.org.* Founded by John D. Rockefeller Jr. in 1951, this preservation and education organization maintains and operates six significant historic sites along the river of which five are in Westchester County: Washington Irving's Sunnyside; Kykuit, the Rockefeller house in Tarrytown; Philipsburg Manor in Sleepy Hollow; the Union Church of Pocantico Hills; and Van Cortlandt Manor in Croton-on-Hudson. Historic Hudson Valley also operates Montgomery Place in Annandale near Bard College. Originally called Sleepy Hollow Restoration, the organization adopted its present name in 1987 as part of an expansion beyond the Tarrytown-Croton area.

**Riverkeeper**. *828 South Broadway, Tarrytown 10591. 800-21-RIVER. www.riverkeeper.org.* Since its creation in 1966 as the Hudson River Fishermen's Association, this environmental watchdog group has monitored the ecology of the river and brought hundreds of successful court cases against polluters.

**Westchester Arts Council**. *31 Mamaroneck Avenue (between Main Street and Martine Avenue), White Plains 10601. 914-428-4220. www.westarts. com.* This is the center for information on upcoming gallery openings, opening nights, concerts, and plays throughout Westchester County. See full description under White Plains, above.

**Westchester County Office of Tourism**. *222 Mamaroneck Avenue, White Plains 10605. 914-995-8500. http://tourism.westchestergov.com.* The Westchester County tourist office provides free maps and guides to hotels, restaurants, shops, and galleries throughout the county and links to other Hudson Valley offices and Web sites of interest to the traveler.

# ROCKLAND COUNTY

New York State's smallest county outside New York City (it is only 176 square miles) has long been associated with artists and writers, who have found here the space to live and work while maintaining close connections with the city just 16 miles downstream. From the high modern novelist William Gaddis, who titled one of his books after the Carpenter's Gothic house he inhabited in Piermont, to the actress Helen Hayes, who started a theater in Nyack, and the photographer Lee Friedlander, who raised his family in New City, artists of all kinds have contributed to an arts-friendly identity that is felt throughout this wedge of riverfront between the New Jersey border and Bear Mountain State Park.

As is happening throughout the Hudson Valley, in recent years communities in Rockland have formed new arts centers that are attracting artists while helping to create audiences for contemporary work. In Garnerville, the GAGA (Garnerville Gallery) Arts Center mounts imaginative shows of contemporary, folk, and performance art in its 20,000-square-foot gallery in a Civil War–era textile mill, while in downtown Nyack the equally ambitious Riverspace Arts has exploded with programming in recent years, bringing world-famous and emerging filmmakers, musicians, dancers, poets, actors, and directors to its stage to introduce new works and reinterpret old ones. (There is even a plan under discussion to rebuild the core of downtown Nyack into an expanded arts complex with Riverspace Arts at its center.) The Arts Council of Rockland, at 7 Perlman Drive in Spring Valley (845-426-3660; www.artscouncilofrockland.org), provides complete listings of arts events throughout the county as well as opportunities for artists.

Architecturally, Nyack is also worth visiting for its abundance of Victorian houses. The painter Edward Hopper grew up in one of them, and the pretty old house is now a thriving arts center providing regular exhibits, poetry readings, backyard jazz concerts, and rooms of Hopper memorabilia. New City, the county seat, was settled by the Dutch in the 1670s, and its native sandstone houses are excellent examples of the traditional build-

*The 1826 Stony Point Lighthouse is the oldest on the river.*

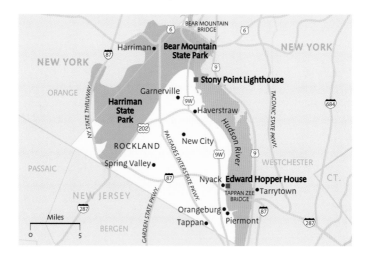

ing styles. The 19th-century Blauvelt farmhouse, also in the Dutch style, is home to the Historical Society of Rockland County, set on seven acres with a museum, a library, and an Anglo-Dutch barn. Completed in 1936, Mary Mobray Clarke's unusual Dutch Garden, behind the County Courthouse in New City, is constructed almost entirely of brick in honor of the county's long history of brick making.

Preservation of the native landscape, whether along the river or among the upland hills, has long been important to Rockland residents, whose county is named for the appearance of its land to its earliest Dutch settlers. The proximity of the Hudson as well as of New York City, and a plethora of raw materials, turned Rockland into a major manufacturing center during the 19th century. Iron was early discovered and mined in the hills that now comprise Harriman and Bear Mountain State Parks. According to the U.S. Geological Survey, by the early 1900s the Highlands mining industry produced 17 percent of the world's iron. Abundant clay in the riverbank at Haverstraw led to a brick-making industry that made the base materials for the construction of New York City. Charging down past Torne Mountain, the Ramapo River provided power and steam for nail manufacturing and a cotton mill.

Spurred by extensive clearing of the county's woodlands, by the beginning of the 20th century a movement had begun to preserve the land along the river. The result was a number of innovative parks including Bear Mountain and Harriman State Parks, Tuxedo Park (see Orange County), and the Palisades Interstate Parkway (see New Jersey). This preservation movement has continued with the transformation of a former army munitions depot into a public marshland and bird sanctuary at Iona Island in Stony Point and the protection of Piermont Marsh in Sparkill as part of the National Estuarine Research Reserve.

British and American armies passed back and forth through Rockland County during the American Revolution, when the county served as a sort of military gateway between northern New York and the central and mid-Atlantic states. George Washington stayed at the De Wint House, in Tappan, no less than four times; and it was in Tappan, in a tavern still in operation today, that the English spy Major John André was imprisoned before his hanging just up the hill on October 2, 1780. "Bear me witness," said the gallant and admired spy after tying his own blindfold, "that I meet my fate like a brave man."

## BEAR MOUNTAIN

**Bear Mountain Bridge**. *National Register*. Carrying Routes 6 and 202 across the Hudson River between Anthony's Nose on the east bank and Bear Mountain State Park on the west, this 1,641-foot-long toll suspension bridge—the longest of its kind in the world when it was completed in 1924—was operated privately before being taken over by the state of New York in 1940. It was here that Sal Paradise waited in vain—in the rain—for a ride on his failed first attempt to hitchhike across the country in Jack Kerouac's *On the Road*.

**Bear Mountain State Park**. *Bear Mountain 10911. 845-786-2701. www.palisadesparksconservancy.org*. Providing a taste of woods and mountains to generations of New York City schoolchildren, this fabled park—once reachable only by riverboat and train—was created in 1909–13 as an alternative to a plan to move Sing Sing Prison to the mountainous site. The park is named for the shape of its highest peak, which is said to resemble a recumbent bear, and its 5,067 acres contain dozens of trails for all abilities, including a section of the Appalachian Trail (contact the New York–New Jersey Trail Conference at 201-512-9348; www.nynjtc.org for maps). The views from the top of Bear Mountain are some of the most spectacular in the state. The park also has a public skating rink, a 40-acre trailside museum and zoo, a merry-go-round, a swimming pool and bathhouse, playing fields, and a guest lodge called the Bear Mountain Inn (National Register). A historical museum on the site of Fort Clinton (taken by the British on October 6, 1777) features exhibits on Native Americans, the American Revolution, and the Boy Scouts.

## GARNERVILLE

**GAGA Arts Center**. *55 West Railroad Avenue, Garnerville 10923. 845-947-7108. www.gagaartscenter.org*. Located in the Garnerville Arts and Industrial Center, a pre–Civil War industrial complex with artists' studios and warehouse space, this thriving arts center hosts exhibits, installations, concerts, and events in its 14,000 square feet of indoor performance space and galleries and its outdoor sculpture and nature walk. GAGA also produces a popular annual arts festival (see Festivals, below). *Opening hours and fees vary; call or visit the Web site for details.*

## HARRIMAN

**Harriman State Park**. *845-786-2701. www.palisadesparksconservancy.org.* It was a landowner in Rockland County, the railroad baron Edward Harriman, his wife, Mary Averell Harriman, and their son, William Averell Harriman, whose donation of 10,000 acres and $1 million in 1910 provided the impetus to create Bear Mountain and Harriman State Parks as an alternative to a state plan to build a prison at the current location of Bear Mountain State Park. The 46,613-acre Harriman Park is one of the largest in New York State, with 31 lakes and 225 miles of marked trails including a section of the Appalachian Trail. Contact the New York–New Jersey Trail conference at 201-512-9348; www.nynjtc.org for maps and guides.

## HAVERSTRAW

Founded in 1666 by Dutch settlers, the village is named after the Dutch word *haverstroo*, or "oat straw," referring to the type of long grass that still grows in marshes along the river. On the shore of Haverstraw Bay in 1780, Benedict Arnold met secretly with Major John André to plan the capture of West Point. The discovery, at about that same time, of large deposits of yellow and blue clay led to a growing brick-making industry in Haverstraw Bay, and by the late 19th century Haverstraw considered itself the "brick-making capital of the world," supplying a large percentage of the bricks used for building in New York City.

**Arts Alliance of Haverstraw**. *91 Broadway (off New Main Street and Route 9W), Haverstraw. 845-786-0253. www.arts-alliance.org.* Headquartered in a historic redbrick firehouse, this gallery and arts center regularly exhibits the work of local and national artists. *The office is open Monday through Friday, 10 am until 5 pm, and the free gallery is open Monday through Friday, 10 am until 5 pm, and Saturday, 11 am until 2 pm.*

**Haverstraw Brick Museum**. *12 Main Street, Haverstraw 10927. 845-947-3505. www.haverstrawbrickmuseum.org.* In the 19th and early 20th centuries, as many as 41 brickyards on Haverstraw Bay produced more than 300 million bricks every year and employing as many as

8,000 workers. *The legacy of this local industry is carefully preserved and explained in this unusual museum, which is open Wednesday, Saturday, and Sunday, 1 pm until 4 pm.*

**Haverstraw King's Daughters Public Library**. *85 Main Street, Haverstraw 10927. 845-429-3445. www.hkdpl.org. National Register.* The oldest public library in Rockland County, the Haverstraw King's Daughters Public Library was chartered in 1895. The library schedules regular book and poetry readings, lectures on many art- and architecture-related topics, and tours of local cultural destinations. *The historic village branch, dating from 1903, is open Monday through Thursday, 10 am until 6 pm, Friday, 10 am until 5:30 pm, and Saturday, 10 am until 5 pm. The new main branch, the modern Rosman Center at 10 West Ramapo Road in Garnerville, is open Monday through Thursday, 10 am until 9 pm, Friday, 10 am until 5:30 pm, Saturday, 10 am until 5 pm, and Sunday, 1 pm until 5 pm; closed Sunday from June 19 until September 4.*

## NEW CITY
The county seat since 1798, this historic farming center was home to the composer Kurt Weill and the playwright Maxwell Anderson. The photographer Lee Friedlander has lived here for many years.

**Dutch Garden**. *21 New Hempstead Road, New City.* Designed by Mary Mobray Clarke, this three-acre memorial to the early Dutch settlers won numerous awards after its construction in 1934–36. Almost entirely constructed of brick wall, including a brick teahouse, a gazebo, an arbor, a bandstand, and the remaining part of an original brick wall, the garden is also meant to remind visitors of the historical role of brick in Rockland's economy (see Haverstraw, above).

**Historical Society of Rockland County/Jacob Blauvelt Farmhouse**. *20 Zukor Road (between Bontecou Lane and Haverstraw Road), New City 10956. 845-634-9629. www.rocklandhistory.org. National Register.* Comprising a seven-acre campus with multiple buildings and landscaped

*The brick teahouse and walls of Mary Mobray Clarke's 1934–36 Dutch Garden in New City were meant to remind visitors of the importance of brick making in Rockland County history.*

grounds, the historical society records the history of this once strong agrarian community. Historical objects and documents are displayed and archived in the History Center Museum, which includes a woodland Indian exhibit and a research library. The Blauvelt House (National Register) from 1832 presents visitors with a window onto life in a vernacular brick farmhouse and the Anglo-Dutch-style Historic Barn from 1865 is home to farm equipment displays and demonstrations. *Open 9:30 am until 5 pm Tuesday through Friday, and 1 pm until 5 pm Saturday and Sunday.*

## NYACK

**Edward Hopper House Art Center**. *82 North Broadway, Nyack 10960. 845-358-0774. www.hopperhouse.org. National Register.* Although the celebrated painter (1882–1967) lived with his wife in New York City and Cape Cod for most of his adult life, he was born and went to school in Nyack, kept his car at the 1858 Queen Anne house where he had grown up and where his sister continued to live, and was buried in Nyack's Oak Hill Cemetery, overlooking the Hudson. Today the house, under the jurisdiction of the Edward Hopper Landmark Preservation Foundation, is both a museum devoted to Hopper and a thriving arts center with juried exhibits, poetry workshops, a jazz series, children's programs, and art classes for adults. *Open Saturday and Sunday, 1 pm until 5 pm.*

**Riverspace Arts**. *119 Main Street, Nyack, NY 10960. 845-348-0741 (main); 845-348-1880 (box office). www.riverspace.org.* This arts center offers a diverse range of adult programs in theater, dance, film, and music and works with schools and community groups to create programs for children and families. *The box office is open Tuesday through Sunday, 12 pm until 6 pm and two hours prior to performances. Fee.*

**Rivertown Film**. *58 Depew Avenue, the Nyack Center, Nyack 10960. 845-353-2568. www.rivertownfilm.org.* Specializing in independent, documentary, and classic films, this nonprofit organization hosts screenings, educational programs, and lectures by filmmakers who live in Rockland County. *Fee.*

## ORANGEBURG

**Camp Shanks World War II Museum**. *South Greenbush Road, Orangeburg 10962. 845-638-5419.* Exhibits, including a re-created barracks, present military life during World War II, when more than one million soldiers passed through here before shipping out to Europe. *Open spring, summer, and fall on Saturday and Sunday, 12 pm until 4 pm.*

## PIERMONT

**Piermont Marsh/Tallman State Park**. *Route 9W, Sparkill (park at Bridge Street in Piermont). 845-889-4745; www.nerrs.noaa.gov/HudsonRiver.* Part of the National Estuarine Research Reserve, the 1,017-acre protected zone along two miles of shoreline south of the Erie Pier in Piermont includes tidal marshes, shallows, and intertidal flats. Uncommon animals include the birds least bittern, osprey, bald eagle, and peregrine falcon and the diamondback terrapin, as well as rare plants such as sedge, button-bush dodder, and saltmarsh bulrush. The 700-acre Tallman State Park (845-359-0544. www.nysparks.state.ny.us/parks) rises along the Palisades above.

**St. Thomas Aquinas College Azarian McCullough Gallery**. *125 Route 340 (at the base of Costello Tower on the campus of St. Thomas Aquinas College), Sparkill 10976. 845-398-4195. www.stac.edu.* Exhibitions of both traditional and contemporary art revolve around the themes of religion and world culture.

## SPRING VALLEY

**Finkelstein Memorial Library**. *24 Chestnut Street (at Route 59), Spring Valley 10977-5594. 845-352-5700. www.finkelsteinlibrary.org.* Founded in 1917, the library hosts free readings and regular art exhibits featuring the work of local artists. *Open Monday through Thursday, 9 am until 9 pm; Friday, 9 am until 6 pm; Saturday, 10 am until 5 pm; and Sunday, 12 pm until 5 pm. On weekends during the summer the library is open on Saturdays, 9 am until 1 pm, and closed on Sundays.*

**Holocaust Museum and Study Center**. *17 South Madison Avenue, Spring Valley 10977. 845-356-2700. www.holocauststudies.org.* Opened in 1988, the museum presents educational programs, lectures, exhibits, teacher training seminars, and commemorative events on the Holocaust. Permanent exhibits combine graphics, montages, artifacts, and audiovisual displays; art exhibits change regularly. *Open Sunday though Thursday, 12 pm until 4 pm. Free.*

**Rockland Conservatory of Music**. *7 Perlman Drive, Spring Valley 10977. 845-356-1522. www.rocklandconservatory.org.* Founded in 1956, this music conservatory provides professional instruction to all ages and skill levels, music therapy, and concerts by students and faculty both on and off campus. *Open Monday through Thursday, 10 am until 9 pm, Friday, 10 am until 7:30 pm, and Saturday, 8:30 am until 3 pm.*

*The Museum at Stony Point Battlefield makes use of reenactments and indoor and outdoor exhibits to commemorate the 1779 capture of the British fort here by Americans under Brigadier General "Mad Anthony" Wayne.*

## STONY POINT

**Iona Island**. *1.5 miles south of the Bear Mountain Bridge traffic circle on Route 9W, Stony Point 10980.* A navy munitions depot during World War I and II and now under the jurisdiction of the Palisades Interstate Park Commission, this 129-acre island and marsh on the west side of the Hudson is an important bird sanctuary and one of four National Estuarine Research Reserves on the Hudson River. Bring binoculars and boots.

**Penguin Players**. *7 Crickettown Road, Stony Point 10980. 845-786-2873. www.penguinrep.org.* Founded in 1977, this small theater company produces plays by contemporary playwrights in a 19th-century barn. *Operates April through September. Fee.*

**Stony Point Battlefield**. *Battlefield Road (off Route 9W), Stony Point 10980. 845-786-2521. www.palisadesparksconservancy.org. National Register.* In 1779 Brigadier General "Mad Anthony" Wayne made a surprise capture of the British fort here, marking an important victory for the Americans. Exhibits in the museum display battle relics and describe the battle; on-site markers elaborate. Guided and self-guided tours and musket/artillery/camplife demonstrations bring historical events to life. *Open April 15 through October 31, Wednesday through Saturday, 10 am until 5 pm; Sunday, 1 pm until 5 pm. Fee.*

*Built in 1700, the DeWint House served as headquarters for General George Washington four times during the American Revolution. It is the oldest surviving structure in Rockland County.*

**Stony Point Lighthouse**. *Stony Point Battlefield, Battlefield Road (off Route 9W), Stony Point 10980. 845-786-2521. www.palisadesparksconservancy .org. National Register.* Built in 1826 to guide ships into the Hudson Highland narrows, this three-story Fresnel-lens lighthouse is the oldest on the Hudson River. It was decommissioned in 1926 and reopened and reactivated in 1995. *Open with the Stony Point Battlefield, April 15 to October 31, Wednesday through Saturday, 10 am until 5 pm, and Sunday, 1 pm until 5 pm. Also open Memorial Day, Independence Day, and Labor Day.*

## TAPPAN

**DeWint House**. *20 Livingston Avenue at Oak Tree Road, Tappan 10983. 845-359-1359. www.dewinthouse.com. National Register.* Serving as headquarters for George Washington on four separate occasions during the American Revolution, this Dutch Colonial farmhouse, built in 1700, is the oldest surviving structure in Rockland County. It was purchased by the New York Masons in 1932 (Washington was himself a Mason) and has been owned by them and open to the public, free of charge, since 1932. *Open daily, 10 am until 4 pm.*

**Old '76 House**. *110 Main Street, Tappan. 845-359-5476. www.76house.com.* Built in 1668, this tavern—one of the oldest in the country and still in operation—was frequented by General Washington during the American Revolution. Here the spy Major John André was imprisoned before his hanging as a British spy October 2, 1780.

*Drawing visitors from up and down the Hudson Valley and performers from around the world, the Hudson Valley Native American Heritage Festival takes place each August in Harriman State Park.*

## WEST NYACK

**Rockland Center for the Arts**. *27 South Greenbush Road, West Nyack 10994. 845-358-0877. www.rocklandartcenter.org.* This multiarts institution houses the Emerson Gallery, the PhotoSpace Gallery, a sculpture park, and the center's School for the Arts, which offers more than 100 courses and workshops a year. *Open Monday, Tuesday, and Friday, 9 am until 5 pm; Wednesday and Thursday, 9 am until 8 pm; and during the fall, winter, and spring only, Saturday, 10 am until 4 pm, and Sunday, 1 pm until 4 pm. Closed weekends in summer.*

### Fairs, Festivals, and Celebrations

**GAGA Arts Festival**. *Garnerville Arts and Industrial Center, 55 Railroad Avenue, Garnerville 10923. 845-947-7108. www.gagaartscenter.org.* June. See listing under Garnerville, above. *Fee.*

**Hudson Valley Native American Heritage Festival**. *Anthony Wayne Recreation Area, Harriman State Park. C/o Redhawk Indian Arts Council, 726 42nd Street, Brooklyn 11232. 718-686-9297. www.redhawkcouncil .org.* Taking place over a weekend in early August, this popular outdoor event in Harriman Park includes Native American artists, performers, and educators demonstrating singing, dancing, drumming, and flute playing and showing works of art. *Fee.*

## Visitor Information

**Arts Council of Rockland**. *7 Perlman Drive (between Pascak and New Clarkstown Roads), Spring Valley 10977. 845-426-3660. www.artscouncil ofrockland.org*. This arts service organization promotes and encourages the arts in Rockland County. The council provides programs, support services, publications, and forums that enhance the cultural life of the county. Some of the council's services include grants for community-based arts projects, art education grants, professional development workshops, an interactive Web site with forums for discussion, a bimonthly newspaper of arts-related articles and opportunities, student scholarships, and a senior visual artist exhibition. *Open Monday through Friday, 8 am until 4 pm.*

**New York–New Jersey Trail Conference**. *156 Ramapo Valley Road (Route 202), Mahwah, NJ 07430. 201-512-9348. www.nynjtc.org*. This federation of hiking clubs, environmental organizations, and individuals, with a membership of more than 100,000, is dedicated to building and maintaining marked hiking trails and protecting related open spaces in the two states. Its maps, available online and at many hiking and outdoor stores, are the best available for many of the parks in the region.

**Palisades Interstate Park Commission**. *Administration Building, Bear Mountain, NY 10911-0427. 845-786-2701. www.palisadesparksconservancy .org*. Formed in 1900, the federally chartered bi-state commission oversees 21 state parks and eight historic sites comprising 110,000 acres in New York and New Jersey. Contact the commission, online or at its headquarters in Bear Mountain State Park, for trail maps and guides.

**Rockland County Tourism**. *18 New Hempstead Road, New City 10956. 845-708-7300. www.rockland.org*. The official county tourist bureau not only provides complete information on restaurants, shopping, hotels, and transportation in Rockland County but has lists of cultural organizations and links to organizations connected with the rest of the Hudson Valley.

# PUTNAM COUNTY

Putnam County's connection to the Hudson River—its views, its village life, its arts scene, and its parks—is close; and with some of the most interesting architecture in the valley it rewards more than one visit. From the Bear Mountain Bridge to Cold Spring, the shore is lined with views and overlooks on the river from village greens and roadside parks, and on waterfront streets the "traffic" nowadays is more in art than in commerce. The pretty Garrison Landing train station, an historic depot dating from 1893, is a busy theater, and across the street exhibits of contemporary art and classes take place at the Garrison Art Center. The restored 19th-century streets of both Garrison Landing and nearby Cold Spring surround easily accessible train stations and draw visitors by train or car for theater events, gallery openings, and abundant antiques stores.

Putnam County is a feast of architecture, from the Greek Revival to the modern, from the secular to the religious. In Carmel, the county seat—15 miles inland from the Hudson on Lake Gleneida— a Greek Revival county courthouse, the second oldest in the state, still functions as a surrogate's court and retains its 19th-century courtroom, while closer to the river (just east of the Taconic State Parkway on Route 301) the largest Buddha in the western hemisphere can be visited inside a striking temple in the style of the Tang Dynasty. Near Garrison are Boscobel Restoration, a historic house that is a prime example of Federal architecture where a famous Shakespeare Festival takes place each summer, and Manitoga, the designer Russell Wright's mid-20th-century home and studio set in a private park that he landscaped himself over many years.

Parks, open space, and gardens are also important parts of the character of Putnam County. One of the largest wetlands in New York State, the Great Swamp, stretches across 6,000 acres of northeastern Putnam and part of Dutchess County. Twenty-four reservoirs feed into the New York City water supply, with the result that more than half of the county is protected by rules governing the watershed. This, together with the efforts of nonprofit organizations, individuals, and state and local govern-

*The view of the Hudson River from the waterfront in Cold Spring is one of the most direct and tranquil in the valley.*

ments to preserve the local environment, has caused thousands of acres to be set aside in such public parks and natural areas as Fahnestalk State Park, Hudson Highlands State Park, and the breathtaking Constitution Marsh. And one of the most stunning gardens in the state, Stonecrop Gardens, has been open in the highlands of Putnam County since 1992.

The state legislature carved Putnam out of Dutchess County in 1812. The county is named for Israel Putnam, a Revolutionary War general who also fought in the French and Indian War. An important center for information and artistic activity of all kinds is the Putnam Arts Council, whose headquarters at 521 Kennicut Hill Road in Mahopac is busy throughout the year with performances, pottery classes, and art and sculpture shows. Visit in person or online for complete information about upcoming events and classes.

## BREWSTER

**Walter Brewster House**. *43 Oak Street, Brewster 10509. 845-279-7429. www.preserveputnam.org. National Register.* Built in 1850 by the founder of the village of Brewster, this restored Greek Revival house is the head-quarters of the local Landmarks Preservation Society. Tours, concerts, and special events take place here throughout the year. The society also oversees the Old Southeast Church and the Doansburg One Room Schoolhouse. *Tours are available May through August, 1 pm until 5 pm on Sunday afternoons.*

**Southeast Museum**. *67 Main Street, Brewster. 845-279-7500. www.southeastmuseum.org.* Located in the former town hall of the township of Southeast, the museum documents the history of the township and the villages it contains, including Brewster. Every year the museum creates a temporary historical exhibit to tell a particular story of cultural significance, based on the museum's permanent collection of quilts, clothing, antique farm and household implements, and assorted Americana. Since 2001 the museum has cosponsored the Brewster Project, a site-specific art installation in Brewster. *Open April until December, Tuesday through Saturday, 10 am until 4 pm. Suggested donation.*

## CARMEL
Situated along the shore of Lake Gleneida in the southeast corner of the county, Carmel has been the county seat since 1812. The town is named for the supposed resemblance of its pleasant rolling, wooded hills to that of the fertile mountain range in northern Israel known as Carmel or "the Garden."

**Chuang Yen Monastery**. *2020 Route 301 (1.7 miles east of the Taconic Parkway), Carmel. 845-225-1819. www.baus.org.* This Buddhist monastery, school, and retreat center is home to a 37-foot statue of the Buddha Vairocana. Designed by C. G. Chen, it is the largest Buddha statue in the western hemisphere. The statue is located inside a remarkable temple in the style of the Tang Dynasty (618 until 907 AD) that also contains lovely bas-reliefs, murals, and 10,000 small Buddha statues, all the work of Chen. The monastery also has one of the only libraries in the United States specializing in Buddhism. *The temple is open to the public April to November, 9 am until 5 pm daily; the library is open on weekdays—call for hours.*

*The Walter Brewster House was built by the founder of the village of Brewster in 1850.*

*The Chuang Yen Monastery in Carmel is the home of a 37-foot statue of the Buddha Vairocana, the largest Buddha statue in the western hemisphere.*

**Putnam County Courthouse**. *44 Gleneida Avenue, Carmel 10512. National Register*. The second oldest in New York State, this Greek Revival courthouse was built in 1814 and is still in use as the county Surrogate's Court. The portico and pillars are a later addition, dating from the 1840s.

**Sybil Ludington Statue**. *Gleneida Avenue, Carmel 10512*. Erected in 1961, the dramatic bronze equestrian statue by Anna Hyatt Huntington commemorates the 40-mile all-night ride of a 16-year-old as she mustered 400 scattered troops for the defense of Danbury on April 26, 1777. Each April, the annual Sybil Ludington 50-Kilometer Footrace, organized by the Taconic Road Runners Club, follows the route of Sybil's ride and ends near the statue.

## COLD SPRING

One of the loveliest spots in the Hudson Valley, with extraordinary views up and down the river from its waterfront park and a number of great places to visit nearby, this village with a 19th-century air has done perhaps the best job of incorporating the train into its daily life: though the tracks run through the center of town, life goes on around them with a unity unmatched elsewhere. Restaurants, small hotels, historic houses, and well-restored storefronts specializing in antiques, clothing, crafts, antique jewelry, and toys all reward an afternoon's stroll and dinner.

**Chapel of Our Lady**. *45 Market Street, Cold Spring. 845-265-5537. www.chapelofourlady.com*. This Greek Revival religious building on a bluff overlooking the Hudson and West Point was consecrated in 1834 as a Roman Catholic church. It fell into disuse during the 20th century but was saved and opened as an ecumenical church in 1977. A popular music series takes place here; call for the schedule.

**Constitution Marsh Wildlife Sanctuary**. *Indian Brook Road (off Route 9D), Cold Spring. 845-265-2601. www.constitutionmarsh.org.* Under the stewardship of the National Audubon Society, this 270-acre tidal marsh two miles south of Cold Spring is an important habitat for birds, fish, and other Hudson River wildlife. An aquarium and exhibits at the visitor center bring flora and fauna up close, but the walk far out onto the marsh on specially designed walkways is breathtaking, with views across the long grasses up and down the Hudson and birds of all kinds making their appearance. *Open daily; visit the Web site for self-guided canoe, kayak, and walking tours.*

**Hudson Highlands State Park**. *Route 9D, Cold Spring 10512. 845-225-7207. www.nysparks.com/parks.* This 6,000-acre park known for its unspoiled woods and dramatic and popular hiking trails is divided among several dramatic sites between Peekskill and Beacon. Its famous 5.5-mile Breakneck Ridge Trail changes altitude by 1,250 feet over the course of just three-quarters of a mile. Because the park is scattered across numerous locations, trail maps and information are available at the centrally located Fahnestock State Park Visitor Center (see below) and at various shops in Cold Spring and Garrison Landing.

*The Greek Revival Chapel of Our Lady in Cold Spring was consecrated in 1834 as a Roman Catholic church. A popular summer music series takes place here.*

*The formal and informal gardens at Stonecrop Gardens, in Cold Spring, flourish above the Hudson Valley in the Hudson Highlands.*

**Putnam Historical Society and Foundry School Museum**. *63 Chestnut Street, Cold Spring. 845-265-4010. www.pchs-fsm.org.* The Foundry School Museum houses a collection of paintings, prints, sculpture, photographs, costumes, tools, furniture, household items, toys, and archives as well as a library with more than 1,000 genealogical records. The museum also presents two temporary exhibitions a year relating to the Hudson Highlands, the Philipstown area, and the West Point Foundry. *Open March through December, Wednesday through Sunday, 11 am until 5 pm. Fee.*

**Stonecrop Gardens**. *81 Stonecrop Lane, Cold Spring. 845-265-2000. www.stonecrop.org.* This astonishing series of formal and informal gardens, all connecting with hedges, waterfalls, paths, ponds, and greenhouses on a 12-acre site in the Hudson Highlands, is the life's work of Anne and Frank Cabot. Originally their home (Frank Cabot is the founder of the Garden Conservancy), they opened it to the public as a horticultural education center in 1992, and with its peaceful, meandering walks and carefully organized bursts of color it is well worth a visit. *Open April 1 through October 31, Monday through Friday and the first and third Saturday of each month, 10 am until 5 pm. Fee.*

## GARRISON
Another charming location, the small village of Garrison Landing, on the river side of the tracks, has some of the best views of West Point from its waterfront park and gazebo.

**Boscobel**. *1601 Route 9D, Garrison-on-Hudson. 845-265-3638. www .boscobel.org. National Register.* The federal architecture and furnishings at this restored 1808 house are considered some of the best examples of the style in the country. Forty-five acres of gardens and scenery offer grand views of the Hudson River and West Point and provide a dramatic and original stage for an annual Shakespeare festival that is revered throughout the valley. *Under the auspices of the nonprofit Friends of Boscobel, guided tours take place Wednesday through Monday, April through October, 10 am until 4:15 pm; November and December, 10 am until 3:15 pm. Fee.*

**Garrison Art Center**. *23 Garrison's Landing (across the street from the MTA Garrison Station), Garrison 10524. 845-424-3960. www.garrisonartcenter .org.* With exhibition space in three 100-year-old buildings in historic Garrison's Landing (National Register), the center presents exhibitions by local artists while also promoting arts education through mentoring programs and annual events such as Summer Arts on the Hudson, an education program for elementary and middle-school age children. *Free.*

**Manitoga/The Russel Wright Design Center**. *584 Route 9D, Garrison. 845-424-3812. www.russelwrightcenter.org. National Register.* The furniture, tableware, and set designer bought woods and a former quarry in Garrison just after World War II, built a house there, and spent the rest of his life, until his death in 1976, sculpting and redesigning the 75-acre property. Named for the "Place of the Great Spirit" in the Algonquin language that was once spoken in these parts, Wright's house is one of

*The Federal architecture and furnishings at Boscobel, a restored 1808 house overlooking the Hudson River and West Point, are considered some of the best examples of the style in the country.*

*The 1893 train station in Garrison is home to the Philipstown Depot Theatre, a popular community performing arts center*

the few 20th-century historic properties open to the public on the east coast. His papers are kept here; an annual awards program and children's summer camp are administered here; and the four miles of hiking trails that Wright created are open daily from dawn to dusk. *Tours of the house and studio take place April through October, Thursday through Monday at 11 am on weekdays and 11 am and 1:30 pm on weekends. Visit the Web site for tour reservations. Fee.*

**Manitou Point Preserve**. *Mystery Point Road, Garrison (2 miles north of Bear Mountain Bridge on Route 9D). 845-473-4440. www.scenichudson .org.* Owned jointly by Scenic Hudson and the Open Space Institute, this 136-acre park contains four miles of trails that wind through woods, marshlands, and a ravine toward the Hudson River. *Open daily, dawn to dusk.*

**Philipstown Depot Theater**. *Garrison's Landing, Lower Station Road, Garrison 10524. 845-424-3900. www.philipstowndepottheatre.org.* Founded in 1996 and located in the 1893 Garrison Train Station, this popular community performing arts center hosts films, plays, readings, musicals, and children's programs. *Fee.*

## KENT

**Fahnestock State Park**. *1498 Route 301 (half a mile west of Taconic State Parkway), Carmel 10512. 845-225-7207. www.nysparks.com/parks.* Sprawling across the center of Putnam County, with land in both Putnam and Dutchess Counties, this 14,086-acre state park contains trails, an outdoor education center, a swimming and boating lake, and a campground. It is named for Clarence Fahnestock, whose brother, Ernest, gave the land to the state as a fraternal memorial in 1929. Maps and other information can be obtained at the visitor center on Route 301 just west of the Taconic State Parkway.

## MAHOPAC

**Belle Levine Art Center/Putnam Arts Council**. *521 Kennicut Hill Road, Mahopac 10541. 845-278-0230. www.putnamartscouncil.com.* (*Note: because of a fire, in 2009 the Putnam Arts Council is operating temporarily from the Lodge building at the Tilly Foster Farm, 100 Route 312, Brewster 10509. 845-216-0636.*) Providing support services to artists and cultural enrichment to the community, the Putnam Arts Council is located in a turn-of-the-20th-century barn that was once the studio of *Mutt and Jeff* cartoonist Bud Fisher. Its Belle Levine Art Center features two galleries and a performance space that host exhibitions, plays, and music performances throughout the year. The council is also home to a photography club, pottery classes, and a gift shop featuring local crafts.

**Carmel Historical Center**. *40 McAlpin Avenue, Mahopac 10541. 845-628-0500.* Located in the 1902 Old Town Hall and operated by the Town of Carmel Historical Society, this museum contains permanent and temporary exhibits on local history and offers programs to school groups and the community. *Open Sundays, May through November, 2 pm until 4 pm.*

**First Presbyterian Church**. *Route 6N and Secor Road, Mahopac 10541. 845-628-2365. www.mahopacchurch.org.* Rebuilt after a fire in 1983, the church was originally built in 1833. The congregation dates from 1752. The tree-of-life stained-glass windows date from the 19th century.

**Our Lady of Kursk Russian Orthodox Church**. *1050 Route 6, Mahopac 10542. 845-628-4975.* The Orthodox church and hermitage dates from 1949, when it became one of many temporary homes of the Kursk-Root Icon—a miracle-working icon found among the roots of a tree near Kursk in the 13th century. Only a copy of the icon remains here (the original is in New York City), but the church—named for the Kursk-Root Hermitage destroyed during the Russian revolution—has been an important American center for the Russian Orthodox community ever since. A festival in honor of the icon takes place here each November 27.

## PATTERSON

**Patterson Environmental Park/Great Swamp**. *South Street (across from the Little Red Schoolhouse), Patterson 12563. 845-855-1917. www.frogs-ny .org.* The second largest freshwater wetland in New York State—twenty miles of habitat for plant, fish, amphibian, and bird life and a critical part of the watershed for New York City's reservoirs—is largely on private land, but this 23-acre town nature preserve provides access to the Great Swamp for hiking, fishing, canoeing, cross-country skiing, bird-watching, and nature observation. Call in advance for canoeing reservations.

### Fairs, Festivals, and Celebrations

**Hudson Valley Shakespeare Festival**. *1601 Route 9D Garrison, NY 10524. 845-265-7858. www.hvshakespeare.org.* Founded in 1987, each summer the festival mounts two full-scale outdoor productions on the grounds of Boscobel in Cold Spring (see above), taking advantage of the lovely outdoor spaces at this restored Federal-style mansion for well-regarded productions. Performances are Wednesday through Sunday evenings during the summer. *Fee.*

**Kursk-Root Festival**. *1050 Route 6, Mahopac 10542. 845-628-4975. Each November 27, at Our Lady of Kursk Russian Orthodox Church* (see Mahopac, above), priests conduct a festival in honor of the 13th-century Kursk-Root Icon that was kept there after World War II and which gave the hermitage its name.

**Putnam County Fair**. *Veterans Memorial Park, Gypsy Trail Road, Carmel. 845-278-6738.* Featuring animals, exhibits, entertainment, and food, the annual fair takes place over three days in late July. Open Friday, 12 pm until 6 pm, Saturday, 10 am until 7 pm, Sunday, 10 am until 6 pm. Admission and parking free.

### Visitor Information

**Preserve Putnam County**. *Whipple House, Gypsy Trail Road, Carmel 10512. 914-843-1422. www.preserveputnam.org.* Also known as the Society for the Preservation of Putnam County Antiquities and Greenways, this non-profit educational organization operates an informative Web site about Putnam County and works to foster preservation of the architecture and environment of the county.

**Putnam Arts Council**. *521 Kennicut Hill Road, Mahopac 10541. 845-278-0230. www.putnamartscouncil.com. (Note: because of a fire, in 2009 the Putnam Arts Council is operating temporarily from the lodge building at*

*The Constitution Marsh Wildlife Sanctuary in Cold Spring provides some of the best views of the river and West Point.*

the Tilly Foster Farm, 100 Route 312, Brewster 10509. 845-216-0636.) This arts service organization provides extensive information about the arts in Putnam County. Please see complete listing under Mahopac, above.

**Putnam Visitors Bureau**. *110 Old Route 6, Building 3, Carmel 10512. 845-225-0381. www.visitputnam.org.* This countywide organization provides listings of hotels, bed-and-breakfasts, special events, and attractions in Putnam County.

# ORANGE COUNTY

The creation of the Storm King Art Center on a former estate in Mountainville in 1960 launched Orange County—and in some ways the Hudson Valley itself—as an important place to view modern art. Preservation has a long history in the county, including the first publicly operated historic site in the United States, Washington's Headquarters in Newburgh, which opened in 1850, and efforts to preserve such natural features as Bear Mountain, Storm King Mountain, and the large tract that became Harriman State Park (see Rockland County). But the addition of a 500-acre sculpture park where great modern work can be viewed in relation to nature helped spark a renewed focus on the arts that spread elsewhere in the valley and continues to this day.

Conservation of Orange County's superb architecture, especially in Newburgh, is a major part of this cultural renaissance. The restoration of Andrew Jackson Davis's 1835 Dutch Reformed Church, at 125 Grand Street in Newburgh, is the centerpiece of an effort by such groups as the Newburgh Preservation Association to ensure that the many rare and wonderful buildings in Newburgh and elsewhere are kept standing and open to the public. The Gomez Mill House on the border between Orange and Ulster Counties in Marlboro, the David Crawford House in Newburgh, Knox's Headquarters in Vails Gate, and Brick House in Montgomery are all in excellent condition and reward a visit not only for their characteristic designs but also for their pleasant gardens and grounds.

Orange County's parks have benefited from the focus on preservation, with the 1897 Downing Park in Newburgh, designed by Frederick Law Olmsted and Calvert Vaux (the architects of Central Park in New York City), a reminder that a well-designed landscape, if properly maintained, only gets better with time. The acquisition of land to create Sterling Forest, an 1,800-acre tract in Tuxedo, in 1998 was the latest in an innovative series of land conservation efforts that also included the saving of Storm King Mountain by Scenic Hudson and others in the 1960s and '70s. As with Rockland County to the south, the larger parks in Orange County and many of the historic sites are owned by New York

*Among the curious architectural details at Knox's Headquarters in Vails Gate are the so-called "Witches' Stairs," wedge-shaped, according to legend, to render them impassable to the curly toes of witches.*

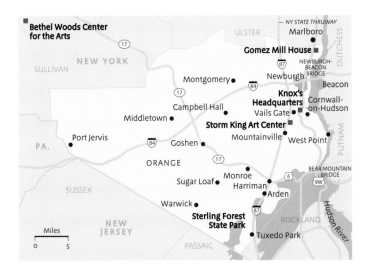

State but administered by the Palisades Interstate Park Commission (see below), itself a model organization created in 1900 to preserve the Palisades and Bear Mountain State Park.

In terms of the contemporary art scene, besides promoting the arts throughout the county, the Orange County Arts Council (845-469-9168; www.ocartscouncil.org—see Resources, below) provides a calendar of gallery and theater openings and operates a Web gallery of local artists. Antiques stores, galleries, fine restaurants, and specialized boutiques can be found in all of the larger towns. The reviving waterfront in Newburgh is alive with restaurants, shops, and music throughout the summer.

One of the original 12 counties established under English rule in 1683, Orange County at first included land that was later split off as Rockland County in 1798. It is named for William III, prince of the Dutch royal house of Orange and king of England, Scotland, and Ireland. The county played host to the successful American army for many months during the winter of 1782–83 while General George Washington awaited word of the signing of the Treaty of Paris ending the war on September 3, 1783. The impressive walls of the U.S. Military Academy rising along the riverbank at West Point—impossible to miss from trains passing along the Putnam County shore across the river—are a reminder that Orange County's long and vibrant history is continuing to be made today.

## ARDEN

**Orange County Historical Society/Clove Furnace**. *21 Clove Furnace Drive (off Arden Road near Route 17), Arden 10910. 845-351-4696.* Founded in 1972, the society operates eight historic buildings on its 51-acre property, publishes cultural guides, and hosts exhibits and educational activities. Among its buildings is an 1854 blast furnace that produced more than 100,000 tons of iron between 1871 and 1881. *The Historical Society is open Monday through Friday, 8 am until 4:30 pm. The furnace can be visited Monday through Friday, 9 am until 11 am and 1 pm until 4 pm. Suggested donation.*

## CAMPBELL HALL

**Hill-Hold**. *Route 416, Campbell Hall. 845-291-2404.* Built in 1769, this stone farmhouse was the home of Thomas Bull and remained in his family for 200 years. It is now a county-run museum on the history of farming in the Hudson Valley. *Open mid-May through early October, Wednesday through Sunday, 10 am until 4 pm. Closed Memorial Day and Labor Day; last tour is 3 pm.*

## CORNWALL-ON-HUDSON

**Hudson Highlands Nature Museum**. *The Boulevard, Cornwall-on-Hudson. 845-534-7781. www.hhnaturemuseum.org.* Chartered in 1959 by the New York State Regents, the museum operates two facilities in the shadow of Storm King Mountain—one called the Wildlife Education Center on the street known as The Boulevard in Cornwall-on-Hudson, and the other, called the Outdoor Discovery Center, on a 177-acre property on scenic Route 9W. Through exhibitions, tours, and community programs, the museum seeks to promote awareness about the cultural and environmental identity of the area known as the Hudson Highlands where the Hudson River cuts through the Appalachian plateau. *The Wildlife Education Center is open Friday and Saturday, 10 am until 4 pm, and Sunday, 12 pm until 4 pm; the Outdoor Discovery Center is open Saturday and Sunday, 12 pm until 4 pm, and other times for workshops and classes. Fee.*

## GOSHEN

**Harness Racing Museum and Hall of Fame**. *240 Main Street (between Erie and Hill Streets), Goshen. 845-294-6330. www.harnessmuseum.com.* A museum dedicated to the specialized American-born sport of Standardbred harness racing (named for the breed), the museum includes collections of historic carts, equipment, and jockey uniforms. Housed in a historic stable in Goshen, the museum's Hall of Fame includes the Hall of Immortals dedicated to influential jockeys and the Hall of Immortal Horses that features models of champion horses. The Peter D. Haughton Library features more than 4,000 books, videos, and documents on the

*An early 20th-century occupant of the Gomez Mill House in Marlboro, the craftsman Dard Hunter, built a paper mill in the shape of a thatch-roofed cottage in Devonshire, England.*

subject of harness racing and a virtual harness race is a major attraction for all ages. *Open daily, 10 am until 5 pm. Free.*

## MARLBORO

**Gomez Mill House**. *11 Mill House Road (off 9W, 5 miles north of New-burgh), Marlboro 12542. 845-236-3126. www.gomez.org. National Register.* Built in 1714, and originally part of a 6,000-acre tract belonging to Luis Moses Gomez, a Sephardic Jew who had fled the Spanish Inquisition, this historic house and museum on the border between Ulster and Orange Counties is the earliest surviving Jewish residence in North America. Among its lovely grounds and gardens (including a particularly gnarled and ancient willow) is a restored early-20th-century paper mill built in the shape of a cottage in Devonshire, England, by the artist and paper maker Dard Hunter, an owner of the house for a time. *Open mid-April through October 31, Wednesday through Sunday, 10 am until 4 pm. Tours begin at 10 am, 11:30 am, 1 pm, and 2:30 pm. Fee.*

## MIDDLETOWN

**Friends of Music**. *115 South Street, Middletown. 10940. 845-343-3049. www.friendsofmusic.net.* This presenting organization hosts approxi-mately two dozen concerts a year in a Victorian mansion on the campus of Orange County Community College. Performances run the gamut from American folk to blues to country and bluegrass with performers ranging from established folk artists to local up-and-comers. *Fee.*

**Paramount Theatre**. *17 South Street, Middletown. 845-346-4195. www.middletownparamount.com.* Restored and opened as a performing arts center by the Arts Council of Orange County in 1985, the theater originally opened as a movie house in 1930. Known for its powerful Wurlitzer organ, the theater hosts shows of ballet, music, drama, and comedy. *The ticket office is open Monday through Friday, 11:30 am until 4:30 pm, and Saturday, 10 am until 1 pm. Fee.*

## MONROE

**Museum Village**. *1010 Route 17M (Museum Village Road, Exit 129 off Route 17), Monroe 10950. 845-782-8248. www.museumvillage.org.* With its 1805 schoolhouse, early drugstore, blacksmith shop, and rustic log cabin, Museum Village documents 19th-century rural life and an early American community. The museum hosts tours, exhibitions, and community events and boasts a natural history museum with exhibits on local geology and the skeleton of a mastodon unearthed in Orange County. *Open April through May, Monday through Friday, by advanced reservation only; Memorial Day through early December, Monday and Tuesday, by advanced group reservation only, and Wednesday through Sunday, 11 am until 4 pm. Closed major holidays. Fee.*

## MONTGOMERY

**Brick House**. *Route 17K, Montgomery 12549. 845-457-4921. www.orangecountygov.com.* Built in 1768 by Nathaniel Hill and still inhabited by his family, this handsome brick house with its colonial and Victorian furnishings is open to the public on weekends between mid-May and mid-October, 10 am until 4 pm, and on other dates for special events. *Fee.*

## MOUNTAINVILLE

**Storm King Art Center**. *Old Pleasant Hill Road (take Route 32 to Orrs Mills Road, follow blue-and-white signs to Storm King Art Center on Old Pleasant Hill Road), Mountainville 10953. 845-534-3115. www.stormking.org.* Taking its name from nearby Storm King Mountain, this sculpture park situated on 500 acres combines sweeping views with more than 100 large-scale sculptures by some of the most important artists of the 20th century—from site-specific pieces by Andy Goldsworthy, Isamu Noguchi, and Richard Serra to acquired work by Mark di Suvero and Louise Nevelson. *Open April through October, Wednesday through Sunday, 11 am until 5:30 pm; November 1 through mid-November, Wednesday through Sunday, 11 am until 5 pm; some summer Saturdays until 8 pm. Closed mid-November through March. Fee.*

*Alexander Calder's* Five Swords *(1976) is one of more than 100 sculptures of all sizes and types placed around the 500 acres of the Storm King Art Center in Mountainville.*

## NEWBURGH

The birthplace of the 19th-century landscape designer Andrew Jackson Downing (1815–52) and the first-rank contemporary artist Ellsworth Kelly (1923–), and for many years one of the Hudson Valley's most important centers of transportation, trade, and manufacturing, this large old city on the bank of the river has begun to renew itself as a cultural force. A strong preservation movement, a growing arts scene, and the extraordinary views and architecture of its houses have been attracting increasing numbers of home buyers, while an extensive historic district (the largest in the state), an Olmsted-designed park, and a thriving restaurant row along the waterfront have been drawing ever more visitors. A new ferry reconnecting Newburgh and Beacon by water links Dia:Beacon and the Beacon arts scene with the restaurants, architecture, and history of Newburgh.

**Ann Street Gallery**. *104 Ann Street, Newburgh 12550. 845-562-6940 ext. 119. www.annstreetgallery.org*. This nonprofit art gallery in a renovated building in downtown Newburgh showcases contemporary art by both emerging and well-known artists. *Open Thursday through Saturday, 11 am until 5 pm. Free.*

**David Crawford House Museum**. *189 Montgomery Street (corner of Clinton and Montgomery Streets, 7 blocks north of Broadway on Grand Street), Newburgh. 845-561-2585. www.newburghhistoricalsociety.com. National Register.* This neoclassical mansion built in 1834 by David Crawford, a local shipbuilder, is the headquarters of the Historical Society of

Newburgh Bay and the Highlands, founded in 1884. The society mounts temporary exhibits from its collections of early Hudson Valley artwork and archival photographs; permanently displays examples from its collection of scale models of sailing and steam-powered vessels; and hosts special programs and events relating to its exhibits and collections. *Open April through October, Sunday, 1 pm until 4 pm, or by appointment.*

**Downing Park**. *Carpenter Avenue at 3rd Street (one block from Route 9W), Newburgh. 845-565-5559. www.newburgh-ny.com/downing. National Register.* The last collaboration by Frederick Law Olmsted and Calvert Vaux (the designers of Central Park in New York City), this lovely 35-acre park was completed in 1897 and is named for Andrew Jackson Downing, the great Newburgh-born landscape architect and horticulturist. A small park building known as the Shelter House, on the side of a duck-filled lake, mounts monthlong art exhibits, and the many gardens, some new and some original to the park, include the only dedicated ornamental daylily garden in New York State. Cormorants, herons, and other exotic birds fish from a rocky island in the lake. *Free.*

**Dutch Reformed Church**. *125 Grand Street (five blocks east of Downing Park at the intersection with 3rd Street), Newburgh 12551. 845-569-8092. www.newburghdrc.org. National Register.* Designed in 1835 by Alexander Jackson Davis, this prominent Greek Revival building—towering alongside the Hudson River for more than 150 years—fell into neglect as its congregation dwindled in the 1960s but has been under restoration in recent years and was declared a National Historic Landmark in 2001. It is considered one of the finest examples of its style in the Hudson Valley and is opened for tours and lectures on select dates throughout the year.

*Named for the Newburgh-born landscape architect and horticulturist Andrew Jackson Downing, Downing Park was the last park that Frederick Law Olmsted and Calvert Vaux designed together.*

*Under restoration but open for tours, the 1835 Dutch Reformed Church in Newburgh is one of architect Alexander Jackson Davis's most famous Greek Revival buildings.*

**Karpeles Manuscript Museum**. *94 Broadway, Newburgh. 845-569-4997. www.karpeles.com.* Located in a former bank on Newburgh's wide central street, this is one of nine linked manuscript museums around the country that together contain the world's largest private collection of rare music, illuminated manuscripts, legal documents, and letters by famous people. In its ground-floor gallery the museum hosts quarterly exhibits of materials from the permanent collection and monthly exhibits of contemporary art by local and national artists. *Open Tuesday through Saturday, 10 am until 4 pm, and Sunday, 12 pm until 4 pm. Free.*

**Newburgh Performing Arts Academy**. *62 Grand Street, Newburgh 12550. 845-562-5650. www.npaainc.org.* Providing intensive instruction in the performing and visual arts for all ages, this community learning center hosts preprofessional courses at its facility on Grand Street, visits community centers and public schools, creates programs for children who are homeschooled, and provides weeklong theater, dance, music, and visual arts classes for young people during the summer. *Fee.*

**Washington's Headquarters State Historic Site**. *84 Liberty Street (corner of Washington Street), Newburgh 12551. 845-562-1195. www.nysparks .com. National Register.* In 1782 and 1783, while the American army awaited the negotiation of the Treaty of Paris in nearby New Windsor, General George Washington set up his headquarters in this simple stone farmhouse belonging to John Hasbrouck. Acquired by New York State and opened to the public in 1850, the house with its lovely grounds and its view across the Hudson is considered the first publicly operated historic site in the United States. It is now managed by the Palisades Interstate Park Commission, though still owned by the State of New York. *Open mid-April through October, Wednesday through Saturday, 10 am until 5 pm; Sunday, 1 pm until 5 pm; and by appointment. Special events take place throughout the year. Fee.*

## PORT JERVIS

The former railroad center and canal town is located on the Delaware River near where the borders of New York, New Jersey, and Pennsylvania meet.

**Minisink Valley Historical Society**. *125-133 West Main Street, Port Jervis 12771. 845-856-2375. www.minisink.org. National Register.* Covering the area between Minisink Ford, New York, and the Delaware Water Gap in New Jersey and Pennsylvania, the society engages in the protection, refurbishment, and interpretation of historic homes and buildings in eight Orange County towns and hamlets and in communities in neighboring states. The society resides in Fort Decker, a stone house built in 1760, with exhibition halls highlighting local history. Founded in 1889, the society engages in genealogical documentation of the area's residents and conducts house tours. *Open Monday through Friday, 9 am until 5 pm; Fort Decker last Saturday of the month, 1 pm until 4 pm May through November. The Archives at the Port Jervis Free Library (see below) are open on Thursdays, 1 pm until 4 pm and by appointment 6 pm until 8 pm.*

**Port Jervis Free Library**. *138 Pike Street, Port Jervis 12771. 845-856-7313. www.rcls.org/ptj.* Opened in 1903, this Carnegie library contains the archives of the Minisink Valley Historical Society (see above) and a complete collection of the works of the novelist Stephen Crane, who lived in Port Jervis and apparently based several characters on local residents. *The library is open Monday, Tuesday, and Thursday, 10 am until 9 pm, and Wednesday and Friday, 10 am until 6 pm.*

## SUGAR LOAF

**Lycian Centre/Kings Theatre Company**. *Kings Highway, Sugar Loaf. 845-469-2287. www.lyciancentre.com.* Founded in 1993, this nonprofit performing arts complex and the resident Kings Theatre Company present concerts, musicals, ballet, drama, children's theater, and art exhibits on their stages and in their high-ceilinged galleries, and host free summer concerts on a three-acre lawn. *The box office is open Tuesday through Saturday, 11 am until 4 pm. Fee.*

## TUXEDO

**Sterling Forest/Frank R. Lautenberg Visitor Center**. *116 Old Forge Road (take Route 84 3.5 miles south from Route 17A), Tuxedo 10987. 845-351-5907. www.nysparks.com.* One of the largest wild forests in New York after the Adirondacks, this 18,200-acre state park is a popular destination for boating, hiking, and hunting. It is home to timber rattlesnakes, bog turtles, and 62 species of butterflies. Overlooking Sterling Lake, the Lautenberg Visitor Center, opened in 2003 and named for the U.S. senator from New Jersey who is credited with securing the funds for acquisition of the park, contains exhibits about the local environment and an auditorium. It also provides information on the new interpretive trail to the Southfields Furnace, a blast furnace dating from the years when this land was a center of iron mining. *The Visitor Center is open 8 am until 4:30 pm daily. Free.*

## VAILS GATE

**Knox's Headquarters State Historic Site**. *Forge Hill Road, Vails Gate 12584. 845-561-5498. www.nysparks.com. National Register.* Major General Henry Knox, George Washington's artillery commander—famous for his role in transporting the cannons from Fort Ticonderoga to Boston at the start of the American Revolution—lived in this 1754 Georgian-style house during several periods of the war. Major General Horatio Gates also lived here during the winter of 1782–83 while the army awaited the war's end at New Windsor Cantonment (see below). The lovely house with its thick walls, period details, and facades in different architectural styles (one side is Georgian, the other Dutch Colonial) originally belonged to a wealthy miller named John Ellison. Knowledgeable tour guides make the house come alive. *Open Memorial Day through Labor Day, Wednesday through Saturday, 10 am until 5 pm; Sunday, 1 pm until 5 pm; other times by appointment. Fee.*

**New Windsor Cantonment/National Purple Heart Hall of Honor**. *Temple Hill Road (Route 300), Vails Gate 12584. 845-561-1765. www.nysparks .com; www.thepurpleheart.com. National Register.* From October 1782 through the cease-fire on April 19, 1783, 7,000 American Revolutionary War troops and their followers lived here in an encampment of nearly 600 log huts that they had built themselves. At this modern-day reconstruction, guides in period costume demonstrate musket drills, blacksmithing, army medicine, and the other daily activities of an 18th-century military camp. Also here is the National Purple Heart Hall of Honor, which collects the stories of recipients of the oldest American military decoration still in use. Originally designed by General Washington toward the end of the war during the period when his troops were camped here, the small purple badge in the shape of a heart (an example is on display here) was the first to honor the common soldier. *The Hall of Honor is also open on Monday through Saturday, 10 am until 5 pm; Sunday 1 pm until 5 pm. New Windsor Cantonment is open April through October, Monday and Wednesday through Saturday, 10 am until 5 pm; Sunday, 1 pm until 5 pm. Closed Tuesdays and Thanksgiving, Christmas, and New Year's Day; open Memorial Day, Independence Day, Labor Day, and Veterans Day. Free.*

## WARWICK

**Dancing Crane Georgian Dance Theater**. *9 DeKay Road, Warwick 10990. 845-986-2638. www.dancingcrane.org.* Founded by Victor Sirelson in Warwick in 1996 to introduce the traditional song and dance of Georgia to American audiences, the troupe holds performances around the state and is composed of both amateur local performers and professionals from the group's namesake country. The company performs at local venues in Orange County and tours throughout the Northeast. *Fee.*

**Pacem in Terris**. *96 Covered Bridge Road (off Francher Road, off Route 94, 3 miles west of Warwick), Warwick. 845-987-9968.* This nonprofit sculpture park is dedicated to the works of Frederick Franck, who created the park over many years before his death in 2008. It is a sort of whimsical garden of sculpture, with paths, trees, and art intermingling in playful and pleasurable ways. Classical music concerts take place on summer weekends. *Open May through October, Saturdays and Sundays, 11 am until 6 pm. Free.*

## WEST POINT

Soldiers manned this strategic point of land on the western shore of the Hudson during the American Revolution, and it has been an important military reservation and training ground ever since. The United States Military Academy opened here in 1802.

**Constitution Island and the Warner House**. *845-446-8676. www.constitutionisland.org.* Although located across from West Point near the eastern shore of the Hudson, this 280-acre island is under the jurisdiction of the United States Military Academy. From the island in 1778 the American army stretched an 80-ton iron chain across the river to West Point with the aim of blocking further British access to the river after the Battle of Saratoga. Historians question whether the chain would have withstood a serious British attempt to break through, but luckily it was never put to the test. Walking trails lead to ruined fortifications and to the restored 19th-century home of Susan Warner, author of the 1850 classic *Wide, Wide World,* and her sister Anna, author of the words to the hymn "Jesus Loves Me." *Boat tours leave from the South Dock at West Point on Wednesdays and Thursdays from June through September. Special Saturday excursions are available during June, July, and August, from Cold Spring only.*

**United States Military Academy**. *Route 9W, West Point. 845-938-2638. www.westpoint.edu. National Register.* Founded in 1802, the world-famous military college still rises fortresslike on the west shore of the

*The United States Military Academy at West Point has shone above the Hudson since 1802. Twenty-five percent of the new lieutenants entering the United States Army graduate from here.*

Hudson, graduating more than 900 new officers annually, or approximately 25 percent of the new lieutenants entering the U.S. Army. The 4,000 members of the Corps of Cadets undergo a rigorous type of intellectual, physical, military, and moral training known as the "West Point Experience." Because of security concerns after the World Trade Center attacks on September 11, 2001, visitors must report to the visitor center inside the main gate and can now tour the campus only by bus. (Because of occasional special events, it is best to call in advance to confirm that tours are running.) Exempt from this restriction is the West Point Museum, which is open to the public without a guide and has exhibits on the history of American wars and the West Point graduates who distinguished themselves in them. Also exempt is the Eisenhower Hall Theatre (845-938-4159; www.eisenhowerhall.com), an on-campus performing arts center and gallery that presents music and theater and art exhibits that are open to the public. *The theater box office is open Monday through Friday, 8 am until 4 pm, and the visitor center and museum are open daily, except Thanksgiving, Christmas, and New Year's Day; visitor center, 9 am until 4:45 pm; museum 10:30 am until 4:15 pm. Free.*

### Fairs and Festivals

**Art Along the Hudson**. *www.artalongthehudson.com*. One weekend each month in selected cities along the Hudson, cultural organizations, restaurants, galleries, and antiques stores stay open late and offer special events and music as part of a yearlong celebration of the arts.

*In Orange County, this recurring festival takes place in Newburgh on the last Saturday of the month, May through October. Free.*

**New York Renaissance Faire**. *Sterling Forest, 600 Route 17A, Tuxedo. 845-351-5171. www.renfair.com.* In this playful re-creation of life in a Renaissance-era village, actors in period costume entertain and instruct in such seminal arts as archery, knife and ax throwing, dart tossing, and Chinese crossbows. Visitors of all ages enjoy the rides, performances, crafts, music, food, and dancing of vanished centuries. Steak on a stake is just the beginning. *Takes place Saturdays and Sundays in August until mid-September and on Labor Day. Fee.*

**Orange County Fair**. *Wisner and Carpenter Avenues, Middletown. 845-343-4826. www.orangecountyfair.com.* Taking place in late July each year on the county fairgrounds, this popular event blends traditional agricultural activities with popular entertainment. *Fee.*

**Warwick Applefest**. *Warwick 10990. 845-987-8300. www.warwickapple fest.com.* On the first Sunday in October each year the town of Warwick becomes an arts and crafts center based on the annual celebration of the fall of the apples. Apple pie baking contests, a quilt raffle, food, music, and shopping make this a popular event. *Free.*

## *Also Nearby*

Fifty-seven miles west of Newburgh on Interstate 84, at the site of the 1969 Woodstock Music Festival in Bethel, NY, is the Bethel Woods Center for the Arts (866-781-2922. www.bethelwoodscenter.org), a state-of-the-art performing arts center opened in 2006 that provides indoor seating for 4,800 and outdoor seating for 12,000 and hosts musicians of all kinds, from the New York Philharmonic, which opened the center in 2006, to Bob Dylan, Joe Cocker, and other rock stars of the 1960s and later. An on-site museum uses film, photographs, text, and artifacts to present the history of the Woodstock Festival and describe its ongoing influence.

Twenty miles north of Bethel, at 48 Main Street in Livingston Manor (at Exit 96 on Route 17), is the Catskill Art Society's CAS Arts Center (845-436-4227; www.catskillartsociety.org), a community multiarts center in this artistic haven in the western Catskills. The CAS Arts Center mounts regular exhibitions in its two galleries; offers classes in drawing, pottery, painting, acting, dance, and more; hosts artist talks, performances, screenings, and other public events; and provides information and a meeting place for artists and art lovers. Open Friday and Saturday, 11 am until 6 pm; Sunday, 11 am until 3 pm.

*Opened in 2006 at the site of the 1969 Woodstock Music Festival, the Bethel Woods Center for the Arts draws thousands each summer for outdoor concerts in the south-western Catskills.*

Fifteen miles southwest of Bethel, at 37 Main Street (at Route 52) in Narrowsburg, is the Delaware Valley Arts Alliance (845-252-7576; www .artsalliancesite.org). Founded in 1976 and located in the Delaware Arts Center (National Register), this arts service organization is home to two galleries, the Gloria Krause Recital Hall and the 165-seat Tusten Theatre. These venues are the site of performing arts series as well as the home of the Delaware Valley opera (845-252-3136; www.dv-opera.org), the Delaware Valley Chamber Orchestra and the annual Jazzfest concert series. The Delaware Valley Arts Alliance also mounts DiGit, a digital video film festival, and Riverfest, a music, art, and environmental festival held on Narrowsburg's Main Street. The gallery is open Tuesday through Saturday, 10 am until 4 pm. Free.

## Visitor Information

**City of Newburgh Tourism**. *83 Broadway, Newburgh 12550. 845-569-7300. www.newburgh-ny.com*. This useful office and Web site offer extensive information on the history of Newburgh, current things to see and do, restaurants, music, and how to get around.

**Newburgh Preservation Association**. *P.O. Box 206, Newburgh 12551. www.preservenewburgh.org*. Founded in 1978, this all-volunteer organization rebuilds, preserves, and promotes the architectural heritage and historic views of Newburgh, provides useful information, and conducts tours.

**Orange County Arts Council**. *23 White Oak Drive, Sugar Loaf 10981. 845-469-9168. www.ocartscouncil.org.* The center for the arts in Orange County is a source of information on arts events and artists; it publishes a cultural calendar, provides links with arts organizations around the county and state, and administers an annual arts awards program.

**Orange County Tourism/Orange Arts**. *124 Main Street, Goshen 10924. 845-615-3860. www.orangetourism.org.* The official county tourist site provides listings of gallery openings and events in the county and is the home of Orange Arts, with extensive information on artists and galleries around the county and workshops.

BARDAVON
BARDAVON BUILDING
BARDAVON
DAN ZANES WYNTON MARSALIS MICKEY HART CLINT BLACK
YOYO MA QUEEN LATIFAH MARTHA GRAHAM CROSBY & NASH
RIVER ARTS FEST
SUZANNE VEGA DAVID
BROMBERG SEPT 15 FREE
DAN ZANES SEPT 29
café PRIMAVERA
PRIMAS PIZZERIA

# DUTCHESS COUNTY

With its famous collection of historic houses overlooking the Hudson River, Dutchess might seem to be a county determined by the architectural and social glories of its past, but in fact this richly storied stretch of land has been in the midst of transformation since its earliest settlement by Dutch farmers in the 17th century, and its lively cultural scene looks both backward and forward in time. It is no coincidence that the largest contemporary art museum in the world, Dia:Beacon, opened in 2003 in the same county as New York State's oldest continuously operating theater, the Bardavon Opera House, which opened in Poughkeepsie in 1869. The county has one of the finest examples of domestic Federal architecture in the United States; Montgomery Place, the only public building by Frank Gehry on the East Coast, the Fisher Center for the Performing Arts at Bard College; and an American rendition of the Palais des Tuileries in Paris in Vassar College's Main Building, designed by James Renwick Jr.

Home to Vassar as well as the Dutchess County Arts Council and the 75-year-old Barrett Art Center, Poughkeepsie is the county seat and cultural center of this busy and interesting stretch of Hudson shoreline. Musicians from Itzhak Perlman to Patti Smith—as well as the Hudson Valley Philharmonic—have performed at Bardavon, and artists ancient and modern are on display at the Frances Lehman Loeb Arts Center at Vassar. The Dutchess County Arts Council, online or at 9 Vassar Street, has up-to-date listings of cultural events, organizations, and resources for artists.

Many residents of the county are proud to trace their ancestry—and often the houses they live in—to ancestors who settled here centuries ago, while others are simply fascinated by the history of the valley. The result is a focus on preservation that has allowed architectural gems from earlier times to be restored and opened to the public. From Springside, Franklin D. Roosevelt's home just north of Poughkeepsie, to Montgomery Place itself, some of the most remarkable private dwellings ever constructed in this country can be visited under the guidance of knowledgeable and often entertaining park rangers and volunteers. Organizations such as Historic Hudson Valley, Scenic

*The Bardavon 1869 Opera House is New York State's oldest continuously operating theater.*

Hudson, and Hudson River Heritage have done a lot to make sure that these houses and the land around them are available to tourists while retaining their historic integrity.

The beauty of the rolling agricultural landscape of Dutchess County has been remarked upon for generations, with 19th-century visitors regularly comparing it to that of the Rhine Valley in Germany (a view reflected in such place-names as Rhinebeck and Rhinecliff). Not just because of the extraordinary popularity of their county fair are residents proud of their agricultural past, but also because agriculture continues to be part of life in these parts. Dutchess County is a growing center of organic farming, and farm tours, farmers' markets, and dairying are a visible part of contemporary life.

Dutchess County organizations are at the forefront of efforts to understand and improve the environment in the Hudson Valley. The Institute for Rivers and Estuaries in Beacon, the Hudson River Research Reserve in Tivoli, and the Hudson River Sloop Clearwater, based in Beacon, all make use of the river as a laboratory, class-room, and rostrum for studying and advocating for river systems. In Millbrook, the Institute of Ecosystem Studies—one of the largest of its kind—turns to the woods and fields of its 1,924-acre sanctu-ary to learn about and promote native plants and ecosystems.

Two prominent educational institutions, Vassar and Bard Colleges, have built museums and theaters that draw musicians, actors, and artists from around the world and help build audiences for cultural events. The Frances Lehman Loeb Art Center at Vassar, designed by Cesar Pelli, shows work from early Renaissance painting to contemporary photography, while Vassar's Powerhouse Theatre regularly introduces new work for the stage. The Center for Curatorial Studies at Bard, designed by Jim Goettsch and Nada Andric, hosts thoughtful exhibits of contemporary art, and whether there for student productions during the year or for the heady mix of summer ballet, opera, drama, jazz, and classical music known as Summerscape, nobody forgets the polished steel rippling off into woods and clouds of Gehry's Fisher Center at Bard.

Dutchess was one of the original 12 counties established by the English administrators of New York in 1683. At first including present-day Putnam as well as parts of Columbia County, it was named in honor of Mary of Modena, Duchess of York, the second wife of James II. (Until the early 19th century, "duchess" was generally spelled with a "t".)

As with most of the Hudson Valley, part of the pleasure of a visit to Dutchess County is simply to stroll up and down the sidewalks of some of the many pleasant villages here—Beacon, Pawling, Rhinebeck, Millerton, Millbrook, Tivoli—tasting the rewards of an hour's quiet browsing in the antiques shops, galleries, bookstores, and artisan shops that deal in everything from new paintings to old masterpieces. Bookstores often feature hard-to-find editions of works by local authors. And the revival of ferry service between Beacon and Newburgh has helped not only to bring commuters across the river to the Newburgh station but to fill the galleries of Beacon and the restaurants of Newburgh with new visitors from across the river.

## AMENIA

**Wethersfield Estate and Gardens**. *214 Pugsley Hill Road, Amenia. 845-373-8037.* Inspired by Italian gardens of the Renaissance, the late Chauncey Stillman built a 10-acre formal garden in the backyard of his 1930s Georgian-style brick house in Amenia that is considered one of the finest New York gardens of the 20th century. From the house, with its collection of art and antiquities, a path leads into a carefully planned oasis with a reflecting pool, hedges, an arborvitae arch, and even a pair of 13th-century recumbent lions. *The gardens are open June through September, Wednesday, Friday, and Saturday, 12 pm until 5 pm; the house by appointment only. Free.*

*Frank Gehry's 2003 Fisher Center for the Performing Arts is one of several cultural institutions at Bard College that draw audiences for performances and exhibits from throughout the region.*

## ANNANDALE-ON-HUDSON

**Bard College**. *Route 9G, Annandale-on-Hudson. 845-758-6822. www .bard.edu.* With one of the lovelier and more dramatic campuses on the Hudson River—a 500-acre estate of large old trees and views of the Catskills—this innovative teaching institution was founded in 1860 as an Episcopal college to prepare young men for the seminary. In the early part of the 20th century the college broadened its curriculum, and later it began admitting women. Today Bard is known for its graduate programs in the arts and music, its experiments in education, and its inviting new buildings for the visual and performing arts:

- Richard B. Fisher Center for the Performing Arts (845-758-7900; www.fishercenter.bard.edu). Frank Gehry's dramatic theater, opened in 2003, is now a regional performing arts center. Every summer, Bard Summerscape explores a major composer's work (see Festivals, below).

- CCS Bard Hessel Museum (845-758-7598; www.bard.edu/ccs). Designed by architects Jim Goettsch and Nada Andric, and with a mission to encourage and explore experimental approaches to the presentation of contemporary visual art, this teaching museum mounts regularly changing exhibits in two connected buildings, the Hessel Museum of Art (which focuses on work from the center's Marieluise Hessel Collection of art created after 1960) and the CCS galleries (which mounts temporary exhibits).

**Montgomery Place**. *Route 9G (3 miles north of the Kingston-Rhinecliff Bridge), Annandale-on-Hudson. 845-758-5461. www.hudsonvalley. org. National Register.* Now under the jurisdiction of Historic Hudson Valley (see Resource Directory), this Federal-style house with its 434 acres of woods, fields, orchards, and gardens is generally considered to be one of the premier examples of Hudson Valley estate life. Built in 1805 by Janet Livingston Montgomery (1743–1828) in memory of her husband, General Richard Montgomery (killed at the Battle of Quebec on December 31, 1775), the house, with its views of the Hudson River and the Catskill Mountains, was later renovated according to plans by the architect Alexander Jackson Davis. Descendants continuously improved the house and grounds, with the landscape architect Andrew Jackson Downing advising on plantings, gardens, lawns, and views. In 1986 the family deeded the property and its historic furnishings to Historic Hudson Valley. *Open May to October, weekends only, 10 am to 5 pm. Fee.*

Surrounded by 434 acres of woods, fields, orchards, and gardens, Montgomery Place, in Annandale-on-Hudson, is one of the best examples of 19th-century Hudson Valley estate life.

*Built in 1874, the Carpenter Gothic St. John the Evangelist Episcopal Church in Barry-town serves as a catalyst for community cultural events.*

## BARRYTOWN

**St. John the Evangelist Episcopal Church**. *1114 River Road (north of Route 199), Barrytown. 845-758-6433. http://stjohnsbarrytown.dioceseny.org.* Built in 1874, this Carpenter Gothic church just north of Route 199 serves as a cultural center for residents of surrounding villages. Local residents who had acted in plays at the church since the 1960s went on to form the nucleus for the Rhinebeck Performing Arts Center (see Rhinebeck, below).

## BEACON

**Bannerman Island**. (Also known as Pollepel Island). *845-831-6346. www.bannermancastle.org. National Register.* This 6.75-acre island about three miles south of Beacon on the eastern shore of the Hudson contains the ruins of a neo-Scottish castle built there by a wealthy arms dealer between 1901 and 1918. Now under the jurisdiction of the New York State Office of Parks, Recreation and Historic Preservation and the nonprofit Bannerman Castle Trust, the island is accessible for tours by canoe and tour boat; visit the Web site or call for more information.

**Beacon Institute for Rivers and Estuaries**. *199 Main Street, Beacon 12508. 845-838-1600. www.thebeaconinstitute.org.* With a mission of research, policy making, and education on rivers, estuaries, and their connection with society, and with offices in Beacon and Troy, this scientific institution with links to major universities and corporations uses the Hudson River as a laboratory for research projects with global applications. Its headquarters in Beacon contains a bookstore and gift shop as well as a gallery with changing exhibits of art and photography on the Hudson and other waterways.

**Dia:Beacon**. *3 Beekman Street, Beacon. 845-440-0100. www.diaart.org. National Register.* Opened in 2003, this vast new space, the largest contemporary art museum in the world, houses the Dia Foundation's important but rarely shown permanent collection. With work by Joseph Beuys, Louise Bourgeois, Walter De Maria, Michael Heizer, Donald Judd, Agnes Martin, Richard Serra, and Andy Warhol, among others, the collection documents the work the foundation patronized, some of which became the most influential work of that important postwar generation. Aside from Dan Flavin's fluorescent sculptures, the museum is lit entirely by natural light diffused through large factory windows and skylights. *Open April through October, Thursday through Monday (closed Tuesdays and Wednesdays), 11 am to 6 pm; November through March, Friday through Monday (closed Tuesdays, Wednesdays, and Thursdays), 11 am to 4 pm. Fee.*

**Hudson River Sloop** *Clearwater*. *724 Wolcott Avenue, Beacon 12508. 845-454-7673. www.clearwater.org. National Register.* Built in 1966 by folksinger Pete Seeger to alert people to the need for Hudson River conservation, and a ubiquitous and reassuring presence along the river

*Familiar to sailors and Amtrak riders, the ruined neo-Scottish castle on Pollepel Island, near Beacon, was built in 1901–18 by the arms dealer Frank Bannerman. The two spans of the Newburgh-Beacon Bridge, behind, opened to traffic in 1963 and 1980.*

*An installation by Imi Knoebel (1940– ) is one of many of all sizes and types in the vast Galleries at Dia:Beacon. Opened in 2003 in a former Nabisco factory, the museum is considered the largest devoted to contemporary art in the world.*

throughout the year, the Hudson River sloop *Clearwater* is a model of the Dutch sloops that plied the river in the 18th and 19th centuries. Docking at towns up and down the Hudson, but based since 2009 on the Beacon waterfront, the much-loved ship offers rides for all ages and classes for everyone from children to master's candidates. The Clearwater organization leads the annual Clearwater Festival, "Our Great Hudson River Revival—The Festival That Saved a River," each summer (see page 10). *Fee.*

**Long Dock Beacon Park**. *Long Dock Road (by the Metro North Station), Beacon. www.scenichudson.org.* One of the features of this 16-acre waterfront park on a former salvage yard and oil storage facility is a terraced deck and boardwalk by the sculptor George Trakas, created in conjunction with Dia:Beacon. *Open dawn to dusk.*

**Madam Brett Park and Homestead**. *50 Van Nydeck Avenue (corner of Teller Avenue, one block off Main Street), Beacon. 845-831-6533. www .hudsonrivervalley.com. National Register.* The Brett family built this traditional Dutch farmhouse in 1709–15 and lived here until 1954, when they sold it to the Daughters of the American Revolution. The oldest house in Dutchess County and still maintained by the Melzingah Chapter of the D.A.R., it is filled with furnishings and architectural details from seven generations of occupancy by a single family. A 12-acre park created by Scenic Hudson connects the house and its grounds along the Fishkill Creek to the Beacon Shoreline Trail, Long Dock Beacon Park, and the Beacon train station.

**Mount Beacon**. *Route 9D (junction with Howland Avenue), Beacon 12508. www.scenichudson.org. National Register.* The site of a signal fire during the American Revolution and later of an incline railway that brought visitors to the summit for dancing and stargazing, this local landmark provides a celebrated view across Beacon, Newburgh, and the Hudson itself to the Shawangunks and the Catskills beyond.

**Mount Gulian Historic Site**. *145 Sterling Street, Beacon. 845-831-8172. www.mountgulian.org. National Register.* This historic house and museum commemorates the colonial Verplanck family, local perspectives on the American Revolution and preindustrial culture. It also sponsors community and school events, including tours and a summer heritage camp for children. *Fee.*

**Newburgh-Beacon Bridge**. *P.O. Box 28, Beacon 12508. 845-831-3700. www .nysba.state.ny.us/bridgepages/NBB/NBBpage/nbb_page.htm.* Carrying NY 52 and Interstate 84 across the Hudson between Beacon and Newburgh, the 1.5-mile-long twin cantilever bridges, completed in 1963 and 1980, replaced a ferry system that dated back to 1743. The curved cantilever spans of the northern (westbound) of the two bridges won it a "most beautiful bridge" award from the American Institute of Steel Construction when it was completed in 1963.

*The sculptor George Trakas designed a section of Long Dock Beacon Park, a 16-acre riverfront park under construction by Scenic Hudson along the river in Beacon.*

## HOPEWELL JUNCTION

**East Fishkill Historical Society**. *68 Kensington Drive, Hopewell Junction NY 12533. 845-227-4136. eastfishkillhistoricalsociety.org.* Established in 1960 by a group of local history buffs, the East Fishkill Historical Society now resides in a late-18th-century Dutch farmhouse that was refurbished in the 1980s. In addition to year-round open houses and special events, the society also organizes an annual Strawberry Festival and hosts exhibitions.

## HYDE PARK

**Culinary Institute of America**. *Route 9, Hyde Park. 845-452-9600. www.ciachef.edu.* Located on the campus of a former Jesuit seminary just up the road from the FDR home, this professional cooking school provides beginning chefs with a superior practical education and shares the fruit of that education with the public through five very different, always interesting restaurants open to the public. For reservations call 845-471-6608. *Fee.*

**Farrand Garden at Bellefield**. *845-229-5320. www.beatrixfarrandgarden.org.* Beatrix Farrand was a pioneering early-20th-century landscape architect, one of the first and most accomplished women in this profession. Her 1912 walled garden at the Bellefield mansion, part of the Roosevelt National Historic Site, is considered one of her finest creations. The planting of its perennial borders creates an unusual sense of space.

**Franklin D. Roosevelt Home and Library**. *4097 Albany Post Road, Hyde Park. 845-229-9115. www.historichydepark.org. National Register.* He served as president of the United States longer than anyone else (four terms, 1933–1945); ushered in the New Deal; presided over the American involvement in World War II; and before all that was a New York State senator (1910–13), an assistant secretary of the navy (1913–19), and governor of New York (1929–32). He was also a lifelong resident of the Hudson Valley, a promoter of local Dutch architectural styles, and a protector of other architectural treasures such as the Vanderbilt Mansion. His family house, his presidential library, his personal retreat, Top Cottage; his wife Eleanor's hideaway and house, Val-Kill; and the Beatrix Farrand Garden at Bellefield are all now owned by the public and overseen by the National Park Service. A new visitor center provides exhibits and films on the Roosevelts and operates a bookstore and café.

- Franklin D. Roosevelt Presidential Library and Museum (www.fdrlibrary.marist.edu). The president himself oversaw the construction of this first of the presidential libraries at his home in Hyde Park and

*The Home of Franklin D. Roosevelt, in Hyde Park, welcomed kings and statesmen during President Roosevelt's four terms in office, and continued to do so years later when President Bill Clinton met here with Boris Yeltsin, the president of Russia, in 1995.*

gathered here the papers from all his years of public service. Before he died he saw that the library—the only one used by a president while still in office—was expanded to accommodate the papers of his wife, Eleanor. The museum is open 9 to 5 daily except Thanksgiving, Christmas, and New Year's Day. There is an admission charge for a combination ticket to the museum and home.

- Home of Franklin D. Roosevelt (www.nps.gov/hofr). It is small wonder that President Bill Clinton chose the house of his Democratic forebearer as the setting for his 1995 meeting with Boris Yeltsin, the president of Russia. The large, comfortable house overlooking the Hudson had welcomed kings and statesmen during Roosevelt's terms in office and was the boyhood home of the author of the New Deal. Filled with memorabilia from Roosevelt's life—including the crippled president's hand-operated elevator—Springwood, as the house was called by Roosevelt's father, also tells the story of one New York family's historic ties to the Hudson Valley. Roosevelt himself and his wife, Eleanor, are buried in the rose garden.

- Top Cottage (www.nps.gov/hofr). In 1938 Roosevelt built this small stone house on a hilltop near his family house as a retreat from the cares of presidential life. Considered one of the very first buildings in the United States designed by a disabled person for his own freedom of movement—and one of the few buildings of any kind designed by an American president while in office—the simple "Dutch Farmhouse" plan dispensed with thresholds and hard-to-reach shelves, keeping all necessary items within easy reach of someone in a wheelchair. On the open porch looking out into the trees FDR entertained family, friends, and distinguished visitors such as Winston Churchill and King George VI and Queen Elizabeth, but he also spent time alone, enjoying a moment's freedom from the stresses of world leadership.

- Val-Kill, Eleanor Roosevelt National Historic Site (845-229-9115; www .nps.gov/elro). Built in 1924 beside a stream two miles east of the Roosevelt estate, this cluster of stone houses became the retreat and, after her husband's death in 1945, the home of the human rights advocate and U.N. delegate whom President Harry Truman called "The First Lady of the World."

**Hyde Park Railroad Station**. *34 River Road, Hyde Park. 845-229-2338. www.hydeparkstation.com. National Register.* Built in 1914 to replace a demolished predecessor and in use until 1958, the abandoned building was purchased from the Town of Hyde Park by the Hudson Valley Railroad Society in 1975 and has been operated as a popular railroad museum ever since.

**St. James Church**. *4526 Albany Post Road, Hyde Park 12538. 845-229-2820. www.stjameshydepark.org. National Register.* The 1844 Episcopal church, the parish of Franklin and Eleanor Roosevelt, is considered an excellent example of the Gothic Revival style.

**Vanderbilt Mansion National Historic Site**. *Route 9, Hyde Park. 845-229-9115. www.nps.gov/vama.* Frederick Vanderbilt may have been the least flamboyant of the grandchildren of Cornelius Vanderbilt, the shipping and railroad magnate who founded the family fortune in the mid-1800s, but you would never know it from the sumptuous weekend place that he and his wife, Louise, completed in Hyde Park in 1899. A triumph of the Beaux Arts style by the architects McKim, Mead & White, the sumptuous house with its Indiana limestone facing and gilt and marble interior was furnished with imported antique rugs and tapestries to create the impression of a European ancestral home. Following the wishes of Louise's niece and heir Margaret Van Alen, who gave the building and its extensive gardens and outbuildings as a national monument after Frederick died in 1938, the house—now under the jurisdiction of the National Park Service—remains virtually unchanged from the way it was when the Vanderbilts lived there. *Open daily, 9 am until 5 pm.*

# MILLBROOK

**Cary Institute of Ecosystem Studies**. *Route 44A, Millbrook. 845-677-5343. www.ecostudies.org*. This ecological research organization studies and protects a 1,924-acre ecosystem lined with trails and dotted with gardens that visitors may access to view the flora and fauna of upstate New York. The institute offers public environmental education programs and sells a variety of items relating to nature and gardening in its shop.

**Innisfree Garden**. *44 Tyrrell Road, Millbrook. 845-677-8000. www.innisfreegarden.org*. This 150-acre garden, influenced by Chinese ideas in landscape design, turns the native New York landscape into a series of pictures, with vistas and landscapes framed in natural and often startling ways. The 40-acre lake is glacial, most of the plant material is native, and the rocks have come from the immediate forest. *Fee.*

**Wing's Castle**. *Bangall Road, Millbrook. 845-677-9085*. Nobody turning onto Route 82 from Route 44 in Millbrook can fail to notice the bizarre castlelike structure on the north side of the road. Built of found and salvaged stones over 23 years by Peter and Toni Wing, this unlikely landmark with its moat and towers is open to the public during the spring, summer, and fall under the supervision of Mr. and Mrs. Wing. *Open May 30 through Christmas, Wednesday through Sunday, 10 am until 5 pm. Fee.*

# PAWLING

This village 24 miles southeast of Poughkeepsie on Route 55 has a growing arts scene with several galleries offering new work by contemporary artists.

**John Kane House**. *126 East Main Street, Pawling. 845-855-9316. www.dutchesstourism.com. National Register*. The headquarters of the Historical Society of Quaker Hill and Pawling, this colonial house with a large Federal-style wing dates from the mid-18th century and was used as a headquarters by General Washington during the American Revolution. It features exhibits on local history and interesting local personalities. *Open Saturday and Sunday, 2 pm until 4 pm, and by appointment. Free.*

**Pawling Concert Series**. *700 Route 22, Pawling 12564. 845-855-3100. www.pawlingconcertseries.org*. Presenting five concerts between September and May, the Pawling Concert Series brings a mixture of classical, jazz, folk, and world music to such popular Pawling locations as All Saints' Chapel and McGraw Pavilion. *Fee.*

## POUGHKEEPSIE

A city of breweries and paper mills during the 19th century, and for more than 100 years, until 1972, the home of Smith Brothers Cough Drops, the Dutchess County seat is best known for its renowned college, Vassar; its opera house, the Bardavon; and its architecture ranging from Art Deco to Italianate, Greek Revival, Romanesque Revival, and Neo-Classical.

**Bardavon 1869 Opera House**. *35 Market Street, Poughkeepsie. 845-473-2072. www.bardavon.org*. A historic performance venue in Poughkeepsie that once brought Mark Twain and Sarah Bernhardt to audiences in the Hudson River Valley, the Bardavon served as a cinema in the 1920s and was saved from demolition in the 1970s. The theater is the home of the Hudson Valley Philharmonic and presents performances by international touring opera companies, comedians, pop music performers, theatrical ensembles, and traveling Broadway shows. In 2006 the Bardavon took over the management of the Ulster Performing Arts Center (UPAC) in Kingston (see Ulster County). *Fee.*

**Barrett Art Center/Dutchess County Art Association**. *55 Noxon Street, Poughkeepsie. 845-471-2550. www.barrettartcenter.org*. Located in the historic home of well-known local painter Thomas Weeks Barrett, the Barrett Art Center has brought arts programming to Poughkeepsie and Dutchess County since 1934. The center hosts an annual juried art exhibition featuring the work of local artists and is home to the Barrett Clay Works and an artists' coop where visitors may purchase works made by local artists and artisans.

**Children's Media Project**. *20 Academy Street, Poughkeepsie 12601. 845-485-4480. www.childrensmediaproject.org. National Register*. An arts and education facility that strives to teach children about media and technology, the Children's Media Project presents film and video exhibitions that address a variety of civic issues at its Digital Café space housed in the Lady Washington Firehouse in downtown Poughkeepsie. Children are also encouraged to attend workshops that teach them how to produce their own films, many of which are screened at the Hamptons International Film Festival and on the project's DROP TV youth-produced television show. *Fee.*

**Cunneen-Hackett Arts Center**. *9 and 12 Vassar Street, Poughkeepsie 12601. 845-486-4571. www.cunneen-hackett.org. National Register.* Located in two restored Victorian buildings near the train station in downtown Poughkeepsie, this multifaceted arts center has a theater and two galleries showing the work of local and regional artists and hosts classes in the performing and visual arts, concerts, plays, readings, and dance performances. *The gallery at 9 Vassar Street is open Monday through Friday, 9 am until 5 pm, and the one at 12 Vassar Street is open on weekends and by appointment. Free.*

**Dutchess County Arts Council**. *9 Vassar Street, Poughkeepsie. 12601. 845-454-3222. www.artsmidhudson.org.* This nonprofit arts service organization was established in 1964 to promote and coordinate cultural activity in the county. It publishes a calendar of events and an art-buying guide on its Web site and a magazine, *ArtsScene*, which lists artists and cultural organizations in Dutchess and Ulster Counties. The council also provides information about grants to artists and art educators, sponsors arts management workshops, and promotes the production and appreciation of art in Dutchess and Ulster Counties.

**Dutchess County Historical Society/Governor Clinton House**. *549 Main Street, Poughkeepsie 12602. 845-471-1630. www.dutchesscountyhistorical society.org. National Register.* Located in the large stone Governor Clinton House (1765), the society has been publishing an annual yearbook of articles on local history since 1914—the oldest continuously published annual in New York State. Known for its publications, educational outreach, and archives, the society hosts an annual conference and a black history lecture series and supervises the maintenance of the nearby Glebe House (1767), another stone house at 635 Main Street. The Clinton and Glebe houses are open for tours by appointment.

**Locust Grove**. *2683 South Road (Route 9), Poughkeepsie 12601. 845-454-4500. www.morsehistoricsite.org. National Register.* In 1847 Samuel F. B. Morse, the inventor of the telegraph, purchased an 1831 Georgian-style house on a bluff overlooking the Hudson. With the help of a friend, the architect Alexander Jackson Davis, Morse enlarged and remodeled the house into a Tuscan-style villa. An admirer of the landscape theories of Andrew Jackson Downing, Morse spent the rest of his life planting and improving the 150-acre estate, creating vistas and lawns that would capture the romantic ideals of the time. After his death the property passed out of his family, but subsequent owners continued to look after it much as Morse had done, and in 1963 it was designated a National Historic Landmark. *Open daily, 10 am until 3 pm, May through November. Fee.*

**Mid-Hudson Bridge**. *P.O. Box 1010, Highland 12528. 845-691-7221.* Carrying Routes 44 and 55 across the river between Poughkeepsie and Highland, this 3,000-foot parallel wire cable suspension bridge was completed in 1930.

**Mid-Hudson Children's Museum**. *75 North Water Street, Poughkeepsie 12601. 845-471-0589. www.mhcm.org.* Geared toward children under the age of 12, this museum mounts exhibitions that pique children's curiosity; offers educational workshops, after-school programs, and live performances by local artists; and houses a planetarium. *Fee.*

**Mill Street Loft**. *455 Maple Street, Poughkeepsie 12601. 845-471-7477. www.millstreetloft.org.* A multidisciplinary arts organization founded in 1981, Mill Street Loft offers art classes and workshops to a wide array of constituents in Poughkeepsie. It promotes intensive arts education through programs such as the Dutchess Arts Camp, Project ABLE, and PASWORD. Mill Street Loft also houses the Tom Adair Dance Video Library.

**New Day Repertory Company**. *29 North Hamilton Street, Poughkeepsie 12602. 845-485-7399.* The company performs four or five productions of classics and new plays each year at its own theater and throughout the Mid-Hudson Valley.

**Springside National Historic Site**. *185 Academy Street (just off Academy Street exit on Route 9), Poughkeepsie. 845-454-2060. www.springside landmark.org. National Register.* The only surviving piece of land in the Hudson Valley directly shaped by the landscape designer Andrew Jackson Downing was the summer property of Matthew Vassar, the founder of Vassar College. Hudson Valley preservationists succeeded in saving the house and 20 acres from development in 1982. Self-guided tour brochures are available at the site or online.

**St. Paul's Episcopal Church**. *161 Mansion Street, Poughkeepsie. 12601. 845-452-8440. www.stpaulspoughkeepsie.org. National Register.* Consecrated in 1873, the Norman Gothic stone Anglican church replaced an earlier building dating from 1837. Its stained-glass windows memorialize parishioners.

**Vassar College**. *124 Raymond Avenue, Poughkeepsie. 845.437.7000. www .vassar.edu. National Register.* Founded in 1861 by Matthew Vassar as a liberal arts college for women, the famous college on the eastern outskirts of Poughkeepsie has long been known for its beautiful campus, its innovative curriculum, and its strong support for the performing and visual arts. It began admitting men in 1969. Its huge Second Empire–style Main Building, designed by James Renwick Jr. (who also designed Grace Church and St. Patrick's Cathedral in Manhattan and the Smithsonian in Washington, D.C.), was thought to enclose more interior space than any other in the country when it opened in 1865.

- Frances Lehman Loeb Arts Center (845-437-5632; www.fllac.vassar .edu). Housed in a 1993 building designed by Cesar Pelli, the Loeb Arts Center was founded in 1864 as the Vassar College Art Gallery. Its permanent collection contains more than 15,000 works including paintings, sculptures, drawings, prints, photographs, and glass and ceramic wares. It is home to the Warburg Collection of Hudson River School paintings, the Magoon Collection of 19th-century British and American art, works by major European and American 20th-century painters, European antiquities, Asian art, and photography. The center presents four or five exhibitions a year.

- Powerhouse Theater (845-437-7235; www.powerhouse.vassar.edu). Started in 1985, Powerhouse Summer Theater takes place in a black box theater created out of an old powerhouse building on the Vassar campus—the building that provided power to the college for a century. A collaboration between Vassar and an established theater company, New York Stage and Film, the program makes use of indoor and outdoor stages and combines the talents of theater professionals and apprentices in incubating new work. The program consists of main stage productions, second stage and workshop productions, play-reading festivals, outdoor productions, studio productions, site-specific plays, and workshops. Call or visit the Web site for the summer schedule.

*120-acre Poets' Walk, in Red Hook, has some of the most dramatic views of the Hudson River and the Catskills beyond.*

*Opened in 1889, the Poughkeepsie-Highland Railroad Bridge was once one of the most important rail connections between New England and the rest of the country. A fire damaged it in 1974, but a nonprofit group, Walkway Over the Hudson, formed to save it and is scheduled to reopen it as a pedestrian bridge in late 2009.*

**Walkway Over the Hudson**. *P.O. Box 889, Poughkeepsie 12602. 845-454-9649. www.walkway.org. National Register.* When the 6,767-foot steel cantilever truss bridge between Poughkeepsie and Highland opened in 1889, its length and design distinguished it as one of the longest of its kind in the world. A fire in 1974 closed the once-important rail connection between New England and the rest of the country, and it sat unused for 35 years until, with the support of state and local government, the visionary nonprofit group Walkway Over the Hudson was formed to restore and reopen it as a pedestrian bridge as part of the quadricentennial celebrations of 2009. The bridge, like the Hudson River sloop *Clearwater*, has come to symbolize for many the resurgence of the Hudson and the interconnectedness of the towns along its banks.

## RED HOOK

The village is said to derive its name from a small peninsula or, in Dutch, *hoek* in the Hudson, notable for its red leaves in the autumn.

**Poets' Walk**. *County Route 103, Red Hook. 845-473-4440. www.scenic hudson.org.* Scenic Hudson created this 120-acre riverfront park on property that is said to have inspired Washington Irving's "Rip Van Winkle." Paths meandering across fields and through woods to the shore offer dramatic views of the Catskills across the Hudson.

**St. John's Reformed Church**. *126 Old Post Road, Red Hook 12571. 845-758-1184. www.stjohnsreformed.org.* The white Carpenter Gothic structure was built in 1871.

## RHINEBECK

The second largest county fair in New York State is one good reason to visit Rhinebeck (see Festivals, below). Another is the Beekman Arms, the nation's oldest continuously operated hotel, which opened its doors in 1766. This turn-of-the-century village with its artists' supplies shop, galleries, antiques stores, and restaurants also has a movie theater specializing in independent and foreign films.

**Burger Hill**. *Route 9G (2.5 miles south of intersection with Route 9), Rhinebeck. www.scenichudson.org.* This 76-acre hilltop park offers great views of the Hudson Valley. *Open during the spring and summer, 9 am until 8:30 pm; during the fall and winter, 9 am until a half hour after sunset.*

**Center for Performing Arts at Rhinebeck**. *Route 308, Rhinebeck. 845-876-3080. www.centerforperformingarts.org.* At this new theater, built in 1998 and shared by several companies, Broadway professionals and local actors join forces in productions of new and classic plays and musicals in a theater shaped like a barn. The center also hosts a child-friendly family series on Saturday mornings. *Fee.*

**Cocoon Theatre**. *6384 Mill Street (Route 9), Rhinebeck 12572. 845-876-6470. www.cocoontheatre.org.* Founded in 1988 as a puppet/dance group, this nonprofit theater for children has grown into a professional studio and theater, offering classes and performance opportunities for people of all ages in theater, puppetry, and dance. *Fee.*

**Ferncliff Forest**. *Between Mount Rutsen and River Roads, Rhinecliff (parking areas along either road). 845-876-3196. http://ferncliff_forest .villageofrhinebeck.info.* This 192-acre old-growth forest preserve and game refuge contains 11 lovely trails and a lookout tower with views of

*An artists' shop in Rhinebeck is one of numerous signs of the vibrant creative life in Dutchess County.*

the Hudson and the Catskills. The property was once a retreat for retired Methodist clergymen.

**Old Rhinebeck Aerodrome**. *9 Norton Road, Rhinebeck. 845-752-3200. www.oldrhinebeck.org.* Dutchess County residents may be accustomed to the drones of ancient aircraft doing battle over Route 199 on weekends, but newcomers are often surprised to look up from the road and see World War I aircraft holding dogfights under the clouds. One of the largest collections of early airplanes in the world, the aerodrome possesses such unusual craft as a 1909 Blériot, the oldest flying aircraft in the United States. Weekend airshows take place from mid-June through mid-October, and the four museum buildings display aircraft from the pioneer era, World War I, and the Lindbergh/barnstorming era. Biplane rides over the Hudson River are available for a fee.

**Rhinebeck Chamber Music Society**. *P.O. Box 465, Rhinebeck 12572. 845-876-2870. www.rhinebeckmusic.org.* The society presents eight concerts a year in Rhinebeck and the surrounding area.

**Upstate Films**. *6415 Montgomery Street, Rhinebeck. 845-876-2515. www.upstatefilms.org.* Since its inception in 1972, this local theater has brought a wide selection of independent and foreign films to Rhinebeck and surrounding areas and has hosted regular lectures by directors and actors. *Fee.*

**Wilderstein**. *330 Morton Road, Route 85, Rhinebeck 12572. 845-876-4818. www.wilderstein.org. National Register.* With riverfront landscaping by Calvert Vaux and interiors designed by Joseph Burr Tiffany, this 35-room Queen Anne mansion (dating from the 1850s but remodeled along its current lines in 1888) was for many years the home of Margaret "Daisy" Suckley, the cousin and sometime romantic friend of Franklin D. Roosevelt. The once opulent house fell on hard times as Miss Suckley's fortune dwindled, but after her death in 1991 at the age of 99 a preservation group began to restore it. Correspondence found under her bed revealed just how close her friendship with President Roosevelt had been. *Fee.*

## STAATSBURGH

**Mills Mansion/Staatsburgh Historic Site**. *Old Post Road, Staatsburgh. 845-889-8851. www.staatsburgh.org. National Register.* In 1895, at the request of Ruth Livingston Mills and her husband, Ogden Mills, the architectural firm of McKim, Mead & White transformed an 1832 Greek Revival house into this Beaux Arts mansion of 65 rooms and 14 bathrooms. The astonishing structure, with its exterior of balustrades and floral swags and its interior of gilt furniture and fine silks and art, was given to the state of New York by Gladys Mills Phipps, the daughter of Ruth and Ogden Mills, in 1938. *It is under the jurisdiction of the New York State Office of Parks, Recreation and Historic Preservation and open April through October, Tuesday through Saturday 10 am until 5 pm, and Sunday 12 pm until 5 pm; January to March, Saturday and Sunday from 11 am until 4 pm. Free.*

## TIVOLI

Antiques stores, galleries, restaurants, and handsome architecture have made Tivoli one of the most popular villages along the Hudson. It is the starting point for a visit to the largest tidal freshwater wetland on the Hudson River, Tivoli Bays (1,722 acres). The view of the Catskills from the parking area for Tivoli Bays is considered one of the county's finest. The village is said to have derived its name from a former estate here called the "Chateau de Tivoli," itself a reference to Hadrian's Villa south of Rome.

**Hudson River Research Reserve, Tivoli Bays Visitor Center**. *Watts dePeyster Fireman's Hall, 1 Tivoli Commons, Village of Tivoli. 845-757-3057. www.dec.ny.gov/lands/4915.html.* Designated as part of a national network of protected estuaries studied by scientists, this two-mile stretch of marshes, mudflats, and tidal swamps between Tivoli and Barrytown provides important habitat for wildlife. The visitor center in the Fireman's Hall in Tivoli contains exhibits and hosts lectures and hands-on education programs about the river and its ecology.

The visitor center is also the starting point for the trail that leads to North Bay.

**Kaatsbaan International Dance Center**. *120 Broadway, Tivoli. 845-757-5106. www.kaatsbaan.org*. A performance facility and school, the Kaatsbaan International Dance Center presents performances by visiting ballet and modern dance companies and offers classes on technique in a variety of dance styles. *Fee.*

**St. Paul's Church**. *39 Woods Road, Tivoli. 12583. 845-757-3131. www.stpaulstivoli.org*. Designed by Lawrence Valk, the lovely stone Episcopal church with its historic cemetery and pipe organ was completed in 1869.

## WAPPINGERS FALLS

**County Players Falls Theatre**. *2681 West Main Street, Wappingers Falls 12590. 845-298-1491. www.countyplayers.org*. This all-volunteer community theater is located in the center of the village of Wappingers Falls.

### Festivals, Fairs, and Celebrations

**Art Along the Hudson**. *www.artalongthehudson.com*. Several weekends a year in selected cities along the river, cultural organizations, restaurants, galleries, and antiques stores stay open late and offer special events and music as part of a yearlong celebration of the arts along the river. In Dutchess County, this recurring festival takes place in Beacon on the second weekend of each month and in Poughkeepsie on a selected weekend every three months. For information about events in Beacon contact 845-546-6222 or www.beaconarts.org and in Poughkeepsie contact the Barrett Art Center at 845-471-2550 or www.barrettartcenter.org.

**Bard Summerscape/Jazz at Bard**. *845-758-7900. www.summerscape.bard.edu; www.bard.edu/jazzatbard*. Taking place each summer in the Bard College Fisher Center for the Performing Arts while school is out, these well-respected programs in music, ballet, drama, and film draw audiences of all ages from throughout the region. Each season offers an ambitious range of styles in which internationally respected artists perform works by major composers, dramatists, and choreographers, often highlighting works by a single artist in different genres.

**Dutchess County Fair**. *6550 Spring Brook Avenue (Route 9), Rhinebeck 12572. 845-876-4001. www.dutchessfair.com*. Taking place during the third week in August, the second largest county fair in New York State (after Buffalo's Erie County Fair) draws more than 500,000 visitors from New

*Waryas Park in Poughkeepsie fills with crafts, art, music and food on the third Saturday of each September during the annual Hudson River Arts Festival.*

England and New York for its annual extravaganza in Rhinebeck. With thousands of farm animals and agricultural and horticultural products on display, the 168-acre fairgrounds also hosts bluegrass performers, crafts shows, art exhibits, and a carnival. During the rest of the year, the Dutchess County Agricultural Society, which runs the fair, puts on other events including a crafts show, antiques shows, a Sheep and Wool Festival, and a Wine and Food Festival. *Open Tuesday through Sunday during fair week, 10 am until 10 pm.*

**Hudson River Arts Festival**. *www.bardavon.org*. This annual fall festival in Waryas Park on the waterfront (where Main Street meets the Hudson) takes place on the third Saturday in September each year and includes musical performances, Hudson River boat cruises on the sloop *Clearwater*, food from local restaurants, activities for children, crafters, fine artists, and the Dutchess County Arts Council's One River Many Streams folk arts festival of performances and demonstrations.

**Vassar College Modfest**. *Poughkeepsie, NY. 124 Raymond Avenue (various locations across campus), Poughkeepsie 12604. 845-437-7294. music.vassar .edu/concerts.html.* A ten-day music series held on the campus each January, Modfest invites vocal groups, chamber musicians, and dancers to perform. *All events are free and open to the public and take place at various locations.*

## Also Nearby

Twenty-five miles east of Poughkeepsie on Route 44—and five from Amenia—New England begins with Litchfield County, Connecticut, whose white clapboard colonial houses, peaceful village greens, and rolling farmland invite a morning's drive. Villages with such names as Kent, Cornwall, and Salisbury are as English as many place-names in the Hudson Valley are Dutch; pleasant restaurants, antiques stores, bookstores, and galleries reward the visitor.

## Visitor Information

**Dutchess County Arts Council**. *9 Vassar Street, Poughkeepsie. 12601. 845-454-3222. www.artsmidhudson.com*. (See entry under "Poughkeepsie," above.) This extremely useful organization not only provides information about the arts in the county but publishes an art-buying guide for visitors and residents, gives grants to artists, and organizes special events.

**Dutchess County Historical Society**. *P.O. Box 88, Poughkeepsie 12602. 845-471-1630. www.dutchesscountyhistoricalsociety.org*. (See entry under "Poughkeepsie," above.)

**Dutchess County Tourism**. *3 Neptune Road, Poughkeepsie 12601. 845-463-4000. www.dutchesstourism.com*. The office provides information on every aspect of the county, from shooting clubs to farm markets to the famous county fair, and has especially useful lists of galleries, arts organizations, and parks.

**Historic Hyde Park**. *4079 Albany Post Road, Hyde Park 12538. www.historichydepark.com*. This Web site run by a consortium of governmental and nonprofit organizations provides a useful overview of attractions and accommodations in Hyde Park.

**Hudson River Heritage**. *P.O. Box 287, Rhinebeck 12572. 845-876-2474. www.hudsonriverheritage.org*. Hudson River Heritage is a preservation organization dedicated to the upkeep of historic homes and landscapes in the Mid-Hudson River Valley from Staatsburgh in Dutchess County to Clermont in Columbia County. It holds an annual County Seats Tour that introduces participants to the architectural import of the region's historic homes and gardens and hosts a number of lectures on topics ranging from local archaeology to ice boating on the Hudson River.

**Hudson River Valley Institute**. *Marist College, 3399 North Road, Poughkeepsie 12601. 845-575-3052. www.hudsonrivervalley.org*. Located at Marist College in Poughkeepsie, the academic arm of the Hudson

*A sculpture garden displays some of the 15,000 works in the collection of the Frances Lehman Loeb Arts Center at Vassar College in Poughkeepsie (page 159).*

River Valley National Heritage Area (see Resource Directory) maintains a digital library and a useful and comprehensive Web site with detailed information on the valley.

**Scenic Hudson**. *One Civic Center Plaza, Suite 200, Poughkeepsie 12601. 845-473-4440. www.scenichudson.org.* The largest environmental group focused on the entire Hudson Valley, this advocacy and preservation organization was founded in 1963 to protect and restore the valley and its landscape. Among its many accomplishments have been the creation, improvement, and operation of 40 parks and preserves along the river, including Poets' Walk in Red Hook, Madam Brett Park and Long Dock Beacon Park in Beacon, and Stockport Flats in Greenport just north of Hudson.

# ULSTER COUNTY

From the formation of the utopian arts and crafts colony known as Byrdcliffe in Woodstock in 1902 to the groundbreaking recordings by Bob Dylan and The Band known as the *Basement Tapes* in West Saugerties 65 years later, Ulster County has kept up a consistent reputation for cultural innovation. Its varied and stunning topography, with lush wetlands along the Hudson, the long fertile valley of Rondout Creek, the soaring heights of the Catskills, and the unexpected vastness of the Shawangunk Ridge, continues to draw artists and nature lovers long after the Hudson River School retreated to the walls of museums.

Today, from Woodstock to New Paltz, and along the river in Kingston and Saugerties, artists continue to perform, create, and teach in such strong and growing institutions as the Woman's Studio Worskshop, the Samuel Dorsky Museum of Art, the Center for Photography in Woodstock, and the Arts Society of Kingston. In the foothills of the Catskills between Woodstock and Saugerties, Harvey Fite's monumental *Opus 40* astonishes visitors with its carefully fitted bluestone walls curving off toward the Hudson Valley, while just outside Woodstock the sounds of chamber music mix with birdcalls in the handmade outdoor music "chapel" of the Maverick Concerts (the longest-running chamber series in the United States).

A popular film festival brings big names and sophisticated audiences to Woodstock each October, and a museum of long-standing, the Woodstock Artists' Association, mounts exuberant exhibits of contemporary art. Farther back from the river, in such Catskill towns as Pine Hill, Phoenicia, Cragsmoor, Arkville, and Margaretville, small arts centers, antiques stores, and galleries host concerts, shows, and street festivals in quirky storefronts and lively community centers.

Two major performing arts centers attract audiences from up and down the Hudson Valley. Idols of the classical, jazz, and pop worlds perform at the indoor Ulster Performing Arts Center in Kingston throughout the year and at the outdoor Belleayre Music Festival at Belleayre Ski Area in High Mount during the summer. No less sophisticated but more intimate spaces such as a United Methodist Church in Saugerties or a wooden concert hall in the

*The 1869 Saugerties Lighthouse has been reopened as a popular bed-and-breakfast.*

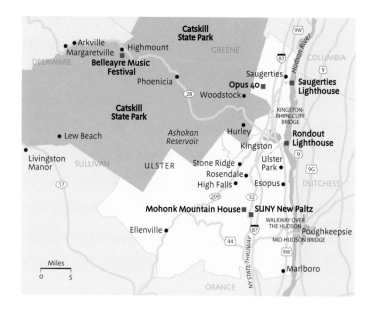

forest outside Woodstock take advantage of unique acoustical settings for such well-regarded series as the Saugerties Pro Musica and the Maverick Concerts.

Settled in 1652 as Wiltwyck, Kingston, the county seat, was one of the first Dutch settlements along the river (the other two being New Netherland—later New York—and Fort Orange—later Albany), and the Dutch architectural legacy remains strong throughout the county. Ancient and lovely stone houses cluster in Hurley and Stone Ridge and in Kingston's own historic center, known as the Stockade District. (Most famous among the houses in the Stockade District is Kingston's Senate House, dating from the 20 years during which Kingston was the first capital of New York State.) Other interesting architecture in Ulster County includes, in New Paltz, a strikingly preserved collection of 17th-, 18th-, and 19th-century French Huguenot houses near the center of town and the lavish 19th-century gardens and architecture of the dramatically situated Mohonk Mountain House, up on the Shawangunk Ridge.

The port district in the downtown or Rondout section of Kingston is the home of museums devoted to boats and trains, restaurants, shops, and galleries—including a gallery devoted exclusively to experimental art known as the Kingston Museum of Contemporary Arts (www.kmoca.org). Like many towns in the valley, Kingston participates in Art Along the Hudson, a celebration of art and artists that takes place on the first Saturday of every month here and on other Saturdays elsewhere. The Arts Society of Kingston at 97 Broadway (845-338-0331; www .askforarts.org) provides complete information on cultural events and places of interest throughout the city and county and mounts a sculpture biennial during odd years, installing sculpture throughout the city in a curated exhibit that treats the entire city as one big gallery.

As a supplier of the stone for New York City's sidewalks and an indirect supplier of the coal for its furnaces, Ulster County flourished as a shipping and railroad center in the 19th century. In recent years, enterprising residents have been finding new uses for the old buildings and industrial sites, reopening a lighthouse as a bed-and-breakfast in Saugerties and creating walking tours along sections of the 108-mile D & H Canal at High Falls, bringing this feat of 19th-century engineering back to life.

## ELLENVILLE

**Shadowland Theatre**. *157 Canal Street (opposite Hermance Street), Ellenville 12428. 845-647-5511. www.shadowlandtheatre.org.* This artistically inventive professional company mounts five productions a year from May to late September. Each season usually includes a mix of classics, notable contemporary works, and new plays. *Open mid-May through late September; performances are Thursday through Sunday. Some winter performances. Fee.*

## HIGH FALLS

**D & H Canal Museum**. *Mohonk Road (Route 6A, one-tenth of a mile west of intersection), High Falls 12440. 845-687-9311. www.canalmuseum.org.* Located in a 19th-century Gothic chapel in a lovely village, the museum examines the history of the 108-mile-long D & H Canal, an important precursor to the Erie Canal. The D & H ran between northeastern Pennsylvania and the Hudson River near Kingston and was in operation for the shipment of anthracite coal to New York City and Canada between 1828 and 1898. The museum's collection includes maps, photographs, and art relating to the canal, its workers, and the booming coal industry that it supported. Guests to the museum may take the Five Locks Tour, which presents 5 of the 108 original locks. *Open May through October, Thursday through Saturday and Monday, 11 am until 5 pm; Sunday, 1 pm until 5 pm. Fee.*

*From intimate recitals to large pop concerts, the Belleayre Music Festival draws thousands high into the Catskills each summer to hear contemporary musical greats.*

## HIGH MOUNT

**Belleayre Music Festival**. *Belleayre Mountain Road (37 miles west of Kingston on Route 28) High Mount. 12441. 845-254-5600 ext. 344. www .belleayremusic.org.* Located high in the Catskills among the green and soaring trails of Belleayre Ski Mountain, this well-regarded series of concerts brings top names in rock, country, jazz, and alternative music to Ulster County each summer. The festival also features theatrical and Broadway-style productions in its covered tent performance area. *Fee.*

## HURLEY

**Elmendorf House/Hurley Heritage Society Museum**. *52 Main Street, Hurley 12443. 845-338-1661. www.hurleyheritagesociety.org. National Register.* Dating from 1783–90, this museum and headquarters of the local Heritage Society offers historical displays and a walking tour pamphlet to the stone houses of Hurley—considered the oldest concentration of privately owned stone houses in the United States. *Open May through October, Saturdays 10 am until 4 pm and Sundays 1 pm until 4 pm; Thanksgiving weekend, Friday, Saturday, and Sunday, 10 am until 4 pm.*

## KINGSTON

This city on a bluff overlooking the Hudson became the first capital of New York State in 1777, though it was supplanted 20 years later by Albany. Settled in 1652 as the Dutch village of Wiltwyck, the city grew from the political center of the mid-Hudson Valley in the 18th century to a manufacturing, trade, and transportation hub in the 19th. Today, roads leading west into the Catskills (Route 28) and southwest along the D & H Canal (Route 209) connect to former sources of trade and current ones of culture. The Kingston Heritage Area Visitor Center (www.ci.kingston. ny.us) and the National Register of Historic Places Travel Itinerary (www. nps.gov/nr/travel/kingston) are excellent places to start for additional information about the city.

**Arts Society of Kingston**. *97 Broadway, Kingston 12401. 845-338-0331. www.askforarts.org.* Made up of visual and performing artists and their supporters, this busy arts center in downtown Kingston hosts monthly exhibits in its two galleries and organizes theater performances, readings, and off-site exhibitions. Special events include an Open Studio Tour each October and the Kingston Sculpture Biennial in odd-numbered years. *Open Thursday through Saturday, 12 pm until 5 pm.*

**Deep Listening Institute**. *77 Cornell Street, Suite 303, Kingston 12402. 845-338-5984. www.deeplistening.org.* Distinguishing between the involuntary nature of hearing and the voluntary act of listening, this organization offers concerts, readings, and discussions in its Deep Listening Space in Kingston. *Its gallery is open Saturday and Sunday, 1 pm until 4 pm and by appointment.*

**Hudson River Maritime Museum**. *50 Rondout Landing, Kingston. 845-338-0071. www.hrmm.org.* Stocked with art and artifacts depicting the maritime history of the Hudson River, this museum near the juncture of Rondout Creek and the Hudson is a gold mine of information on boats

of every kind, from iceboats to steamboats; local industries along the river; and discoverers, sailors, ferry captains, and just about anyone else who happened to ply the waters on a regular basis. All this is presented in picture and object (including a complete iceboat), exhibits, pamphlets, and a Web site. *Open May through October, Thursday through Monday, 12 pm until 6 pm. Fee.*

*Among the boats collected at the Hudson River Maritime Museum in Kingston is a set of Hudson River iceboats.*

**Kingston Museum of Contemporary Arts**. *103 Abeel Street, Kingston 12401. www.kmoca.org.* Located in the downtown or Rondout section of Kingston near Rondout Creek, this museum devoted to outsider art and work with a strong social commentary mounts a new exhibit each month and hosts film screenings, readings, and live music.

**Kingston-Rhinecliff Bridge**. *P.O. Box 1400, Kingston 12401. 845-336-8181. http://nysba.state.ny.us.* Carrying Route 199 across the river between Kingston and Rhinecliff township, the 7,793-foot underdeck truss bridge opened in 1957, replacing a ferry whose crossing was one of the oldest on the river.

**Kingston Senate House and Museum**. *296 Fair Street, Kingston 12401. 845-338-2786. www.nysparks.state.ny.us/sites. National Register.* In 1777, when Kingston became the state capital during the American Revolution, the stone house of Abraham Van Gaasbeek, a Kingston merchant, became the meeting place of New York's first senate. The state acquired the property in 1887 in recognition of its role and it has been a museum ever since. In 1927 the state constructed a two-story museum building to contain its growing collection of art and historical objects including paintings by John Vanderlyn of Kingston and other members of his family, dating from the 1720s through the 1870s, and by Ammi Phillips, Joseph Tubby, James Bard, and Thomas Sully. (John Vanderlyn's *Panoramic View of the Palace and Gardens of Versailles* is permanently installed in a specially designed circular room in the American Wing at the Metropolitan Museum of Art in New York City.) *Open April 7 through October 31, Monday, Wednesday, and Saturday, 10 am until 5 pm, and Sunday, 11 am until 5 pm. Also open Memorial Day, Independence Day, and Labor Day and year-round by appointment. Fee.*

**Old Dutch Church**. *272 Wall Street (in the Stockade District), Kingston. 845-338-6759. National Register.* The Renaissance Revival bluestone church, designed by Minard Lafever, was built in 1852 for a Dutch Reformed congregation that dates back to the founding of Kingston in 1659. The church often has organ recitals during the week in the warmer months.

**Rondout Lighthouse**. *National Register.* Completed in 1915 and one of the youngest on the river, the lighthouse is owned by the City of Kingston but operated and maintained by the Hudson River Maritime Museum (see above). *Tours take place from Memorial Day to Labor Day, Saturdays, Sundays, and holiday Mondays.*

*When Kingston briefly became the New York State capital in 1777, the stone house of Abraham Van Gaasbeek, a Kingston merchant, became the meeting place of New York's first senate*

**Stockade District**. *National Register.* Bounded by Washington and Clinton Avenues and Main and North Front Streets, Kingston. The historical nucleus of Kingston was originally enclosed within a stockade fence as a protection against raids by the local Esopus Indians. Rendered obsolete by a treaty in 1664, the fence lasted until the end of the 17th century but many of the limestone-and-mortar fieldstone houses within it still stand. A pamphlet published by the Friends of Historic Kingston (845-339-0720; www.fohk.org) provides information on 32 locations of interest within the district and a map of an easy walking tour.

**Trolley Museum of New York**. *89 East Strand, Kingston 12402. 845-331-3399. www.tmny.org.* Created in 1955, this museum on the site of the original Delaware & Hudson Railroad yards displays trolley, subway, and rapid transit cars from the United States and Europe and operates a one-and-a-half-mile excursion ride illustrating the history of rail transportation and its role in the Hudson Valley. *Open Memorial Day through Columbus Day, Saturdays, Sundays, and holidays, 12 pm until 5 pm.*

**Ulster Performing Arts Center**. *601 Broadway (between O'Neil and Cornell Streets), Kingston 12401. 845-339-6088. www.upac.org.* One of the prominent arts organizations in the Hudson Valley, this 1,500-seat concert hall and theater attracts well-known performers from throughout the country and world. *The box office is open Monday through Friday, 9:30 am until 5 pm, and Saturday, 11 am until 3 pm. Fee.*

*The Hasbrouck House is one of a group of 17th-century Huguenot dwellings in New Paltz maintained by the Huegenot Historical Society.*

## NEW PALTZ

Settled in 1677 by a group of Huguenots escaping Catholic persecution in Europe, this old farming village on the Wallkill, at the foot of the Shawangunk Mountains, retains a unique charm based on its largely intact street of original 17th-century houses, its magnificent rural setting in apple fields leading off to rugged cliffs, and the lively presence of the college at New Paltz, a branch of the State University of New York known for its focus on the fine and performing arts. For more information on the town itself, visit www.newpaltz.org.

**Huguenot Historical Society**. *18 Broadhead Avenue (at Route 32), New Paltz 12561. 845-255-1660. www.huguenotstreet.org. National Register.* Dating from 1687, this complex of historic homes, church, and military fort bears the traces of a settlement of French Protestants who came to America to escape religious persecution. Three of the houses have been furnished to reflect 18th-century lifestyles, while others reflect the fashion for colonial revival and the changing agricultural practices of the 19th century. *Tours take place May through October, Tuesday through Sunday, 10 am until 5 pm, and in other seasons by appointment. Huguenot Street is open year-round.*

**Mohonk Mountain House**. *1000 Mountain Rest Road (6 miles outside New Paltz), New Paltz 12561. 845-255-1000. www.mohonk.com. National Register.* This great hotel, dating from 1869 and one of the few remaining 19th-century American grand hotels, has long been distinguished for its architectural grandeur, its dramatic setting on a lake on the Shawangunk Ridge, its extensive and well-maintained Victorian gardens (including a maze), its early environmental awareness, and its history. The views from high points around the hotel are some of the most far-reaching and dramatic in the state. From 1883 until 1916, one of the founders, Albert Smiley (whose family still runs the hotel), sponsored the annual

Lake Mohonk Conference of Friends of the Indian, bringing government officials, university professors, philanthropists, and Indian leaders together to discuss the conditions of Native Americans and suggest ways to improve their lives. Annexed to the 2,200 acres of fields, gardens, and woods around the hotel are another 6,500 acres of the Mohonk Preserve, a unique privately owned public treasure (see below).

**Mohonk Preserve**. *3197 Route 44/55, Gardiner 12525. 845-255-0919 www .mohonkpreserve.org.* Established in 1963 by the owners of the Mohonk Mountain House and some guests, the 6,500-acre park is the state's largest nonprofit nature preserve. More than 100 miles of trails and carriage roads allow hiking, running, mountain biking, horseback riding, and cross-country skiing. The famous cliffs here known as the "Gunks" are sought out by rock climbers from around the world. A visitor center offers trail information, exhibits on local wildlife and geology, a butterfly garden, a sensory trail, and a nature trail. *Fee for nonmembers.*

**SUNY New Paltz**. *75 South Manheim Boulevard, New Paltz 12561.* Started in 1833 as the New Paltz Academy, this college of the State University of New York is renowned for its offerings in the visual and performing arts and very much gives New Paltz the exciting atmosphere of a college town. Its public arts offerings include:

*Long distinguished for its architectural grandeur and its dramatic setting in the Shawangunks, the Mohonk Mountain House, in New Paltz, is one of the few remaining 19th century grand hotels still in operation.*

- The Samuel Dorsky Museum of Art (845-257-3844; www.newpaltz.edu/ museum). Opened in 2000 to house the university's expanding collection, the 17,000-square-foot museum displays work from all periods. Areas of specialization within the permanent collection include 20th-century prints and paintings, decorative art, photographs, Asian art, and pre-Columbian artifacts. In addition to exhibits, the museum also offers tours, workshops, and a lecture series. *Open Wednesday through Saturday, 11 am until 5 pm, and Sunday, 1 pm until 5 pm.*

- Theatre Arts Mainstage Season (845-257-3880; www.newpaltz.edu/ artnews). The theater department mounts four to six shows in its two venues between October and April. Student-directed works take place in the Black Box Studio.

- The college is also home to the Piano Summer Institute and Festival (www.newpaltz.edu/piano), an intensive summer teaching program devoted solely to the piano.

**Unison Arts and Learning Center**. *68 Mountain Rest Road (on Mountain Rest Road half a mile west of Springtown Road), New Paltz 12561. 845-255-1559. www.unisonarts.org.* This multidisciplinary arts center hosts performances of jazz, blues, folk, classical, new music, theater, and dance. The center also houses a gallery and an outdoor sculpture garden. *The office is open Monday through Friday, 10 am until 5 pm; classes take place daily, 10 am until 10 pm.*

## ROSENDALE
**Women's Studio Workshop**. *722 Binnewater Lane (near Breezy Hill Road), Rosendale 12472. 845-658-9133. www.wsworkshop.org.* Established in 1974 by four women seeking to create an alternative space for female artists, this nonprofit organization holds several exhibitions each year in its Binnewater Arts Center gallery and an annual Summer Arts Institute that invites artists to create new works. *Open Monday through Friday, 10 am until 5 pm; weekends by appointment. Free.*

## SAUGERTIES
***Opus 40/Quarryman's Museum***. *50 Fite Road (off Route 212 via Glasco Turnpike and Highwoods Road), Saugerties. 845-246-3400. www.opus40 .org. National Register.* From 1939 until his death in 1976, the sculptor Harvey Fite transformed an abandoned quarry into this monumental sculpture composed of thousands of blocks of bluestone cut and fit together by hand. Fite had originally intended the swirling six-acre structure to be a showcase for his smaller pieces but came to realize that the structure was a sculpture in itself. The Quarryman's Museum displays the unusual tools Fite used to create his work. The site is now overseen by a

*From 1939 until his death in 1976, the sculptor Harvey Fite transformed an abandoned bluestone quarry near Saugerties into a monumental sculpture known as* Opus 40.

nonprofit organization. *Open Memorial Day weekend through Columbus Day weekend, Friday, Saturday, Sunday, and holiday Mondays, 11:30 am until 6 pm.*

**Saugerties Lighthouse**. *168 Lighthouse Drive (on the Hudson River), Saugerties 12477. 845-247-0656. www.saugertieslighthouse.com. National Register.* Built in 1869, the redbrick lighthouse at the mouth of Esopus Creek was restored during the late 1980s by the Saugerties Lighthouse Conservancy and reopened in 1990 as a museum and bed-and-breakfast. *Open year-round; reachable by a half-mile trail from the parking lot or by boat. Fee.*

**Saugerties Pro Musica**. *United Methodist Church (corner of Washington Avenue and Post Street), Saugerties. 845-679-5733 or 845-246-5021. www .saugertiespromusica.org.* This nonprofit organization mounts Sunday afternoon concerts in the fall and spring.

## STONE RIDGE
**Bevier House Museum/Ulster County Historical Society**. *Route 209 (6 miles west of intersection with Route 28), Stone Ridge. 845-338-5614. www.bevierhousemuseum.org. National Register.* Built in the 1780s, this historic house and museum—the headquarters of the Ulster County Historical Society—was inhabited by a single family for 223 years before

its transfer to the society in 1938. The museum contains well-preserved artifacts and period furniture depicting the long and varied history of the house and region. *Open June through September, Thursday through Sunday, 1 pm until 5 pm. Fee.*

**High Meadow Arts**. *Route 209, Stone Ridge 12484. 845-687-4855. www.highmeadowarts.org.* This school and arts center offers drama, singing, modern dance, music composition, visual arts, and video and media production to children and adults throughout the year. Instructors include local artists and educators from Marbletown, Rosendale, Kingston, Woodstock, Kripplebush, and New Paltz. *Fee.*

**SUNY Ulster**. *Cottekill Road, Stone Ridge 12484. 845.687.5000. www.sunyulster.edu.* This two-year college of the State University of New York hosts exhibits of local and nationally known artists in the Muroff-Kotler Visual Arts Gallery in Vanderlyn Hall (845-687-5113; open Monday through Friday, 11 am until 3 pm and by appointment), and stages student and professional theatrical productions, concerts, dance presentations, poetry readings, and guest lectures each semester in the 500-seat John Quimby Theater (845-687-7127). *Fee.*

## ULSTER PARK
**Esopus Meadows Lighthouse, Lighthouse Park**. *River Road (east of Route 9W), Ulster Park. 845-297-1569. www.esopusmeadowslighthouse.org. National Register.* Built in 1871 to mark a mudflat on the west side of the river known as the Esopus Meadows, the wooden lighthouse (the only wooden lighthouse still standing on the river) fell into disrepair after the automation of its light in 1965 but was restored and reopened as a museum and working lighthouse in 2002. The Save Esopus Lighthouse Commission offers occasional tours.

## WOODSTOCK
Even though the Woodstock Festival did not take place in the town of Woodstock (it was actually 65 miles southwest on a farm in Sullivan County, now the Bethel Woods Center for the Arts; see Orange County) this Ulster County town keeps the 1960s alive with a determined mix of record shops, crafts stores, galleries, funky restaurants, and more traditional hardware stores and banks. The formation of the Byrdcliffe artists' colony in 1902, the Maverick Concerts in 1916, and the Woodstock Artists' Association in 1920—all of which are alive and well today—began a tradition of support for the arts that continues with more recent additions such as the Center for Photography, the Woodstock Fringe Festival, and a monthly art celebration throughout the town on the second Saturday of each month.

**Byrdcliffe Arts Colony**. *National Register*. The Englishman Ralph Radcliffe Whitehead started a utopian Arts and Crafts community for woodworkers, potters, weavers, photographers, and painters on the hill on the north side of Woodstock in 1902. A new generation of artists is back and, under the management of the Byrdcliffe Guild, this venerable institution with its lovely houses, studios, and performance spaces scattered through the woods remains one of the oldest summer arts residency programs in the country. The grounds are open to the public dawn to dusk, and tours are available through the Byrdcliffe Guild (see below) on Saturdays.

**Byrdcliffe Guild**. *34 Tinker Street (near the Village Green), Woodstock 12498. 845-679-2079. www.woodstockguild.org*. Established in 1939, the guild houses the Kleinert/James Arts Center, a performance venue, and the Fleur de Lis Gallery, an exhibition space for local artists. It also offers a variety of classes and is steward of the Byrdcliffe Arts Colony (see above). *The guild is open Monday through Friday, 10 am until 5 pm; the gallery, Friday through Sunday, 12 pm until 5 pm. Fee.*

**Center for Photography at Woodstock**. *59 Tinker Street, Woodstock. 845-679-9957. www.cpw.org*. This arts center devoted to photography mounts up to six exhibitions a year of work by photographic artists from all over the state and world and offers workshops, lectures, and classes by some of the most distinguished names in photography. It also publishes the magazine *Photography Quarterly. Open Wednesday through Sunday, 12 pm until 5 pm. Free.*

**Karma Triyana Dharmachakra**. *Meads Mountain Road, Woodstock. 845-679-5906. www.kagyu.org*. Built in the 1980s, this monastery following the Karma Kagyu form of Tibetan Buddhism welcomes visitors to its main shrine room, which has a hand-painted ceiling by resident artist Thinley Chojor and lovely statuary including a revered statue of the Buddha. Public tours are Saturdays and Sundays at 1:30 pm (call in advance).

**Maverick Concerts**. *Maverick Road, Woodstock. 845-679-8217. www.maverickconcerts.org. National Register*. First organized in 1916 by the poet and novelist Hervey White, and taking place on Saturday evenings and Sunday afternoons in a "music chapel" hand-built by White and others, these outdoor summer concerts by some of the great musicians of the world are part of the longest continuously running chamber music series in the United States. Renowned for its acoustics, the concert hall, open to the sounds of the woods but providing cover from the rain, is a superb place to appreciate this most challenging and exciting form.

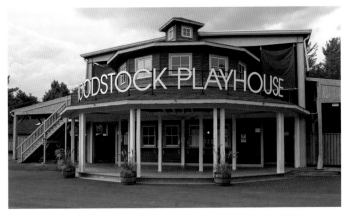

*The semienclosed Woodstock Playhouse is the home of the Bird-on-a-Cliff Theatre Company.*

Free children's concerts are also offered. Concerts take place from the end of June until early September.

**Woodstock Artists' Association and Museum**. *28 Tinker Street (near the Village Green), Woodstock 12498. 845-679-2940. www.woodstockart .org.* Founded in 1920, and one of the most important arts institutions in the county, this exhibition space and meeting place is home to an ever growing collection of art by local artists and hosts literary readings, video screenings, symposia, and lectures. *Open Friday through Monday, 12 pm until 5 pm.*

**Woodstock Playhouse**. *Mill Hill Road (at the junction of Routes 212 and 375), Woodstock 12498. 845-679-4101. www.woodstockplayhouse.org.* This semienclosed performance space hosts a range of groups from classical musicians to rock bands and is the home of the Bird-on-a-Cliff Theatre Company, which produces two plays there each summer. *Fee.*

**Woodstock Poetry Society**. *Town Hall, 76 Tinker Street, Woodstock.* Founded in 1996, the society puts on a reading on the second Saturday of every month in the Woodstock Town Hall as part of the local arts day, usually featuring two established poets and an open mike.

## Fairs, Festivals, and Celebrations

**Art Along the Hudson**. www.artalongthehudson.com. One weekend each month in selected cities along the river, cultural organizations, restaurants, galleries, and antiques stores stay open late and offer special events and music as part of a yearlong celebration of the arts along the river. The festival takes place in Kingston on the first Saturday of every month and in other cities along the Hudson on other Saturdays. The Arts Society of Kingston (www.askforarts.org) has the full schedule.

**Jazz in the Valley**. P.O. Box 148, West Park 12493. 845-384-6350. www .transartinc.org. This annual concert series takes place on the last Sunday in August at Williams Lake near Rosendale and welcomes many of the biggest names in jazz to Ulster County.

**Kingston Jazz Festival**. 518-945-2669. www.planetarts.org. Taking place at City Hall and in the Rondout neighborhood, this two-day event brings national and international jazz musicians together with such local groups as the Kingston High School Jazz Ensemble.

**Ulster County Fair/Art and Crafts Fair**. Libertyville Road, New Paltz. 845-255-1380. www.ulstercountyfair.com. Run by the Ulster County Agricultural Society since 1886, this popular annual event takes place at the beginning of August. A tractor pull and a beauty pageant are among the popular events. The fairgrounds are also the site for the annual Woodstock/New Paltz Arts and Crafts Fair (845-679-8087).

**Woodstock Film Festival**. P.O. Box 1406, 86 Mill Hill Road, Woodstock 12498. 845-679-4265. www.woodstockfilmfestival.com. Founded in 2000, the Woodstock Film Festival attracts films, filmmakers, and celebrities to the Hudson River Valley for five days each October. New and recently released features, documentaries, and shorts are screened in venues including Tinker Street Cinema and Bearsville in Woodstock, Upstate Films in Rhinebeck, and the Catskill Mountain Foundation Theatre in Hunter. The festival also programs year-round events in local venues such as Inquiring Minds Gallery in Saugerties and the Woodstock Town Hall. Festival runs late September to early October.

**Woodstock Fringe Festival of Theater and Song**. P.O. Box 157, Lake Hill 12448. 845-810-0123. www.woodstockfringe.org. Performing throughout August in the Byrdcliffe Theater at Byrdcliffe, this professional perform-ing arts organization presents new and experimental theater and musical works including plays, performance art, and opera.


## Also Nearby

Twenty-five miles west of Kingston on Route 28, Phoenicia, a small but busy town on the Esopus Creek, is home, among other things, to the Empire State Railway Museum (845.688.7501; www.esrm.com), a former station house of the Ulster & Delaware Railroad that was built

*With its bookstores, galleries, antiques stores, and historical society, the Village of Saugerties draws visitors throughout the year.*

in 1899 and is listed on the National Register of Historic Places. Exhibits of photographs, artifacts, and films and several restored railroad cars illuminate the history of the powerful little trains that brought visitors up to the great Catskills hotels and carried out bluestone, wood, and other products for shipment on the Hudson. Open weekends and holidays, Memorial Day through Columbus Day, 11 am until 4 pm.

Twenty miles farther west of Phoenicia, in the tiny hamlet of Arkville, is the Catskill Center for Conservation and Development (845-586-2611; www.catskillcenter.org), an environmental and community development organization that hosts five exhibits a year of drawing, painting, photography, sculpture, and fine crafts in its Erpf Gallery. Two miles farther is Margaretville, a busy village with galleries, crafts stores, restaurants, and cafés.

## Visitor Information

**City of Kingston Visitor Centers**. *www.ci.kingston.ny.us*. The city operates two fully staffed information centers with maps, guides, and brochures to Kingston, Ulster County, and the Hudson Valley, one at 20 Broadway in the downtown or Rondout section (845-331-7517) and another at 308 Clinton Avenue near the Senate House uptown (845-331-9506).

**Transart and Cultural Services**. *P.O. Box 148, West Park 12493. 845-384-6350. www.transartinc.org.* Seeking to promote the arts of Africa and the African diaspora, TRANSART curates exhibitions, organizes performing arts programs, and conducts cultural awareness projects in venues throughout the Hudson Valley. Each August, the group sponsors the Jazz in the Valley festival at Williams Lake near Rosendale, an event that welcomes many of the biggest names in jazz music to the area. Last Sunday in August.

**Ulster County Tourism**. *10 Westbrook Lane, Kingston 12401. 800-342-5826. www.ulstertourism.info.* With information on hotels, restaurants, and things to do and see throughout the year, this office (and the Web site) is a good place to start when planning a trip.

# COLUMBIA COUNTY

Poets, composers, and other artists have been moving to Columbia County in recent years, drawn by the pastoral landscape, the lively cultural scene, and an artistic tradition that dates back to well before Frederic Edwin Church began building his Persian-style house near Hudson in 1870. With the Catskill Mountains rising like a dark wall to the west and the Berkshires to the east, this enclave of rolling farmland and ancient villages is home to a diverse and knowledgeable population that supports and understands the arts.

The former whaling port (and county seat) of Hudson has been reborn as one of the cultural capitals of the Hudson Valley, drawing visitors from New York City as well as Albany, Massachusetts, Connecticut, and points west and south to its antiques stores, galleries, restaurants, bookstores, an auction and an opera house, several theaters, even a museum of firefighting. One of the oldest planned cities in the United States, Hudson retains a unity in its Federal, Greek Revival, and Victorian architecture that makes its central avenue Warren Street a kind of museum of American architectural history. Something is always happening along Warren and the surrounding streets, whether it be music at the Hudson Opera House, an avant-garde theater troupe at Time & Space Limited, or Shakespeare at Stageworks/Hudson. Visit the Columbia County Council on the Arts, online or at 209 Warren Street, for up-to-the-minute information on openings, screenings, performances, and festivals including the Hudson ArtsWalk each fall and the oldest county fair in the state.

Some of the most interesting art in the United States is being produced along the back roads of this county 100 miles north of New York City and 35 south of Albany. Well-conceived venues such as the Fields Sculpture Park in Ghent or the Spencertown Academy, a former teacher training academy turned gallery and performance space in Spencertown, have helped spur a burst in artistic activity not seen since the founding of the Hudson River School. When the poet Edna St. Vincent Millay moved to Columbia County in 1939, little did she realize that three-quarters

*Since 1874 the Second Empire Hudson-Athens Lighthouse has warned ships away from the Middle Ground Flats, connecting Columbia and Greene Counties with a sense of a shared maritime institution.*

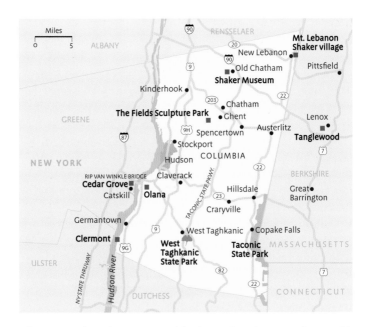

of a century later her 600-acre blueberry farm in Austerlitz would become a thriving international artists' colony, nurturing the talents of dozens of artists in numerous disciplines each year.

Chatham is a lively place, with excellent restaurants, galleries, stores, and a film festival. The hamlet of Old Chatham has a museum devoted entirely to the heritage of the Shakers. The performing arts thrive here at such popular theaters as the Mac-Haydn and the Ghent Playhouse, three miles from the center of Chatham. At the Crandell Theatre in Chatham, the Chatham Film Club screens art films alongside more mainstream features as part of the annual Film Columbia festival.

Former president Martin Van Buren was born in Columbia County, and Lindenwald, the house where he spent his later years, is one of several distinguished historic houses in the county, ranging from Clermont, the former estate of the Livingston family in Germantown, to the Federal-style James Vanderpoel House in Kinderhook. The Staats House, built circa 1660 on Stockport Creek, a stone's throw from the Hudson River, is one of the oldest still-inhabited houses in New York if not the nation. The Columbia County Historical Society oversees a fair number of these houses and hosts creative exhibitions in the former Masonic Lodge that is its headquarters in Kinderhook.

Columbia County connects to Greene County, across the

river, by more than just the Rip Van Winkle Bridge and a shared lighthouse. Numerous events, from ongoing collaborations between Cedar Grove—the Thomas Cole house in Catskill—and Olana, the house of Frederic Edwin Church just across the river, and between the Greene and Columbia County Arts Councils, to weekend tours of the Hudson-Athens Lighthouse, celebrate the symbiotic and historic relationship between the two riverbanks.

Columbia County has a thriving year-round trade at commercial galleries and antiques stores, both in Hudson and in outlying towns. In Hudson itself, a five-block stretch of Warren Street draws knowledgeable browsers from four states and beyond for everything from the latest in contemporary art and sculpture to 18th-century American furniture and antiquarian books. The Web sites www.hudsonantiques.net and www.hudson artgalleries.com provide complete information on the more than 65 antiques shops and 25 galleries in town, and visit the Columbia County Tourism office for listings of special events in town such as the annual WinterWalk, which draws hundreds of people to the streets of Hudson every December. Chatham also has its share of shops and galleries, and a drive on almost any road in the county will lead past some small but interesting and unexpected dealer.

*Settled in the late 18th century as a whaling port, Hudson is now an important center of art and antiques. The unified mix of Federal, Greek Revival, and Victorian architecture along its central avenue, Warren Street, makes it a kind of museum of American architectural history.*

## AUSTERLITZ

**Steepletop/Millay Colony for the Arts**. *East Hill Road, Austerlitz. www .millaysociety.org; www.millaycolony.org. National Register.* Although the former home of the poet Edna St. Vincent Millay is not open to the public, the Edna St. Vincent Millay Society and the Millay Colony for the Arts independently offer public programs on the property where the Pulitzer Prize–winning poet and her husband, Eugen Boissevain, lived from 1925 until 1950. Visitors are invited to stroll on the grounds, hike on the Poetry Trail, visit Millay's grave site and enjoy the 600 acres of beautiful landscapes that inspired Millay's poetry. The Millay Poetry Trail is a wood road leading to the Millay family grave sites with Millay's nature poems posted along it. Art at Steepletop is a summer Saturday extravaganza of readings, concerts and exhibits by graduates of the artists' colony. Millay Colony artists also put on concerts, readings, and exhibits at such well-known Columbia County spaces as the Hudson Opera House and the Spencertown Academy (see below). For more information on Edna St. Vincent Millay in Columbia County, the Millay Society, and the artists' colony, visit the Web sites above.

## CHATHAM

**Chatham Film Club**. *518-766-5892. www.thechathamfilmclub.com.* The Chatham Film Club brings the latest art, independent, and foreign films to the Crandell Theatre in Chatham (see below) once a month and hosts the Film Columbia film festival each October. A three-day event, the festival has premiered films that have gone on to receive national and international acclaim. *Fee.*

**Crandell Theatre**. Main Street, Chatham. *518-392-3331. www.crandell theatre.com.* Columbia County's oldest and largest theater has remained basically unchanged since Walter S. Crandell built it in 1926 as a vaudeville house. Today the Spanish-style brick and stucco theater, which seats 534, is used primarily to screen contemporary films. It is also home to the Chatham Film Club (see above), which hosts a popular festival of cutting-edge documentary and art films each fall. *Fee.*

**Mac-Haydn Theatre**. *Route 203, Chatham. 518-392-9292. www.machaydn theatre.org.* Established in 1969 by two women devoted to the theater, this professional organization in Chatham presents seven mainstage and four children's productions each summer in its intimate theater-in-the-round. *Fee.*

## CLAVERACK

**Reformed Dutch Church of Claverack**. *Route 9H, Claverack 12513. 518-851-3811. National Register.* The simple and elegant building dates from

1767, though it was enlarged during the 19th century. The congregation is one of the oldest in the county and dates from 1726.

## COPAKE FALLS

**Taconic State Park**. *Route 344, Copake Falls, NY 12517. 518-329-3993. nysparks.state.ny.us/parks.* The oldest state park in the Taconic Region is 5,000 acres and home to Bash-Bish falls, a famous cascade often painted by members of the Hudson River School. Located along 11 miles of the Taconic Mountain Range and sharing a border with Massachusetts and Connecticut, the park has two developed areas, Copake Falls and Rudd Pond. The terrain along its extensive trail system varies from easy to challenging and offers spectacular views. Open year-round, sunrise to sunset. *The campground is open the first Friday in May through the first weekend in December. The winterized Greenwich Cabin area, a short drive to local ski resorts, is open year-round.*

## CRARYVILLE

**Taconic Hills Performing Arts Center**. *73 County Route 11A (4 miles east of the Taconic Parkway Claverack/Hillsdale exit), Craryville. 518-325-0457. www.taconichills.k12.ny.us/community/PA.* Housed in a state-of-the-art 950-seat auditorium built in 1999, the Taconic Hills Performing Arts Center is run by—and located on the campus of—the Taconic Hills Central School district in Craryville. The center hosts a wide variety of theatrical, musical, and dance performances, in addition to lectures and cultural events throughout the year. In the warm months, many performances are held in an outdoor amphitheater in close proximity to the main theater. *Fee.*

## GERMANTOWN

**Clermont**. *One Clermont Avenue, Germantown 12526. 518-537-4240. www.friendsofclermont.org. National Register.* The incredible view of the river and the Catskills is one reason Robert Livingston Jr. (1688–1775) named his brick Georgian-style house Clermont when it was completed in 1750. Because of the family's support of the American Revolution, the British burned the house during their march up the river in 1777, but the family rebuilt it and ended up living on the spot for seven successive generations, until 1964. It was Robert R. Livingston Jr. (1746–1813)—drafter of the Declaration of Independence, chancellor of the State of New York, and minister to France—who financed his son-in-law Robert Fulton's first steamboat, known to history as the *Clermont*. Today the house, on its 500-acre historic landscape, appears much as it did in the early 20th century, when the estate was the home of the last two generations to occupy the property: Mr. and Mrs. John Henry Livingston and their daughters, Honoria and Janet. *Open April through*

*DeWitt Godfrey's* Picker (2004) *is part of the ever-expanding collection of contemporary sculpture at the 300-acre Fields Sculpture Park at Omi International Arts Center in Ghent.*

*September, Tuesday through Sunday, 11 am until 5 pm; October, Friday through Sunday, 11 am until 4 pm; and November and December, Saturday and Sunday, 11 am until 4 pm. Fee.*

## GHENT

**The Fields Sculpture Park at Omi International Arts Center**. *1405 County Route 22, Ghent. 518-392-4747. www.artomi.org/fields.htm.* Omi International Arts Center is a not-for-profit residency program for international visual artists, writers, musicians, and dancers. It is also home to the Fields Sculpture Park, a 300-acre park with an ever-expanding collection of sculptures by contemporary artists from around the globe. Guests are invited to stroll across the property's changing terrain as they view sculptures by Carl Andre, Beverly Pepper, Nina Katchadourian, Robert Grosvenor, and dozens of other renowned sculptors as well as an array of emerging ones. A new visitor center—the first certified green building in Columbia County—has indoor galleries for sculpture as well as a shop, a café, and restrooms. Artists in residency at Omi give regular readings and open houses. *The park is open seven days a week from dawn to dusk. The visitor center is open mid-May through October, Sunday, Monday, and Thursday, 10 am until 5 pm, and Friday and Saturday, 10 am until 6 pm; November through mid-May, Saturdays and some other days (check Web site), 10 am until 5 pm. Free.*

**Ghent Playhouse**. *Ghent. 518-392-6264. www.ghentplayhouse.org.* After two decades of providing community theater in local halls, auditoriums, churches, and restaurants, the Columbia Civic Players moved into the former Ghent Town Hall in 1988, purchasing the building from the town in 2001. Local audiences flock to the renovated space for performances by amateur and semiprofessional actors throughout the year. *Fee.*

**Walking the Dog Theater**. *39 Oak Hill Rd. Ghent, NY 12075. 518-392-0131. www.wtdtheater.org.* Focused on staging Shakespeare's plays and collaborating with local artists to create new kinds of theater events, this production company has given more than 700 performances and more than 170 workshops on three continents. *Fee.*

## GREENPORT

**Olana**. *5720 Route 9G, Greenport. 518-828-0135. www.olana.org. National Register.* The painter Frederic Edwin Church was the best-known pupil of Thomas Cole, the founder of the Hudson River School. Fascinated by the Hudson Valley since his initial painting expeditions to the Catskills with Cole in the 1840s, Church returned with his new wife, Isabel, in 1860 and began constructing his Persian-style villa on a hilltop near Hudson ten years later. Based on designs that the Churches brought back from their extensive travels in the Middle East, and constructed over a period of more than 20 years according to Church's precise but evolving vision, the unusual and beautifully decorated house overlooks a breathtaking stretch of the Hudson River as well as the Catskill Mountains and the Taconic Hills. Happily, today not only the house and Church's extensive collection of art and furniture but 250 acres of lawns, ponds, and trails planted and designed by Church are owned by the State of New York and open to the public. *The property, jointly operated by the state and the*

*nonprofit Olana Partnership, is open daily, 8 am to sunset; and tours of the house (fee) take place Tuesday through Sunday, 10 am to 5 pm from April through mid-November, and Friday through Sunday, 11 am to 4 pm from mid-November through the end of March.*

*Visible from miles around on its hilltop near Hudson, Frederic Edwin Church's Persian-style Olana remains the emotional and architectural center of the Hudson River School in the valley.*

## HUDSON

**American Museum of Firefighting**. *117 Harry Howard Avenue, Hudson. 518-822-1875. www.fasnyfiremuseum.com.* The Firemen's Association of the State of New York created the Museum of Firefighting on the grounds of the Firemen's Home in 1925 to safeguard the heritage of volunteer firefighting in New York State. It contains one of the largest collections of firefighting apparatus, equipment, gear, and memorabilia in the world. Old-time fire trucks, tools, badges, uniforms—even firemen's hats— remind one of how much—and how little—has changed in the fighting of fires. Staff and retired volunteer firefighters lead tours. *Open daily, 10 am until 5 pm. Free.*

**Columbia County Council on the Arts**. *209 Warren Street, Hudson 12534. 518-671-6213. www.artscolumbia.org.* Housed in a historic storefront, the Columbia County Council on the Arts hosts exhibitions by local artists throughout the year. The council organizes numerous events and shows as well, including tours of artists' studios, the Riders Mills Historical Association Fence Show (a regional juried art show), and the 10-day multidisciplinary Hudson ArtsWalk (see Festivals, below). *Open Monday through Friday, 9:30 am until 5 pm, and Saturday, 11 am until 5 pm.*

**First Presbyterian Church**. *369 Warren Street, Hudson 12534. 518-828-4275.* One of the distinctive sights of Hudson, this large stone edifice with its four-sided clock tower was originally built in 1837. It was substantially redesigned in 1877 and the clock tower was added in 1905. (The clock is still maintained by the city and wound once a week.) Nearly closed in 1993, the church was saved by the Friends of the First Presbyterian Church and has been maintained by them ever since.

**Hudson-Athens Lighthouse**. *The middle of the Hudson River. 518-828-5294. www.hudsonathenslighthouse.org. National Register.* Warning ships away from the Middle Ground Flats—once a shallows, now a long island in the river—since 1874, this Second Empire–style lighthouse is still controlled by the U.S. Coast Guard but is owned and maintained by the Hudson-Athens Lighthouse Preservation Society, which provides tours from July through October. Boats leave from Hudson and Athens.

**Hudson Opera House**. *327 Warren Street, Hudson. 518-822-1438. www.hudsonoperahouse.org.* A nonprofit group has turned the former Hudson City Hall (1855) into a thriving center for numerous artistic activities, with more than 700 programs and events for people of all ages throughout the year, including exhibitions, lectures, readings, workshops, concerts, and after-school programs. The building itself is of

*The former Hudson City Hall has been transformed into a thriving arts center known as the Hudson Opera House.*

historical interest not only because Frederic Church and Sanford Gifford showed their paintings here, but the performance hall on the second floor (scheduled to open in 2010) is one of the oldest surviving theaters in New York State. *Open daily, 12 pm until 5 pm.*

**Stageworks/Hudson**. *41 Cross Street, Hudson 12534. 518-828-7843. www.stageworkstheater.org.* The only Actors' Equity theater in Columbia County, founded in Hudson in 1993, the company produces three mainstage productions a year as well as an annual festival of new plays and two programs for children. *Fee.*

**Time & Space Limited**. *434 Columbia Street, Hudson (1 block north of Warren Street, between 4th and 5th, and a few blocks West of Route 9). 518-822-8448. www.timeandspace.org.* Through its original theater, art exhibits, youth programs, independent film screenings, performances, youth events, readings, and talks, this unusual organization has become a catalyst for culture in Columbia County, encouraging innovation and broad public participation in everything from opera to photography. *Open Thursdays through Sunday evenings. Fee.*

## KINDERHOOK

**Columbia County Historical Society**. *5 Albany Avenue, Kinderhook 12106. 518-758-9265. www.cchsny.org.* Operating a museum and three historic buildings in Kinderhook, the society is housed in a 1916 Masonic Temple and offers exhibitions of artwork and treasures from its vast collection of historic objects and documents. The society also owns and operates

*Built circa 1820, the James Vanderpoel House in Kinderhook is recognized for its Federal architecture.*

(see below) the Luykas Van Alen House, the 1818 James Vanderpoel House, and the Ichabod Crane Schoolhouse. *Open Monday and Thursday through Saturday, 10 am until 4 pm, and Sunday, 12 pm until 4 pm.*

**Ichabod Crane Schoolhouse**. *Route 9H, just south of Kinderhook (on the grounds of the Luykas Van Alen House). 518-758-9265. www.cchsny.org.* The circa 1850 one-room schoolhouse was moved some years ago to the property of the Luykas Van Alen House (see below—same hours and joint admission). It takes its name from the schoolmaster in the Washington Irving tale "The Legend of Sleepy Hollow." According to the Columbia County Historical Society, which oversees both houses, the schoolmaster is modeled on Jesse Merwin, the teacher at the school when Irving visited here.

**James Vanderpoel House**. *Broad Street (Route 9), just off the village square, Kinderhook. 518-758-9265. www.cchsny.org.* Built circa 1820, the James Vanderpoel House is a superb example of Federal architecture. The simplicity of its brickwork, combined with a Chippendale-style balustrade, Palladian windows, and graceful front- and back-door fanlights, give it refined elegance. *It is open 10 am to 4 pm Thursday through Saturday and 1 pm until 4 pm Sunday between Memorial Day and Labor Day weekends. Guided tours. Fee.*

**Lindenwald**. *1013 Old Post Road (2 miles from the village), Kinderhook 12106. 518-758-9689. www.nps.gov/mava.* As eighth president—the first born under the U.S. flag and the only president who was not a native speaker of English—Martin Van Buren (1782–1862) continued the era of Jacksonian Democracy. A visit to his house in Kinderhook (which reopened after renovations in 2007) usually includes a tour of his 36-room mansion, but all sorts of events and activities are offered on the 220-acre property throughout the season, and a trail through land adjacent to the house is punctuated with signs describing life in Van Buren's time. *Open mid-May to the end of October and under the jurisdiction of the National Park Service. Fee.*

**Luykas Van Alen House**. *Route 9H, just south of Kinderhook. 518-758-9265. www.cchsny.org. National Register.* Designated a National Historic Landmark in 1968, the Luykas Van Alen House is a restored house museum representing 18th-century rural Dutch farm life. Featuring parapet gables, Dutch doors, and entrance stoops, it stands as a testament to traditional Dutch architecture in the Hudson River Valley. *Open Memorial Day through Labor Day, Friday and Saturday, 10 am until 4 pm, and Sunday, 1 pm until 4 pm. Fee.*

**St. Paul's Episcopal Church of Kinderhook**. *6 Sylvester Street, Kinderhook. 518-758-6271. http://stpauls.kinderhookny.us.* Designed by Richard Upjohn, this Gothic Revival Episcopal church was built in 1851.

## NEW LEBANON

**Mount Lebanon Shaker Village**. *Darrow Road, New Lebanon 12125. 518-794-9100. www.mountlebanonshakervillage.org. National Register.* For 160 years, the Shakers at Mount Lebanon led the largest and most successful utopian communal society in America. With more than 6,000 acres and 100 buildings, Mount Lebanon Shaker Village was a driving force in the agricultural, industrial, commercial, and institutional activities of its day. With the industrial revolution and the naturally declining population of the celibate community, the Shaker membership dwindled and communities consolidated and closed. The last seven Shakers left Mount Lebanon in 1947. Most of this historic and architecturally significant village is in the hands of the Darrow School and a Sufi community, but the North Family house and several outbuildings—including the famous Great Stone Barn, measuring 50 feet wide, 4 stories high, and nearly 200 feet long—are open to the public under the jurisdiction of the Shaker Museum and Library in Old Chatham (see below). The Shaker Museum and Library eventually plans to move its vast collection of Shaker memorabilia to the Mount Lebanon site. Visitors may experience the acoustical pleasures of the Shaker Tannery at Mount Lebanon by attend-

ing one of the Tannery Pond Concerts (see below), featuring world-class chamber groups in an unusual and intimate setting.

*Kinderhook native Martin Van Buren, the eighth president of the United States, moved into Lindenwald soon after leaving the White House in 1841.*

*As it has been from days when Shakers grew seeds and tilled the soil here, Old Chatham—and much of the Hudson Valley—is still connected to the land through a rich farming and agricultural life.*

**Tannery Pond Concerts**. *Darrow Road, New Lebanon. 888-820-9441. www.tannerypondconcerts.org. National Register.* Between May and October since 1991, this small organization has been producing six or seven chamber concerts annually in the acoustically resonant Shaker Tannery in the Mount Lebanon Shaker Village on the grounds of the Darrow School. *Fee.*

**Theater Barn**. *654 Route 20, New Lebanon 12125. 518-794-8989. www .theaterbarn.com.* Between mid-June and late October, the theatrical presenter in New Lebanon organizes eight mainstage plays and musicals. *Fee.*

## OLD CHATHAM
**Shaker Museum and Library**. *88 Shaker Museum Road, Old Chatham. 518-794-9100. www.shakermuseumandlibrary.org.* At its height in the 19th century the Shaker religion was a thriving sect, with 19 settlements in the United States. Living in celibate communities of male and female converts under the direction of male and female elders, the Shakers received their name from the dances that were a central part of their ceremonies. They were famous for their premodern designs for architecture and everyday utensils as well as for packaged seeds, furniture, and innovations in cooking and farming; they invented such everyday devices as the circular saw and the screw propeller. Columbia County is fortunate to be one of the main repositories for the legacy of this nearly vanished but not forgotten religious sect, thanks to the efforts of the Shaker Museum and Library to preserve and display Shaker artifacts. Established in 1950

*In Spencertown, a schoolhouse dating from 1840 is now an arts center and gallery.*

near the charming village of Old Chatham, the museum holds more than 18,500 articles from Shaker communities in New Hampshire, Maine, and Massachusetts, including buckets, clocks, and agricultural and medical equipment. The permanent collection is on view throughout the year, and temporary exhibitions regularly highlight parts of the collection as well as aspects of Shaker life. Eventually, the museum plans to move its entire collection to the Great Stone Barn and other buildings under its jurisdiction at the Shaker Village in New Lebanon (see above). *Open late May until late October, Wednesday through Monday, 10 am until 5 pm. Fee.*

## SPENCERTOWN

**Spencertown Academy**. *Route 203, Spencertown. 518-292-3693. www.spencertownacademy.org. National Register.* Located in an 1840s-era schoolhouse, this multidisciplinary arts institution presents performances of classical and traditional music, theater, film, and readings in its auditorium, hosts regular exhibitions in its two galleries, and offers classes in art, writing, ballet, and crafts.

**Taconic Sculpture Park and Gallery**. *Stever Hill Road (off Route 203), Spencertown. 518-392-5757. www.fairpoint.net/~kanwit/.* A 19-foot cement head of a woman, visible from the Taconic State Parkway, is one of the 40 whimsical stone and concrete pieces that sculptor Roy Kanwit has arranged in his field overlooking the Hudson Valley and the Catskills. *Open weekends, 9 to 5, and by appointment.*

## STOCKPORT

**Church of St. John the Evangelist**. *107 County Route 25, Stockport. 518-828-3925. www.stjohnstockport.com. National Register.* The oldest Episcopal Church building in Columbia County, consecrated on July 3,

1847, was designed after the architecture of the Anglican Church in Stockport, England. Its annual Dutch Supper dates back nearly 100 years.

## WEST TAGHKANIC

**Lake Taghkanic State Park**. *Taconic State Parkway, West Taghkanic. 518-851-3631. nysparks.state.ny.us/parks*. The lovely hills and forests along the Taconic State Parkway are home to a variety of recreational activities centered on a lake. The park has tent and trailer campsites and cabin and cottage camping facilities, two beaches, picnic grounds, and a boat launch. In addition, the park has hiking, biking, and cross-country ski and snowmobile trails. Ice skating and ice fishing are permitted when conditions merit.

## *Festivals, Fairs, and Celebrations*

**ArtsWalk**. *Hudson and vicinity. www.artscolumbia.org/events.html*. Organized by the Columbia County Council on the Arts each fall, this 10-day festival celebrates and draws attention to the community of performing, visual, and literary artists at work in Columbia County and the variety of venues for the sale and display of art. In the past, ArtsWalk exhibits have included works of both "undiscovered" local artists and more famous county residents such as Richard Artschwager. The CCCA also hosts a studio tour in May and the Rider's Mills Schoolhouse Fence Show in September.

**Black Arts Festival**. *Operation Unite, Hudson. 518-828-3612*. A parade down Warren Street, an afternoon of food, entertainment, and arts and crafts, and an evening Gospel and R&B Song Festival are highlights of this popular one-day event that takes place every August in Hudson.

**Celebration of Celts**. *Columbia County Fairgrounds, Chatham. www.celebrationofcelts.com*. Founded in 2004, and taking place in early May each year, this two-day total immersion in Celtic culture, music, dance, history, and heritage has grown to be the largest pan-Celtic event on the East Coast. Knights in action, a piping competition, a parade of Celts, a Celtic pub, even a Single Malt Whisky Seminar combine with great music to draw thousands to Chatham—a reminder that more than one-third of the population of the United States can claim Celtic heritage.

**Columbia County Fair**. *Chatham. 518-758-1811. www.columbiafair.com*. The oldest county fair in New York State takes place Labor Day weekend at the fairgrounds just off Route 66 in Chatham. The fair celebrates the joys, skill, and hard work of farming, quilting, weaving, riding, cooking, and other arts and crafts. More than 300 exhibition and competition categories cover a wide range of agricultural and homemaking arts.

**Falcon Ridge Folk Festival**. *860-364-0366. www.falconridgefolk.com*. Taking place on a farm at the foot of the Berkshires in July, this huge event draws as many as 50 performers from around the country for four days of folk music and dance each year.


## Also Nearby

Bordering Columbia County is the historically significant, culturally rich Berkshire County in Massachusetts, which is said to have the greatest concentration of summer theater in America. Visit the thriving center of Great Barrington—30 miles from Hudson and only 12 from Hillsdale—for galleries, antiques stores, and restaurants, then wander through the gardens, listen to a concert, or tour the rooms at Edith Wharton's villa The Mount in nearby Lenox (www.edithwharton.org). Lenox is also home to Tanglewood (www.tanglewood.org), the music center where the Boston Symphony Orchestra has performed almost every summer since 1937. Jacob's Pillow in Lee (www.jacobspillow.org) is the only dance institution to be named a National Historic Landmark. In Pittsfield, volunteers lead tours of Arrowhead (www.mobydick.org), the house looking out on Mount Greylock where Herman Melville wrote *Moby-Dick* and entertained Nathaniel Hawthorne.


## Visitor Information

**Columbia County Council on the Arts**. *209 Warren Street, Hudson 12534. 518-671-6213. www.artscolumbia.org*. This is the center for all arts-related information in the county (see full listing under Hudson, above).

**Columbia County Tourism**. *401 State Street, Hudson 12534. 518-828-3375. http://bestcountryroads.com*. With a full calendar of events, lists of museums, galleries, parks, and historic sites, and information on everything from bird-watching to car rentals, this office and Web site are good places to start when planning a trip to Columbia County. The office is open Monday through Friday, 8:30 am until 4 pm.

**Columbia Land Conservancy**. *49 Main Street, Chatham, 12037. 518-392-5252. www.clctrust.org*. The Columbia Land Conservancy hosts a variety of workshops and educational lectures on the topics of environmental protection and agriculture in addition to many nature-themed tours of the rural landscape of Columbia County. Its annual Full Moon Coyote Ramble is a nighttime walk through the Greenport Conservation Area that includes tales of local legends and a group howl into the night sky.

# GREENE COUNTY

More than any other county along the Hudson, Greene retains the wild, mountainous flavor that inspired the generation of artists known as the Hudson River School. On summer evenings, as if in a painting by Thomas Cole or Frederic Edwin Church, shadows from the high peaks of the Catskills still boldly descend across the river into Columbia and Dutchess Counties, and sun streaks through the winding mountain valleys around Tannersville, Hunter, and Windham.

The recent restoration of Cedar Grove, the house where Cole lived and worked—directly across the river from Olana, Church's house in Columbia County—and the preservation of the forest and trails around South Lake and the site of the famed Catskill Mountain House in Haines Falls have put many of the haunts of those 19th-century painters, poets, and novelists in easy reach of the 21st-century traveler. Efforts by the National Park Service Rivers and Trails Program, Cedar Grove: Thomas Cole National Historic Site, and other groups to bring attention to the artistic heritage of the Hudson Valley have resulted in such useful guides as the Hudson River School Art Trail (www.thomascole.org/trail), a brochure and online guide published by Cedar Grove, showing access points to many of the Hudson River School sites along the river, particularly in Greene County.

Openings, festivals, concerts, and readings take place throughout the year in Catskill, the historic river town that is the county seat. With a gallery and performance space at 398 Main Street, the Greene County Council on the Arts (www.greenearts.org) provides up-to-date listings of events in Catskill, nearby Athens, and other locations along the river and in the mountains. A number of popular ski resorts are near Hunter and Windham, and these towns are increasingly sought out for their year-round cultural offerings, including a popular Chamber Music Festival in Windham and an array of shows, exhibits, and lectures under the auspices of the Catskill Mountain Foundation in Hunter and Tannersville.

Greene County was created from Albany and Ulster Counties in 1800 but settlement began more than a century earlier. A farm

*The 260-foot double waterfall known as Kaaterskill Falls was a favorite subject of the Hudson River School painters. A visit to the site today is still as treacherous and rewarding as it was for them.*

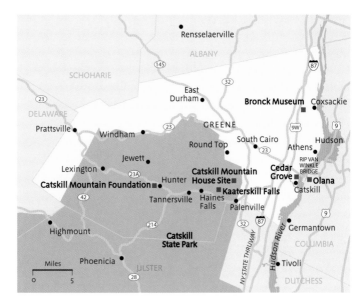

begun by Pieter Bronck in Coxsackie in the 1660s, and lived on by seven later generations of his family, is now an extensive historical museum and the headquarters of the Greene County Historical Society. Before the advent of railroads and the Erie Canal, commerce passed along the trails and roads of the county to and from western New York, and riverfront towns such as Catskill and Athens became important centers of trade. Bark from hemlock stands in the Catskills provided the raw material for a booming tanning industry, and one highly successful tanner, Zadock Pratt, made a fortune, became a U.S. congressman, and built a stately home in Prattsville that is now a museum of northern Catskills history (see Also Nearby, below).

## ATHENS

Athens once shared a symbiotic relationship with Hudson, the city directly across the river that is the seat of Columbia County. Hudson, a whaling port, was incorporated in 1785, and Athens, a center of shipbuilding, followed soon thereafter, in 1815. Ferries plied between the two cities from the time of the American Revolution until shortly after the erection of the Rip Van Winkle Bridge in 1935. Athens and Hudson continue to celebrate their common interest in the Hudson-Athens Lighthouse.

**Athens Cultural Center**. *24 Second Street, Athens 12015. 518-945-2136. www.athensculturalcenter.org. National Register.* An Egyptian Revival storefront a few blocks from the river is home to this busy arts center offering exhibits of work by regional artists, displays of vintage photographs and postcards, regional wine and food tastings, and free art classes for all ages. *Open weekends, 1 pm until 4 pm. Free.*

**Hudson-Athens Lighthouse**. *The Hudson River. 518-828-5294. www .hudsonathenslighthouse.org.* (see page 194 above). Boats leave from Hudson and Athens.

## CATSKILL

The wooden statue of Rip Van Winkle on Main Street reminds the visitor that this lively village of renovated storefronts, galleries, and shops is a sort of cultural bridge between the river and the mountains. It was at the landing here, in what is now Catskill Point Park, that passengers disembarked for the journey up to Kaaterskill Falls and the Catskill Mountain House, and today Route 23A still snakes up through the cliffs and cloves of Kaaterskill Creek to the mountain attractions of Haines Falls, Tannersville, and Hunter.

**Catskill Point Park**. *One Main Street, Catskill 12414. 518-943-3400.* With its exhibition hall and historic signs, this riverfront park at the foot of Main Street is popular among visitors and residents for its farmers' and artisans' markets, its spring shad festival, and its intimate views of the Hudson.

*The tiny village of Athens has changed little since its inception as a shipbuilding town across the river from Hudson in 1815.*

*With weekly farmers' markets in its wharf building, summer concerts, and an annual Shad Festival, Catskill Point Park in Catskill is typical of efforts by municipalities up and down the Hudson Valley to reconnect with the waterfront.*

**Cedar Grove: Thomas Cole National Historic Site**. *218 Spring Street (near the western entrance to the Rip Van Winkle Bridge), Catskill. 518-943-7465. www.thomascole.org. National Register.* The house and studio where the founder of the Hudson River School of painting lived and worked was opened to the public as a historic site in 2001. With its Cole memorabilia (including Cole's thoughtfully reproduced studio), its period furnishings, its knowledgeable tour guides, and its grand view of the Catskills to the west, the 1815 Federal-style house provides a sense of what life was like here for the painter and his family. *Open May through October, Thursday through Sunday, 10 am until 4 pm; Memorial Day, Labor Day, Columbus Day, and Independence Day, 1 pm until 4 pm (last tour begins at 3 pm); other times by appointment. Fee.*

**Dutchmen's Landing**. *East end of Main Street, Catskill 12414.* The best starting place for the Greene County Council on the Arts walking tour of riverside sites, the park has a view across the river of Olana, a playground, a gazebo, picnic tables, and a boat launch. The town of Catskill sponsors concerts here every Thursday during the summer.

**Greene County Council on the Arts**. *398 Main Street, Catskill. 518-943-3400. www.greenearts.org.* Since 1975 the council has been supporting the arts of the Catskill region through exhibitions of local artists' work, lectures, musical performances, poetry readings, information services, and grants. The council maintains two year-round gallery spaces, the GCCA Catskill Gallery in downtown Catskill and the

*Cedar Grove, the house and studio in Catskill where Thomas Cole lived and worked, was opened to the public as a historic site in 2001.*

GCCA Mountaintop Gallery in the resort town of Windham. *The Catskill Gallery, located on Main Street between Thompson and William Streets, is open Monday through Saturday, 10 am until 5 pm; the Mountaintop Gallery, on Main Street in Windham, is open Friday to Monday, 10 am until 5 pm.*

**RamsHorn-Livingston Sanctuary**. *Grandview Avenue, Catskill 12414. http://ny.audubon.org.* Jointly owned by Scenic Hudson and Audubon New York (see Resource Directory), this 480-acre nature sanctuary provides access by foot and canoe to the largest tidal swamp forest in the northern Hudson River estuary—and to the Hudson itself. *Open dawn to dusk.*

**Rip Van Winkle Bridge**. *P.O. Box 286, Catskill 12412. 518-943-2360. www.nysba.state.ny.us.* Completed in 1935, and carrying Route 23 across the Hudson from Catskill, in Greene County, to Hudson, in Columbia County, this 5,041-foot cantilever toll bridge was originally supposed to pass through part of the Thomas Cole property at Cedar Grove. Negotiations with Cole's descendants led the New York State Department of Public Works to reroute the bridge just north of the property. The Dutch Colonial–style toll booths and administration building are a local design touch.

*Connecting Catskill, in Greene County, with Hudson, in Columbia, the Rip Van Winkle Bridge was originally supposed to pass through the Thomas Cole Property at Cedar Grove.*

## COXSACKIE

**Bronck Museum/Greene County Historical Society**. *385 Pieter Bronck Road, Coxsackie. 518-731-6490. www.gchistory.org.* One of the oldest surviving dwellings in upstate New York, the 1663 Bronck House (National Register) is one of several unusual buildings that make up the county historical museum and serve as the headquarters for the county historical society. A thirteen-sided barn dating from 1830—the oldest documented multisided barn in the state—is another. Eight generations of the Bronck family (the same one that gave a name to the New York City borough) inhabited the property before it came to the society. The society also operates a research library. *Open Memorial Day weekend through mid-October, Wednesday through Friday, 12 pm until 4 pm; Saturdays and Monday holidays, 10 am until 4 pm; Sundays, 1 pm until 4 pm; and Memorial Day, Labor Day, and Columbus Day, 1 pm until 4 pm (last tour at 3:30 pm daily).*

**Four Mile Point Preserve**. *Four Mile Point Road (off Route 385, 8 miles north of the Rip Van Winkle Bridge), Coxsackie 12051. www.scenichudson .org.* Excellent views of the river, a quiet pond, and trails are features of this 7.6-acre preserve under the jurisdiction of Scenic Hudson (see Resource Directory), the Town of Coxsackie, and the Greene County Soil and Water Conservation District. *Open dawn to dusk.*

## EAST DURHAM

**Durham Center Museum**. *Route 145, East Durham 12423. 518-239-8461.* This museum in an 1825 schoolhouse on the historic Susquehanna Turnpike is packed with Catskills memorabilia (including parts of the columns of the Catskill Mountain House), folk art, and local history. *Open Memorial Day through Columbus Day, Thursday through Sunday, 1 pm until 4 pm; genealogical library open in winter by appointment.*

**Irish American Heritage Museum**. *2267 State Route 145, East Durham 12423. 518-634-7497. www.Irishamericanheritagemuseum.org.* Dedicated to the history of the Irish in America, and located next to the Michael J. Quill Irish Cultural and Sports Centre, the museum exhibits artifacts from its permanent collection to help bring the heritage of Irish Americans to a wider audience. *Open Memorial Day weekend through Labor Day weekend, Wednesday through Sunday, 12 pm until 4 pm. Fee.*

**Michael J. Quill Irish Cultural and Sports Centre**. *2119 State Route 145 (quarter mile from Weldon House), East Durham 12423. 518-634-2286. www.east-durham.org.* This Irish cultural organization sponsors the annual Irish Arts Week and the traditional Irish Music Festival (see Festivals, below) at venues in East Durham, as well as educational programming in support of the strong local Irish traditions and heritage.

*A thirteen-sided barn, the oldest of its kind in New York State, is one of the architectural and historical curiosities at the Bronck Museum in Coxsackie.*

## HAINES FALLS

**Site of the Catskill Mountain House**. *North South Lake Campground (off County Route 18—O'Hara Road), Haines Falls 12436. 518-357-2234. www .dec.ny.gov.* The famed hotel with its columned porch overlooking the Hudson Valley remained open for an astonishing 127 years and stood empty for an additional 23 before the New York State Department of Environmental Conservation burned it to the ground in 1963. The place where it stood and other lookouts along the breathtaking Catskill Escarpment can be visited by trail from the North South Lake Campground in Haines Falls. *Seasonal fee.*

**Kaaterskill Falls**. *Route 23A at Kaaterskill Creek (3.5 miles west of Palenville), Haines Falls. www.thomascole.org/trail.* "In the Kaaterskill," wrote Thomas Cole in his *Essay on American Scenery* (1836), "we have a stream, diminutive indeed, but throwing itself headlong over a fearful precipice into a deep gorge of the densely wooded mountains—and possessing a singular feature in the vast arched cave that extends beneath and behind the cataract." The 260-foot double waterfall loved by Cole, William Cullen Bryant, James Fenimore Cooper, Washington Irving, and others is considered the tallest in New York State. It is accessible from a parking lot on the west side of a hairpin turn on Route 23A, about 3.5 miles west of Palenville. A sign marks the start of the steep, rocky half-mile trail; use caution as the shoulders of the road are narrow and the visibility poor, and the hike itself, though short, is strenuous.

**Mountain Top Historical Society**. *Route 23A, Haines Falls 12436. 518-589-6657. www.mths.org.* Based in a lovingly-restored Ulster &

*The view from the site of the Catskill Mountain House is still as large and picturesque as in the days when Thomas Cole, Sanford Robinson Gifford, and others painted it.*

*Hudson River School painters depicted South Lake, near Haines Falls, in many different kinds of light.*

Delaware train station, the society studies the art, literature, history, culture, folklore, legends, and environment of the section of the Catskills known as "Mountain Top." Public exhibits, lectures, meetings and hikes cover such topics and places of interest as the Catskill Mountain House, Kaaterskill Falls, and other subjects.

## HUNTER

**Catskill Mountain Foundation**. *7970 Main Street (Route 23A), Hunter 12442. 518-263-4908. www.catskillmtn.org.* This multifaceted organization in a busy new complex in downtown Hunter runs two farms at separate locations that promote a kind of farming known as natural agriculture; hosts literary programs and performing arts events; and houses a gallery, a performing arts center, a cinema, and a bookstore. *The gallery, specializing in "everything from outsider art to 6th-century Japanese scrolls," and with many local crafts, is open Friday through Monday, 10 am until 5 pm.*

**Pleshakov Piano Museum**. *Route 23A (Main Street), Hunter 12442. 518-263-3333. www.pleshakov.com.* With regularly scheduled concerts on period instruments, the museum exhibits pianos from the days of Michelangelo to the days of Mozart and Beethoven, Chopin and Liszt. *Tours by appointment. Fee.*

*An exhibition at the Catskill Mountain Foundation Gallery in Hunter featured the paintings of George A. Peterson.*

## JEWETT

**St. John the Baptist Ukrainian Catholic Church/Ukrainian Culture Center**. *Ukraine Road (5 miles west of Hunter on Route 23A), Hunter 12442. 518-263-3862. www.brama.com/stjohn; www.grazhdamusicandart.org.* Built in 1962 in the traditional timber blockwork style of the Ukrainian Carpathian Mountain highlanders, with a lovely hand-carved interior, the center is both a cultural meeting place for the community and a well-regarded example of traditional Ukrainian Church architecture. Each summer the church welcomes visitors to its *grazhda*, or parish hall, for cultural events including lectures, folk art courses and exhibits, classical music concerts, and literary evenings. *The shop and art exhibits are open Tuesday through Friday, 12 pm until 4 pm; Saturday, 10 am until 2 pm and 6 pm until 8 pm; and Sunday, 11:30 am until 2 pm.*

## ROUND TOP

**Altamura Center for Arts and Culture**. *404 Winter Clove Road, Round Top 12473. 518-622-0070. www.altocanto.org.* Founded in 2000 by Carmela and Leonard Altamura, this performing arts center works to promote understanding among world peoples through the study of music. The center offers regular public performances, runs a summer music festival, and offers "Encounters with the Masters," an immersion in operatic literature, performance, and Italian culture with prestigious faculty from such venerable Italian institutions such as La Scala. *Call or visit the Web site for program dates. Fee.*

## SOUTH CAIRO

**Mahayana Buddhist Temple**. *Ira Vail Road, South Cairo 12482.*
*518-622-3619.* About seven miles west of Catskill on Route 23, this
retreat center was founded in 1971 and welcomes the public to enjoy its
architecture and its meditation retreats.

## TANNERSVILLE

**Mountaintop Arboretum**. *Route 23C, Tannersville. 518-589-3903.*
*www.mtarbor.org.* Located at 2,500 feet above see level, this 10-acre
high-altitude nature preserve and garden was opened in 1977 as a
living museum of native trees, shrubs, and flowers alongside exotic
transplants. In its meadows, woodlands, and gardens the arboretum
offers lectures and programs on nature, the arts, and local history; bird
walks; medicinal plant foraging; and the popular Hudson Valley Ramble
fall foliage walk.

**Orpheum Performing Arts Center**. *Main Street, Tannersville.*
*518-263-4908.* The Catskill Mountain Foundation (see Hunter, above)
has redesigned and rebuilt the venerable local theater following plans
by Hugh Hardy, who also designed the Glimmerglass Opera House in

*Built in 1962 in the traditional timber blockwork style of the Ukrainian Carpathian
Mountain highlanders, the Ukrainian Catholic Church in Jewett is also a cultural
center hosting lectures, folk art courses and exhibitions, classical music concerts, and
literary evenings.*

Cooperstown and renovated the BAM Harvey Theater in Brooklyn and the New Victory Theater on 42nd Street in Manhattan. *The theater is scheduled to reopen for the summer season of 2010. Fee.*

## Festivals, Fairs, and Celebrations

**Catskill Mountain Renaissance Faire**. *Angelo Canna Town Park, Mountain Avenue, Cairo. 518-622-9164. www.caironychamber.com*. Taking place in August in Cairo's town park, the two-day fair features magic, dragons, juggling, jousting, music, falcons, and food. Open 11 am until 6 pm each day.

**Grey Fox Bluegrass Festival**. *County Route 22, between Oak Hill and Durham. 888-946-8495; 315-724-4473. www.greyfoxbluegrass.com*. This venerable festival, which had taken place in mid-July in Columbia County since 1976, moved to a new location in Greene County in 2008. The festival features four performance stages and three learning tents, camping, and great music.

**Hunter Mountain Festivals**. *Hunter Ski Mountain. Off Route 23A, Hunter 12442. 1-800-HUNTERMTN. www.huntermtn.com*. During two weekends every August, the steep, green ski slopes of Hunter Mountain are taken over by singers, dancers, and merrymakers enjoying the traditional food and music of their Irish and German ancestors. The German Alps Festival features traditional German music, German American foods, Schuhplatt-ler Dancers, and various children's activities. The CelticFestival includes a bagpipe competition followed by a mass march of hundreds of pipers and drummers descending the mountain in unison. After the march the procession plays as one at the base of the mountain.

**Irish Festivals**. The Michael J. Quill Irish Cultural and Sports Centre in East Durham (518-634-2286; www.east-durham.org) sponsors three major events during the summer: a two-day Irish Festival over Memorial Day weekend; the weeklong Irish Arts Week in mid-July; and a step dance festival in August.

**Windham Chamber Music Festival**. *5379 Main Street (State Route 23), Windham.  518-734-3868. www.windhammusic.com*. Started by the violinist Magdalena Golczewski and the baritone Robert Manno of the Metropolitan Opera in 1997, this ongoing series of concerts of new and classic chamber pieces takes place each summer in a restored 1826 church with excellent acoustics.

## Also Nearby

About 35 miles west of Catskill on Route 23 is Prattsville, home of the Zadock Pratt Museum and Pratt's Rocks (518-299-3395; www.prattmuseum.com). The homestead of the founder of Prattsville is now a museum on the history and culture of the mid-19th-century northern Catskills. With its indigenous stands of hemlock, this area was once a center for tanning. A short climb leads to Pratt's Rocks, where Pratt left carvings commemorating important moments in his life. Open Memorial Day through Columbus Day, Thursday through Sunday, 1 pm until 5 pm, and in December for holiday events.

## Visitor Information

**Greene County Council on the Arts**. *398 Main Street, Catskill. 518-943-3400. www.greenearts.org*. (See listing under Catskill, above.)

**Greene County Historical Society**. *385 Pieter Bronck Road, Coxsackie. 518-731-6490. www.gchistory.org*. (See listing for Bronck Museum under Coxsackie, above.)

**Greene County Tourism**. *P.O. Box 527, Catskill, NY. 518-943-3223. www.greenetourism.com*. The official county tourist agency is a good place to start for information on food and lodging, hours and schedules, suggested itineraries, and upcoming events.

# ALBANY COUNTY

The influence of government is strong in New York State's capital, visible from afar in the modernist marble buildings of the Governor Nelson Rockefeller Empire State Plaza, towering in the center of town, and from within the New York State Capitol building itself, one of the masterpieces of 19th-century municipal architecture, whose chambers, staircases, and porticos swirl with pleasing forms and rare materials put together over 32 years under the direction of five architects. Over many years the State of New York has encouraged cultural endeavors large and small, and the results show in the museums, galleries, and performance spaces, the collections of art and historical materials, the parks, the historic houses, and the government buildings of Albany and its satellite cities of Troy, Rensselaer, Schenectady, and Saratoga Springs.

Architecturally, Albany is one of the most interesting places in the Hudson Valley. From General Philip Schuyler's large and comfortable brick Georgian house on the south side of town, built in 1761, to the elegant new Hudson River Way Pedestrian Bridge, finished in 2002, which crosses six lanes of I-787 traffic to reconnect downtown Albany with its waterfront, the city has adorned itself with a lavishness and sophistication that makes it much more than a provincial capital. Aside from the Capitol building, the single most dramatic effort to ensure Albany's architectural prominence was Empire State Plaza, completed in 1978. The plaza includes the stately Cultural Education Center, the Erastus Corning Tower—the tallest building in the state outside New York City—and the Egg, an oval theater in the spirit of master architect Wallace Harrison's other late-20th-century tours de force, the United Nations and the Metropolitan Opera building at Lincoln Center. Other architectural landmarks in Albany include Henry Hobson Richardson's 1883 Albany City Hall, Olmsted and Vaux's Washington Park, Philip Hooker's 1789 First Church of Albany, Edward Durrell Stone's mid-1960s University at Albany campus, and the new Atrium of the Albany Institute of History and Art, completed in 2001.

In the visual arts, Albany's cultural institutions have impressive holdings of both the art of the past and modern and contemporary work. To its extensive array of Hudson River School and

*Designed by Henry Hobson Richardson, Albany City Hall was completed in 1883. Musicians play concerts on the carillon atop its 220-foot tower each summer.*

other American paintings the Albany Institute of History and Art has recently been adding new work by contemporary artists as part of an aggressive acquisitions program. Amassed under Governor Nelson Rockefeller's eye, the Empire State Plaza's collection of modern painting and sculpture—on view in the underground concourse and throughout the complex—is one of the most impressive in the country. The University at Albany, the Albany Center Gallery, the Olpaca Gallery at Sage College, and the Massry Center gallery at the College of St. Rose all present regularly changing exhibits of contemporary work.

The performing arts can be enjoyed both indoors and out-doors. Washington Park, designed by Frederick Law Olmsted and Calvert Vaux, the creators of Central Park in New York City, and the newer and very busy Albany Riverfront Park both come alive every summer with free theater, jazz, folk, and pop music in their grassy performance spaces. The Albany Civic and Steamer No. 10 theatres—both in former firehouses—specialize in community theater, and both new and classical plays take place at the Capi-tal Repertory. The Albany Symphony Orchestra plays regularly at the historic Palace Theatre, and the new recital hall at the Massry Center for the Arts, at the College of St. Rose, hosts regular chamber performances. Between sporting events, popular music concerts take place at the 17,500-seat Times-Union Center.

Dutch traders began settling the place we now call Albany in 1624, naming it Fort Orange. The trading post and growing town remained under Dutch control until 1664, when the English took possession and renamed it for James, Duke of York and Albany. Dutch influence remained strong, and though Albany became an American city, at least in spirit, after the Battle of Saratoga in 1777, and became the state capital in 1797, its citizens stayed true to their Dutch heritage and continue to celebrate it today in an annual Tulip Festival and dozens of streets with such names as Ten Broeck Place, Bogardus Road, Van Schaick Avenue, and Peyster Street.

Noted by Charles Dickens, when he passed through in 1842, as a "large and busy town," this cosmopolitan city took advantage of its connections to Manhattan, the eastern seaboard, and Europe by the Hudson River, to the Midwest by the Mohawk River and its valley, and to Canada by Lake George and Lake Champlain to retain its importance as a trading center. The introduction of Robert Fulton's steamboat in 1807, the openings of the Champlain Canal in 1823 and the Erie Canal in 1825, and the arrival of railroads in the 1830s and 1840s brought grace and style as well as business to what has always been a city at the crossroads. Like any successful city, it was a place not just of merchants and politicians but also of artists and artisans—actors, singers, painters, sculptors, stonemasons, carpenters, gardeners, weavers, potters, and silversmiths.

The Albany Heritage Area Visitors Center, with offices at 25 Quackenbush Square, is a good place to start for information on openings, performances, and other events. As part of the First Fridays program, shops, galleries, museums, and restaurants stay open late once a month in a citywide celebration of the arts. The sweeping space of the Empire State Plaza is busy with outdoor concerts and events in the warmer months and ice skating in the winter. Part of the pleasure of a visit to Albany is to explore some of the older streets with their quirky shops, antiques shops, galleries, and small restaurants. A good place to start is Lark Street, a block away from Washington Park, often called the Greenwich Village of Albany. Small shops, boutiques, commercial galleries, and antiques stores line the streets, and every September the city pays tribute to the district with a popular street fair called Larkfest.

Albany has a close relationship with its neighboring cities and counties, and the capital's cultural institutions attract audiences from Troy, Rensselaer, Schenectady, Hudson, and Saratoga Springs and, in turn, help swell the audiences in these places and beyond.

## ALBANY

**Albany Center Gallery**. *39 Columbia Street, Albany 12207. 518-462-4775. www.albanycentergallery.org.* Opened in 1977, this regional gallery presents at least seven exhibitions a year, including the Mohawk Hudson Regional Invitational, and participates with performing arts organizations to present an Art in Education program. Works exhibited include painting, drawing, sculpture, photography, printing, fiber arts, video, mixed media, installation, and artist-made books. *Open Tuesday through Saturday, 12 pm until 5 pm. Free.*

**Albany City Hall and Carillon**. *24 Eagle Street, Albany 12207. 518-434-5100. www.albanyny.org. National Register.* Designed by Henry Hobson Richardson, the graceful building that is Albany's seat of local government was completed in 1883. In a room at the top of its 220-foot tower is the first municipal carillon in the United States, installed in 1926. Restored and enlarged during the city's tricentennial in 1986, the concert-class, 49-bell instrument is played by guest and local performers at midday concerts during June and July. *For performance schedules, contact 518-434-8036 or www.albanycarillon.org.*

**Albany Civic Theater**. *235 Second Avenue, Albany. 518-462-1297. www.albanycivictheater.org.* Located in a former firehouse, this 126-seat community theater produces plays throughout the year, stages readings of new works, and puts on children's performances and other special events.

**Albany Heritage Area Visitors Center**. *25 Quackenbush Square (corner of Broadway and Clinton Avenue), Albany. 518-434-0405. www.albany .org.* Brochures and staff answer questions about the city and region. An orientation show and exhibits present the history of Albany. There is also a gift shop and planetarium. *Open Monday through Friday, 9 am until 4 pm; Saturday and Sunday, 10 am until 4 pm.*

**Albany Institute of History and Art**. *125 Washington Avenue, Albany. 518-463-4478. www.albanyinstitute.org. National Register.* Founded in 1791, this museum, one of the oldest in the United States, is dedicated to the history, art, and culture of Albany and the upper Hudson Valley. Collecting and exhibiting paintings, sculpture, furniture, publications, ceramics, silver, and other materials that document the city's influence on American history, the museum has a substantial collection of paintings, sketches, and memorabilia by Hudson River School artists and a trove of works by contemporary artists working in the region. In addition to ongoing installations of its permanent collection, the institute hosts a variety of relevant temporary exhibitions. In 2001 its handsome 1908

*The Palace Theater is home to the Albany Symphony Orchestra and hosts performances of ballet, music, movies, and comedy.*

Renaissance-style brick-and-limestone building, designed by Albert W. Fuller and William B. Pitcher, was enhanced and expanded according to a design by Solomon+Bauer Architects to include a glass atrium and new second-floor galleries. *Open Wednesday through Saturday, 10 am until 5 pm, and Sunday, 12 pm until 5 pm. Fee.*

**Albany Riverfront Park**. *Across the Hudson River Way Pedestrian Bridge. 518-434-0405. www.albany.org.* An 800-seat amphitheater in this popular local park brings people to the river for concert series such as the Albany Riverfront Jazz Festival, Alive at Five, and the Father's Day Pops Concert (see Festivals, below). An exhibit in the visitor center explains the Hudson River's tides; there are also a bike trail and a boat launch.

**Albany Symphony Orchestra**. *19 Clinton Avenue, Albany. 518-465-4755.* The Albany Symphony Orchestra presents performances of well-loved favorites alongside new or lesser-known works at venues in the capital region, including the Troy Savings Bank Music Hall in Troy, the Palace Theatre in Albany, and Canfield Casino in Saratoga Springs. In addition to evening concerts, the orchestra also organizes afternoon family concerts and classes for adults. *Fee.*

**Capital Repertory Theater**. *111 North Pearl Street, Albany. 518-445-7469. www.capitalrep.org.* Developing new work and reviving the classics, this professional company performs 270 times a year at its space on North Pearl Street, and conducts educational programs, apprentice training for young professionals, discussion groups, and special events. *Fee.*

**Cathedral of All Saints**. *62 South Swan Street, Albany 12210. 518-465-1342. www.cathedralofallsaints.org. National Register.* Begun in 1884 on a design by R. W. Gibson and still incomplete, this High Gothic Episcopal cathedral in the shadow of the New York State Education Building is the seat of the Episcopal Diocese of Albany.

**College of St. Rose/Massry Center for the Arts**. *1002 Madison Avenue, Albany 12203. 518-454-5102. www.strose.edu.* Completed in 2008, this 46,000-square-foot arts center provides a new state-of-the-art gallery and recital hall for this respected Albany educational institution. The Esther Massry Gallery (518-484-3902) presents a regular series of exhibits and programs in contemporary fine arts and design, featuring the work of nationally recognized contemporary artists as well as students and faculty. The 400-seat Picotte Recital Hall is designed acoustically to accommodate everything from a single performer to a full orchestra. *Fee.*

**eba Dance Theatre**. *351 Hudson Avenue (at Lark Street), Albany 12210. 518-465-9916.* This Albany-based group presents dance performances in New York State venues. It also holds classes at its eba Center for Dance and Movement, hosts performances at the eba Theatre, and mounts small gallery shows at the eba Visual Arts Gallery.

**Empire State Plaza**. *Madison Avenue and Swan, State, and Eagle Streets (Empire Plaza Exit from I-787), Albany. 518-474-2418. www.ogs.state.ny.us.* One of the best times to visit Empire State Plaza is at sunset, when the vast scale of the buildings, with their white marble reflecting in three oblong pools, brings to mind not the vestiges of a Dutch colonial city transformed by the industrial revolution but Rockefeller Center, the United Nations, and Lincoln Center. This is not surprising, since the architect of the 98-acre complex of government office buildings and cultural institutions, Wallace K. Harrison, was also responsible for those

other complexes. It is said that when he first became governor in 1959, Nelson A. Rockefeller was embarrassed to bring visitors through the changing streets of New York State's capital. To do better, and to deal with a shortage of office space for state

*Visible from miles around Albany, Empire State Plaza is both the governmental and the cultural nexus of the state capital.*

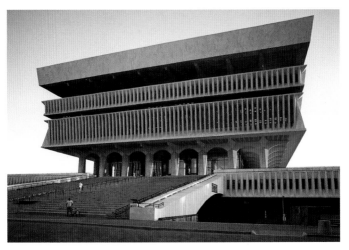

*The New York State Museum, at the end of Empire State Plaza, is a vast repository of documents and objects related to New York State, an important center of research, and a museum with thoughtful, changing exhibits.*

workers, he commissioned Harrison to create something impressive and magnificent.

- New York State Museum, Library and Archives. *Empire State Plaza, Albany. 518-474-5877. www.nysm.nysed.gov.* This vast repository of letters, maps, plans, photographs, rocks, bones, and other objects, all relating to New York State, was founded in 1836 as the State Geological and Natural History Survey, dedicated to promoting inquiry and advancing knowledge in the fields of geology, biology, anthropology, and history. Important scholarship, including the ongoing translation of the Archives of New Netherland (12,000 pages of Dutch colonial papers from 1638 until 1664), takes place here, and changing exhibitions document particular areas of research, such as Harlem in the 1920s, the Adirondack landscape, or the fossil remains of the Cohoes mastodon, a prehistoric mammal related to the woolly mammoth.

- The Empire State Plaza Art Collection. *518-473-7521. www.ogs.state. ny.us.* Governor Rockefeller's mother, Abby Aldrich Rockefeller, was a founder of the Museum of Modern Art in New York City, and the governor was himself a collector of new work being produced during the 1950s and '60s. With the help of advisers from MoMA the governor put together a collection of 92 paintings, sculptures, and tapestries—permanently on view on the concourse level of the plaza as well as in the buildings and outdoors around the plaza itself—now belonging to the people of New York. Especially strong in the abstract expressionists of the time, the collection is a virtual who's who of the big names of the period—Helen Frankenthaler, Donald Judd, Robert Motherwell, Isamu Noguchi, David Smith. *Open from 6 am to 6 pm daily. Works in the Erastus Corning Tower can be seen 6 am until 6 pm Monday through Friday. Free.*

- The Egg. *518-473-1845. www.theegg.org.* Completed in 1978, 12 years after construction began and a year before the death of Governor Rockefeller, this unique performing arts center was the pièce de résistance of Empire State Plaza and of Governor Rockefeller's vision for the architectural renaissance of downtown Albany—an inverted dome perched on a pedestal whose unexpected shape serves the architectural function of breaking up the rigid parallels of the other buildings and the social one of drawing the curious to the center of town for cultural events. The perfectly smooth Egg actually contains two theaters whose superb acoustics, calm lighting, and comfortable seating accommodate a year-round schedule of musical theater, dance performances, concerts, chamber concerts, cabarets, lectures, multimedia presentations, solo performances, and children's programs. *Fee.*

- New York State Capitol. Washington Avenue and State Street, Albany. *518-474-2418. www.assembly.state.ny.us. National Register.* The five-story granite building was built over the course of 32 years at a cost of $25 million, twice that of the U.S. Capitol. It was the grandest and most sumptuous state capitol building in the United States when it was completed in 1899. Architects Thomas Fuller, Leopold Eidlitz, Henry Hobson Richardson, Frederick Law Olmsted, and Isaac Perry all contributed to the job. The staircases with their elaborate carvings, the richly decorated and comfortable Assembly and Senate chambers, and the Executive Red Room with its mahogany, oak, and gold leaf all reward a visit. *Guided tours take place Monday through Friday, 10, 12, 2, 3, and 3:45, and Saturdays, 11, 1, and 3. Closed holidays. Free.*

**Executive Mansion**. *138 Eagle Street, Albany. 518-473-7521. www.ogs.state .ny.us. National Register.* The Queen Anne house a few blocks from the Capitol has been the home of New York's

*With its extraordinary carvings and lavish columns, Henry Hobson Richardson's Great Western Staircase in the Capitol cost a million dollars by the time it was completed in 1897.*

*Imported from Holland in 1656, the hand-carved pulpit in Philip Hooker's 1789 First Church in Albany is said to be the oldest of its kind in the United States.*

governors and their families since 1875. *Tours of the architecture, furnishings, and art take place on Thursdays, 10 am until 2 pm. Reservations must be made two weeks in advance. Free.*

**First Church in Albany**. *110 North Pearl Street, Albany. 518-463-4449. www.firstchurchinalbany.org. National Register.* Built in 1789 for a congregation dating back to 1642, the Dutch Reformed church was designed by Philip Hooker, with stained-glass windows by Louis Comfort Tiffany. The hand-carved pulpit was imported from Holland in 1656 and is considered the oldest of its kind in the United States.

**Historic Cherry Hill**. *523 1/2 S. Pearl Street, Albany. 518-434-4791. www.historiccherryhill.org. National Register.* Built in 1787 for the Rensselaer family, this Georgian home set on five acres in Albany offers visitors a glimpse into 18th- and 19th-century households, with large collections of antique furniture, silver, books, and other cultural artifacts. *Fee.*

**Hudson River Way**. Crossing the six lanes of I-787 and the tracks of the Canadian Pacific Railroad, this footbridge connecting Broadway with Albany Riverfront Park was opened in 2002. Trompe l'oeil paintings on the lampposts depict scenes from Albany's history. Inscribed bricks record the personal messages of more then 10,000 donors to the bridge project.

**Lark Street**. *Two blocks west of Empire State Plaza and one east of Washington Park.* A mixture of bars and clubs (gay and straight), galleries, clothing and antiques stores, restaurants, and jewelry shops in blocks of 19th-century brownstones have given the street and surrounding neighborhood a reputation as the Greenwich Village of Albany. Here begin the monthly First Friday arts celebrations, and here vendors and musicians draw crowds during the annual Larkfest in September (see Festivals, below).

**Old Songs**. *37 South Main Street, Voorheesville 12186. 518-765-2815. www.oldsongs.org.* Traditional music and dance are kept alive by this Albany presenting organization. From September through May, Old Songs presents a series of monthly concerts and contra dances. In May it hosts a fiddlers' reunion, and in June a three-day festival. It also hosts music and dance classes.

**Opalka Gallery/Sage College of Albany**. *Albany. 518-292-7742. www.sage .edu/opalka.* This 7,400-square-foot gallery and lecture hall on the Albany campus of this college based in Troy puts on exhibits and lectures for students and the public. Concentrating on work by artists from outside the region, the gallery often features multidisciplinary projects and readings, recitals, and symposia in conjunction with its shows. *Open during the academic year Monday through Friday, 10 am until 4:30 pm; Monday through Thursday evenings, 6 pm until 8 pm; and Sundays, 12 pm until 4 pm. During the summer, Monday through Friday, 10 am until 4 pm and by appointment.*

**Palace Theatre**. *19 Clinton Avenue, Albany 12207. 518-465-3335. www.palacealbany.com. National Register.* This historic theater opened in 1931 and is home to the Albany Symphony Orchestra (see above) and regularly hosts performances of ballet, movies, concerts, comedy, and song.

**Park Playhouse**. *Washington Park, Albany 12201. 518-434-2035. www.parkplayhouse.com.* Founded in 1989, this nonprofit organiza-

tion produces free performances throughout the summer of musicals in the outdoor amphitheater in Albany's largest park and runs a theater education program for young people.

**Schuyler Mansion**. *32 Catherine Street, Albany. 518-434-0834. www.nysparks .state.ny.us/sites. National Register.* This

*The statue of Philip Schuyler outside Albany City Hall honors upstate New York's most famous citizen during the American Revolution, and one of the state's first two U.S. senators.*

large brick Georgian-style house, built in 1761, was the home of Philip Schuyler, the wealthy landowner who became a revolutionary and was appointed a major general by George Washington and put in charge of the northern campaign. He served later as one of the first two U.S. senators from New York. *Open for tours April through October, Wednesday through Sunday, 11 am until 5 pm. Tours begin on the hour. Also open on Tuesdays in June, July, and August, and November through March by appointment only, Monday through Friday, 10 am until 4 pm. Group tours by appointment year-round.*

**St. Peter's Church**. *107 State Street, Albany. 518-434-3502. www.stpeters churchalbany.org. National Register.* With its lovely stained-glass windows and mosaic floor, this Gothic Revival Episcopal church was built by Richard Upjohn in 1859.

**Steamer No. 10 Theatre**. *500 Western Avenue (intersection of Allen Street, Western Avenue, and Madison Avenue), Albany 12203. 518-438-5503. www.steamer10theatre.org.* Opened in 1991 in an 1891 brick firehouse that once contained a steam-powered municipal fire engine, this eclectic theater presents five productions a year in its 120-seat space. The company tours schools and offers workshops.

**Ten Broeck Mansion**. *9 Ten Broeck Place, Albany. 518-436-9826. www .tenbroeckmansion.org. National Register.* Built in 1798 by General Abraham Ten Broeck and his wife, Elizabeth Van Rensselaer, this Federal-style house is the headquarters of the Albany County Historical Association. Lawns, gardens, and views of the Hudson River made the house one of the finest in the city for 150 years, and since taking on its stewardship in 1948 the association has worked to keep up that reputation. Ten Broeck himself, a fifth-generation descendant of original Dutch settlers, played a prominent role in the Battle of Saratoga and was a state senator and judge in Albany. *Open for tours May through December, Thursday and Friday, 10 am until 4 pm, and Saturday and Sunday, 1 pm to 4 pm. Fee.*

**Times-Union Center**. *51 South Pearl Street. 518-487-2000. www.times unioncenter-albany.com.* Frank Sinatra was the first to perform when Albany County's sports and entertainment center opened in 1990, and since then the facility has hosted such diverse attractions as the Rolling Stones, Ringling Brothers and Barnum & Bailey Circus, the Albany River Rats hockey team, and the Siena Saints college basketball team. Drawing audiences from a wide area, the center seats between 6,000 and 17,500, depending on the layout of the seats. (Formerly called the Pepsi Arena, the facility was renamed for Albany's largest newspaper in 2007.) *The box office is open from Memorial Day until Labor Day, Monday through Friday,*

*10 am until 5 pm, and Saturdays and Sundays when events are taking place; and from Labor Day until Memorial Day, Monday through Friday, 10 am until 6 pm, Saturdays, 10 am until 3 pm, and Sundays when events are taking place.*

**University at Albany Art Museum**. *400 Washington Avenue, Albany. 518-442-4035. www.albany.edu/museum.* Willem de Kooning, Ellsworth Kelly, and Louise Nevelson are just some of the diverse artists represented in the collections of this contemporary art museum opened in 1967 on the campus of the State University of New York at Albany. The museum produces six to eight exhibits a year in its 9,000-square-foot space designed by the modernist architect Edward Durrell Stone. *Open Tuesday through Friday, 10 am until 5 pm; Saturday and Sunday, 12 pm until 4 pm. Free.*

**Upstate Artists Guild**. *247 Lark Street, Albany. 518-426-3501. www .upstateartistsguild.org.* Begun in 2004, this nonprofit gallery and art education center hosts classes, workshops, and exhibits and organizes the monthly First Friday arts appreciation days (see below).

**USS *Slater* Destroyer Escort Historical Museum**. *Broadway/Quay, Albany. 518-431-1943. www.ussslater.org. National Register.* A nonprofit preservation group has devoted itself to restoring a World War II navy destroyer, the USS *Slater*—the only one of its kind still afloat in the United States— docked along the river in Albany. Hour-long tours cover the history and workings of the ship and ongoing restoration by volunteer navy veterans and local craftsmen. *Open April through November, Wednesday through Sunday, 10 am until 4 pm. Fee. Overnight camping on board the ship is available for youth groups.*

**WAMC Performing Arts Studio**. *318 Central Avenue, Albany 12206. 518-465-5233. www.wamcarts.org.* WAMC, 90.3 FM, one of the Northeast's largest public radio stations, is based in Albany, sending its cultural programming to 22 counties in the state. WAMC's Performing Arts Studio is a popular place to enjoy live performances throughout the year. *Fee.*

**Washington Park**. *www.washingtonparkconservancy.com. National Register.* Open in 1871 on land that had been a cemetery and parade ground, and designed by Frederick Law Olmsted and Calvert Vaux, the creators of Central Park in New York City, this 90-acre sanctuary of gardens, lawns, and trees is Albany's flagship park. Notable monuments in the park include a Robert Burns statue by Charles Calverley (1888) and a dramatic bronze fountain with a figure of Moses by J. Massey Rhind (1893). The park is surrounded by interesting brick and stone mansions, apartment houses, and other architecture of note including the 1900

*Ninety-acre Washington Park was designed by Frederick Law Olmsted and Calvert Vaux, the creators of Central Park in New York City.*

Dutch Renaissance Revival Nelson A. Rockefeller Institute of Government and the 1883 First Presbyterian Church of Albany. Taking place here annually are Tulip, Latin, Italian, and Winter Festivals (see below), free outdoor performances at the Park Playhouse (see above), and other special events and entertainments.

## COHOES

This old manufacturing city is located about eight miles north of Empire State Plaza at the actual junction of the Mohawk and Hudson Rivers.

**Cohoes Music Hall**. *58 Remsen Street, Cohoes 12047. 518-237-5858. www.cohoesmusichall.com.* Built in 1874 and popular among many early celebrities including Buffalo Bill Cody, John Philip Sousa, and Colonel Tom Thumb and his wife, this historic music hall was restored and reopened in 1975 as a nonprofit musical theater. *Fee.*

**Erie Canal**. *200 Southern Boulevard, Albany 12201 (administration). 518-237-7000. www.nyscanals.gov.* One of the great engineering feats of the 19th century, this 363-mile canal connecting the Hudson River at Cohoes with Buffalo, on the shore of Lake Erie in western New York, allowed commerce to pass between New York City and the Midwest, helped spur settlement of the American West, and ensured New York City's dominance as a trading port. Enlarged and moved more directly to the rivers whose courses they followed between 1905 and 1918, the canal and its tributaries—the Champlain, the Oswego, and the Cayuga-Seneca—fell into disuse for commercial purposes during the second half of the 20th century and are used today primarily for pleasure boating and historic tours under the jurisdiction of New York State Canals (see Resource Directory).

**Peebles Island State Park**. *Delaware Avenue (from Ontario Street on Van Schaick Island), Cohoes. 518-237-7000 ext. 220. www.nysparks.com.* Located 12 miles north of Albany, this 138-acre island at the confluence of the Mohawk and Hudson Rivers offers close-up views of the two great rivers of New York State as they converge for the long journey to New York Harbor. The island contains earthworks designed by the engineer Thaddeus Kosciuszko during the American Revolution and a visitor center with restrooms and historical information.

**Van Schaick Mansion**. *Van Schaick Avenue, Cohoes. 518-235-2699. www .vanschaickmansion.org. National Register.* Located just across the Hudson from the Herman Melville house in Lansingburgh, this 1755 Dutch Colonial farmhouse is where General Philip Schuyler turned over command of the Northern Army to General Horatio Gates a few days before the Battle of Saratoga. *Open by appointment.*

## COLONIE

**Albany International Airport—Arts and Culture Program**. *737 Albany-Shaker Road, Albany 12211. 518-242-2241. www.albanyairport.com.* Dating from its reopening after substantial renovations in 1998, the Albany airport has hosted a comprehensive and competitive exhibition program in its new terminal featuring the work of artists and museums in the Hudson Valley and national traveling exhibitions. Exhibits make use of an airport concourse, glass cases throughout the terminal, and a dedicated 2,500-square-foot gallery. *The gallery is open 7 am until 11 pm daily. Free.*

**Pruyn House**. *207 Old Niskayuna Road, Newtonville 12128. 518-783-1435. www.colonie.org/pruyn. National Register.* Built in 1830 for the land agent of Stephen Van Rensselaer III, the last patroon, this mixed Federal and Greek Revival farmhouse now serves as a cultural center for the township of Colonie. Ten outbuildings, some original and some relocated from elsewhere, include a restored barn and schoolhouse. *Open Monday through Friday, 9 am until 4:30 pm. Free.*

**Shaker Heritage Society**. *875 Watervliet Shaker Road, Colonie 12211. 518-456-7890. www.shakerheritage.org. National Register.* Located across the street from Albany International Airport, this 770-acre historic site was the first Shaker community in the United States. Eight Shaker buildings, fields, an apple orchard, a pond, a nature preserve, and a Shaker cemetery preserve the heritage of mother Ann Lee, the founder of the sect, who is buried here. The society offers tours of the buildings and the historic district, craft courses, workshops, lectures, and numerous annual events throughout the year. *Open February through October, Tues-*

*The American Shakers got their start in the Hudson Valley and dominated the region's agriculture, industry, and architecture for many years. The Shaker Heritage Society in Colonie has been restoring the first Shaker community in the United States—located across the street from the Albany International Airport.*

*day through Saturday, 9:30 am until 4 pm, and November and December, Monday through Saturday, 10 am until 4 pm. Fee.*

## RENSSELAERVILLE
Located in the rocky hills about 25 miles southwest of Albany, this lovely late-18th-century agricultural hamlet is a museum in itself. Isolation through 200 years of industrial growth elsewhere in the state left its architecture largely intact, and the result is a level of period detail and an overall harmony of effect that make the place unusual among New York State towns and well worth a visit. *National Register.*

## WATERVLIET
**Watervliet Arsenal**. *Route 32, Watervliet 12189. 518-266-5805. www.wva .army.mil. National Register.* Founded in 1813, this historic arsenal across the Hudson from Troy has been manufacturing large-caliber cannons for the U.S. Army since 1887. The guns still manufactured here provide the firepower for the army's main battlefield tank, the M1A1 Abrams. *Open Sunday through Thursday, 10 am until 3 pm.*

## Festivals, Fairs, and Celebrations
**Alive at Five**. *518-434-2032. www.albanyevents.org*. National, regional, and local musicians perform changing genres of music in this free summer concert series in Albany Riverfront Park (see above). Refreshments available.

**At the Plaza Summer Series**. *(518) 473-0559. www.ogs.state.ny.us*. Organized by the state Office of General Services, five free festivals take place from late June until August at Empire State Plaza: Fabulous Fourth of July, Kids Day, Plazafest, African American Family Day, and the Food Festival. There is also a Wednesday night concert series.

**Columbus Parade and Italian Festival**. *Washington Park. 518.641-7518. www.columbusdayalbanyny.com*. At 1 pm on the Saturday of Columbus Day weekend the large parade sets off, following Western Avenue to Robin Street and into Washington Park. There, food, drinks, and dancing continue until 5 o'clock. Rain or shine! *Magnifico!* Organized by the City of Albany Office of Special Events.

**First Friday**. *518-434-3861. www.1stfridayalbany.org*. On the first Friday of every month, the Upstate Artists Guild organizes a citywide evening out to celebrate the arts and artists of Albany. Galleries plan openings and special one-night shows; museums, antiques stores, and other shops stay open late; restaurants fling their doors wide; and live entertainment takes place on multiple stages around town.

**Larkfest**. *Lark Street. 518-434-3861. www.larkstreet.org*. Albany's biggest street festival takes place on a Saturday in September, with live music and entertainment, family activities, vendors of all kinds, and food from local restaurants. *10:30 am until 5:30 pm.*

**Latin Fest**. *www.albanylatinfest.com. 518-434-2032*. Taking place in Washington Park on the last Saturday in August, this all-day extravaganza of music, food, arts and crafts, and children's rides celebrates the Hispanic cultural heritage. *Open 11 am until 6 pm.*

**Riverfront Jazz Festival**. *518-434-2032. www.albanyevents.org*. This one-day free event in early September in Albany Riverfront Park features distinguished local and national performers.

**Tulip Festival**. *Washington Park. 518-434-2032 www.albanyevents.org*. A popular annual event since 1949, this three-day festival in Washington Park (see above) each May marks the start of spring and honors Albany's Dutch heritage. Events include a Tulip Queen Coronation, a Royal Tulip Ball, music, and children's activities.

## Also Nearby

Eighteen miles northwest of Albany along the Mohawk River is Schenectady, a famous old industrial town with a wonderful old theater. Built as a vaudeville house in 1926, Proctor's Theater (518-382-3884; www.proctors.org) was saved from the wrecking ball in 1979 and has subsequently expanded and taken on a new life as a popular regional performing arts center. *National Register.*

Farther afield, Cooperstown, on Otsego Lake 60 miles west of Albany, is home to the National Baseball Hall of Fame (607-547-7200; www.baseballhalloffame.org), the Fenimore Art Museum (607-547-1400; www.fenimoreartmuseum.org), which has a well-regarded collection of American paintings, folk art, and Native American art; the Farmers' Museum (607-547-1450; www.farmersmuseum.org), a unique collection of upstate buildings from the 1840s and an old-style working farm; and Glimmerglass Opera (607-547-5704; www.glimmerglass.org), the internationally recognized company that has brought opera and opera lovers to Cooperstown every year since 1975. *National Register.*

## Visitor Information

**Albany County Convention and Visitors Bureau**. *25 Quackenbush Square, Albany 12207. 518-434-1217. www.albany.org.* This busy tourist office and cultural center is a great place to start for information on current events at museums, galleries, theaters, and performing arts centers in Albany and the surrounding region, and for help with hotels, restaurants, and transportation in Albany.

*Half Moon*/**New Netherland Museum**. *P.O. Box 10609, Albany 12201. 518-443-1609. www.newnetherland.org.* A reproduction, built in 1989, of the 85-foot square-rigged yacht that Henry Hudson sailed into New York Harbor and up the Hudson River in 1609, the *Half Moon* serves as a traveling museum, docking at cities up and down the Hudson and providing tours below and above deck and classes on the history of New Netherlands.

**Historic Albany Foundation**. *89 Lexington Avenue, Albany 12206. 518-465-0876. www.historic-albany.org.* Founded in 1974 to promote the architectural preservation of historic homes and buildings in the Capital District, the Historic Albany Foundation offers a wide array of programs relating to architectural history, including public lectures and area house tours. The foundation also maintains a large reference library for architecture lovers and would-be do-it-yourselfers as well as the Architectural Parts Warehouse, a nonprofit shop in downtown Albany that sells salvaged architectural elements.

**Parks & Trails New York**. *29 Elk Street, Albany 12207. 518-434-1583. www.ptny.org.* An advocacy and promotion organization based in Albany, Parks & Trails New York provides information on over 90 multiuse trails across the state. The group organizes bike tours of the Erie Canalway and Hudson River Valley and provides detailed maps of the state's abundant greenway and park system.

# RENSSELAER COUNTY

The opening of Rensselaer Polytechnic Institute's Experimental Media and Performing Arts Center (EMPAC) in 2008 put Troy back on the map as one of the most interesting places in the Hudson Valley. Already recognized for its striking 19th-century architecture, its strong educational institutions, and its rich offerings in music and the visual arts, this old manufacturing city reestablished its claim as a cultural leader with the unveiling of Nicholas Grimshaw's whimsical contemporary arts center focused on the crossover of technology and high art.

Located along the east bank of the Hudson River near the junction of the Erie and Champlain Canals, Troy is the seat of Rensselaer County and was for many years one of the economic and cultural engines of the capital region. During the 19th century the city made a name for itself as a manufacturer of church bells, cast-iron stoves, horseshoes, and other iron products, and later came to be known as the "Collar City" for its factories producing shirts, shirt-collars, and shirt-cuffs. The enormous profits from these technologically advanced companies found their way into local arts institutions such as the 1895 Troy Savings Bank Music Hall, a lovely concert hall above a bank whose acoustics are still admired by recording musicians almost 150 years later.

Today, Troy institutions old and new are drawing audiences for new-media performances and daring renditions of classical work, and preservation groups are culling from streets, archives, and the land itself the record of the city's architectural and industrial heritage. Blocks of spacious and often strikingly designed brownstones, office buildings, and storefronts have attracted artists, families, and filmmakers looking for intact 19th-century urban settings. Acres of specialized plants and warehouses, their redbrick forms stretching south along the Hudson, have made the outlying districts a sort of museum of industrial-age architecture.

Exhibiting contemporary artists from throughout the Hudson Valley in its gallery, the Arts Center for the Capital Region, at 265 River Street in downtown Troy (www.artscenteronline.org), is a

*The Experimental Media and Performing Arts Center at Rensselaer Polytechnic Institute reflects a long history of technological experimentation in Troy, one of the most important cities for education, manufacturing, and the arts on the Hudson River.*

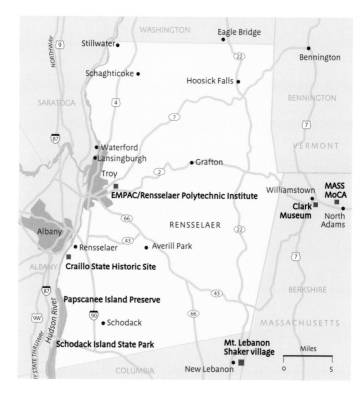

great source of information on cultural events not only in Troy, but in Albany and Schenectady as well. Information on chamber concerts at the Emma Willard School, musicals at the Sand Lake Center for the Arts in Averill Park, or performances at the Experimental Media and Performing Arts Center can all be found here. The RiverSpark Visitor Center, next to City Hall at 251 River Street in Troy (www.troyvisitorcenter.org), is a good place to start for any kind of tour.

One distinctive feature of Troy's remarkable history is its concentration of educational institutions for women. Since the reformer Emma Willard established the country's first secondary school for girls here in 1814, education has been a thriving business in Rensselaer County. Stephen Van Rensselaer, the sixth in a line of Dutch patroons dating back to the 17th century, founded Rensselaer Polytechnic Institute, the first technological university in the United States, in Troy in 1824. Partly inspired by Emma Willard, Margaret Olivia Slocum Sage, the widow of the financier Russell Sage, started the Russell Sage College for Women in Troy in 1916. With talented faculties, diverse students, and architecturally interesting campuses, these institutions are an important part of the cultural fabric of the county and of the capital region as a whole.

The county takes its name from the Dutch pearl and diamond merchant Kiliaen Van Rensselaer, the first patroon (a sort of feudal lord in the Dutch system), who bought land along both sides of the Hudson as an investment in 1629. Five subsequent generations of his family collected rents from as many as 3,000 tenant farmers on an estate of approximately 1,200 square miles before the patroonship dissolved upon Stephen Van Rensselaer III's death in 1839. Crailo State Historic Site, the restored Van Rensselaer family home in Rensselaer, is now a museum.

Downtown Troy and the other communities of Rensselaer County reward an afternoon's browsing and wandering. A two-block stretch of River Street in Troy, known as the Antiques District, is filled with antiques stores; in addition, several new galleries specialize in contemporary art. Troy has even made a public event of browsing, organizing an annual Victorian Stroll (see Festivals, below) through the historic and shopping districts in early December each year. Each June, upward of 40,000 people gather along 4th Street to watch the annual Flag Day Parade, considered the largest observance of this day in the country.

## AVERILL PARK
**Sand Lake Center for the Arts**. *2880 NY 43, Averill Park 12018. 518-674-2007. www.slca-ctp.org.* Opened in 2003 in a historic (1833) church,

*The Sand Lake Center for the Arts opened in 2003 in an 1833 church in Averill Park.*

and located a few miles inland from the Hudson River, this thriving community theater and arts center hosts regular art shows, music and dance performances, and theater productions by the local Circle Theatre Players. Children's programs include a Kids' Arts Day and Kids for Kids Theatre.

## GRAFTON

**Grafton Lakes State Park**. *61 North Long Pond Road, Grafton. 12082. 518-279-1155. www.nysparks.com.* This 2,357-acre state park on the ridge between the Hudson and Taconic Valleys has 25 miles of trails for hiking, bicycling, horseback riding, and cross-country skiing. Its five ponds are popular with fishermen and boaters. *Open year-round.*

## LANSINGBURGH

In 1847 this community just north of Troy permitted its school district to raise money through taxes, creating one of the first free schools in the state. Among the famous residents of the village was Herman Melville, who went to school at the Lansingsburgh Academy at the corner of 4th Avenue and 114th Street, graduating with a degree in surveying and engineering. The 1820 brick schoolhouse is on the National Register and is now an arts center and a branch of the Troy Public Library. The house where Melville lived from 1838 until 1847, and where he wrote his first two novels, *Typee* and *Omoo*, at Number Two 114th Street, at the corner of First Avenue, is also on the National Register and is the headquarters of the Lansingburgh Historical Society (518-235-3501).

## RENSSELAER

**Crailo State Historic Site**. *9½ Riverside Avenue, Rensselaer 12144. 518-463-8738. www.nysparks.com.* A state museum of colonial history since 1924, this 18th-century house was once part of Rensselaerwyck, the large estate of the Van Rensselaer family on both sides of the Hudson. Exhibits and guided tours tell the story of the early Dutch inhabitants of the region. *Open April through October, Wednesday through Sunday (and Tuesdays, June through August), 11 am until 5 pm; November through March, by appointment only, Monday through Friday, 11 am until 4 pm.*

**Rensselaer Rail Station**. *525 East Street, Rensselaer 12144.* Operated by the Capital District Transportation Authority, this busy Amtrak station serving Albany and Rensselaer Counties is a major rail hub, with trains bound north for Montreal, west for Chicago, south for New York City, and east for Boston. The bright, high station building was completed in 2002, replacing a smaller nearby structure dating from 1968.

*In this house overlooking the Hudson River in Lansingburgh, now North Troy, where he lived with his family from 1838 until 1847, the young Herman Melville completed his first two novels,* Typee *and* Omoo.

**St. John's Roman Catholic Church**. *50 Herrick Street, Rensselaer 12144. 518-463-4401.* Completed in 1891, and replacing an earlier structure destroyed by fire, this landmark Catholic church a few blocks east of the Rensselaer Rail Station is a distinctive sight on the east side of the Hudson, famous for its tower and blue beehive dome.

## SCHODACK

Just a few miles apart, two parks on the Hudson, one run by New York State and the other by Rensselaer County, offer miles of hiking, biking, and cross-country ski trails on the waterfront:

- The 156-acre Papscanee Island Preserve (Route 9J at Staats Island Road, Schodack 12033; 518-270-2888; www.rensselaercounty.org) is a county park with six miles of hiking trails along two miles of shoreline. It is open dawn to dusk.

- The 1,052-acre Schodack Island State Park (1 Schodack Way, Schodack 12033; 518-732-0187; www.nysparks.state.ny.us/parks) is a bird sanctuary and protected estuary along seven miles of the river. It is home to bald eagles, blue herons, and many other species. Picnicking, biking, volleyball, horseshoes, kayaking, and canoeing are encouraged.

## TROY

**Arts Center of the Capital Region**. *265 River Street, Troy 12180. 518-273-0552. www.artscenteronline.org*. With a reach extending beyond Rensselaer to Albany and Schenectady Counties, this major exhibition, studio, and teaching facility hosts shows by national and local artists and provides studio space, classes, and lectures for artists of all ages. Among many popular events, the annual Fence Show open to local artists is a regular draw in the Capital Region. *The gallery is open Monday through Thursday, 11 am until 7 pm; Friday through Saturday, 9 am until 5 pm; and Sunday, noon until 4 pm. Free.*

**Beacon Institute for Rivers and Estuaries**. *270 River Street, Troy 12180. 518-273-3215. www.thebeaconinstitute.org*. With a mission of research, policy making, and education on rivers, estuaries, and their connection with society, and with offices in Beacon and Troy, this scientific institution with links to major universities and corporations uses the Hudson River as a laboratory for research projects with global applications. Its research center in Troy focuses on the watershed, communities, and people extending from the Capital District northward.

**Bush Memorial Center**. *Corner of Congress and First Streets, Troy 12180. 518-244-2000. www.sage.edu*. Constructed as a Presbyterian church in 1836, and used as a lecture and concert hall by Russell Sage College since 1975, this Greek Revival temple on the Sage College campus is one of what is thought to be only ten surviving churches by the architect James Harrison Dakin. It is distinguished by several Tiffany windows and the ionic columns and pilasters in its main hall.

**Children's Museum of Science and Technology**. *250 Jordan Road, Rensselaer Technology Park, Troy 12180. 518-235-2120. www.cmost.org*. Through its planetarium and interactive exhibits, the museum introduces children to science, history, and the arts. A special exhibit on the Hudson River provides a virtual tour of the river from its source at Lake Tear of the Clouds in the Adirondacks to New York Harbor. *Open September through June, Thursday through Sunday, 10 am until 5 pm. Fee.*

**Emma Willard School**. *285 Pawling Avenue, Troy 12180. 518-833-1300. www.emmawillard.org. National Register*. The educational reformer Emma Willard founded what remains the oldest American secondary school for girls here in 1814. The wonderful gargoyle-covered Collegiate Gothic buildings of the "new campus" on the hill above Troy date from 1910. The school presents regular public performances of music, dance, and theater by students and professionals. The organization Friends

*James Harrison Dakin's Greek Revival Bush Memorial Center at Russell Sage College was constructed as a Presbyterian Church in 1836 but is now used mainly for concerts and lectures.*

of Chamber Music (see Visitor Information, below) organizes regular chamber music concerts in Kiggins Hall. *The Dietel Art Gallery, part of the music, art, and library complex, exhibits professional as well as student and faculty work and is open Monday through Friday, 9 am until 7 pm, and weekends, 10 am until 5 pm, when school is in session.*

**Fulton Street Gallery**. *408 Fulton Street, Troy 12180. 518-274-8464. www.fultonstreetgallery.org.* Founded in 1997, this nonprofit gallery produces two international, two regional, and several solo and small group exhibits of contemporary art each year, and organizes workshops and residencies for artists in schools. *Free.*

**New York State Theatre Institute**. *Main box office: 37 First Street, Troy 12180. 518-274-3256. www.nysti.org.* This well-respected theater mounts a full season of classic plays for family and school audiences in the Schacht Fine Arts Center at Russell Sage College. *The box office is open Monday through Friday, 9 am until 4 pm. Fee.*

**Rensselaer County Historical Society**. *57 Second Street, Troy 12180. 518-272-7232. www.rchsonline.org. National Register.* Located in downtown Troy in two adjacent town houses, the Rensselaer Historical Society has been documenting and exhibiting the history of the region since 1927. In addition to regular exhibitions and area house tours, the society

*Built in 1827, the white marble Hart-Cluett House in downtown Troy was owned by just two families before its transfer to the Rensselaer County Historical Society in 1927.*

also is home to a full research library. Its architecturally significant, white marble Hart-Cluett House was built in 1827 as a gift from New York City merchant and banker William Howard for his only child, Betsey. Purchased by the Cluetts, a wealthy industrial family in the shirt collar business, the house was passed on to the society in 1927 by the Cluett family upon Betsey's death. With many of its original furnishings and most of its original interior structure intact, the house is one of the finest examples in the Hudson Valley of an important late-Federal-period house.

**Rensselaer Polytechnic Institute**. *110 Eighth Street, Troy 12180. 518-276-6216. www.rpi.edu.* With its world-famous faculty, its high-tech labs, and its practical goal of integrating knowledge, culture, and industry, the country's oldest (founded in 1824) technological university has long attracted some of the brightest minds in the country to its campus of mixed Georgian and modern architecture on the hill above Troy. Its experimental arts program, known as iEAR or Integrated Electronic Arts at Rensselaer (West Hall, Room 107; 518-276-4778; www.arts.rpi.edu), was founded in 1985 and capitalizes on the university's technology focus while exploring innovations in computer music, video art, image processing techniques, and performance. The program received a significant boost with the completion, in 2008 of:

- Experimental Media and Performing Arts Center (518-276-4133; www.empac.rpi.edu). This extraordinary glass building designed by the English architect Nicholas Grimshaw combines in one great space a concert hall, a theater, and two studios designed to accommodate both the most traditional and the most technologically advanced music, dance, theater, film, and electronic media. The 1,200-seat Concert Hall—a pod of curved cedar planks seemingly suspended inside a larger glass box—was designed for both traditional orchestras and performances that involve electronically generated sound and

*Completed in 2008, the Experimental Media and Performing Arts Center at Rensselaer Polytechnic Institute combines in one glossy, glassy space a concert hall, a theater, and two studios, all designed to accommodate the most traditional and the most technologically advanced performances.*

video projection. The theater, with a 40 by 80 foot stage and flexible seating and orchestra pit, was designed for both professional and student productions and can accommodate projection screens and loudspeakers to create virtual environments. A major addition to the cityscape of Troy, EMPAC dominates the hill above the city and has a commanding view of the Capital Region. Fee.

**RiverSpark Visitor Center**. *251 River Street, Troy 12180. 518-270-8667. www.troyvisitorcenter.org*. New York State has designated a stretch of land at the intersection of the Hudson and Mohawk Rivers, including Cohoes, Colonie, Green Island, Troy, Waterford, and Watervliet, as a Heritage Corridor—the first of 17 such places in the state. Called RiverSpark because water was such a defining feature of its history, this corridor, which reaches into three counties, is introduced and explained through exhibits, brochures, and talks, at this visitor center on the north side of City Hall in Troy.

**Russell Sage College**. *45 Ferry Street, Troy 12180. 518-244-2000. www.sage.edu*. Founded in 1916, this highly respected women's college has expanded in recent years to include a coeducational campus in Albany, a graduate school, and an adult education school. Among its cultural offerings in Troy are numerous concerts, performances, lectures, and exhibits on its historic campus on First and Second Streets (see New York State Theater Institute, above).

**Sanctuary for Independent Media**. *3361 Sixth Avenue, Troy 12180. 518-272-2390. www.thesanctuaryforindependentmedia.org.* Located in a former church, this telecommunications production facility dedicated to media arts hosts screenings and performances and provides production facilities, training in media production, and a meeting space for artists, activists, and independent media makers. *Suggested donation.*

**Troy Gas Light Company Gasholder House**. *Fifth Avenue and Jefferson Street, South Troy. www.siahq.org. National Register.* The round brick building, designed by Frederick Sabbaton, is one of the most distinctive buildings in Troy. Built in 1873, it is one of the largest remaining structures in America built to protect an iron gas tank from the weather. Inside, under the domed roof and cupola, a tank storing gas for illuminating the city rose and fell on a track according to the volume it contained. A sketch of the building is the logo for the Society for Industrial Archaeology. *The building is privately owned and not open to the public.*

**Troy Savings Bank Music Hall**. *32 2nd Street, Troy 12180. 518-273-0038. www.troymusichall.org. National Register.* Famous well beyond the capital region for its acoustics, this 1875 Italian Renaissance–style music hall above a bank—one of the most innovative buildings of its time—has

*The round brick Gasholder House of the Troy Gas Light Company was built in 1873 and is one of the largest remaining structures built to protect an iron gas tank from the weather.*

*A concert hall above a bank, the 1875 Troy Savings Bank Music Hall is famous well beyond the capital region for its acoustics.*

a full range of performances by musicians from classical to pop, from orchestras to chamber groups and soloists, throughout the year. *The box office is open 10 am until 5 pm Monday through Friday. Fee.*

**Uncle Sam's Gravesite/Oakwood Cemetery**. *50 101st Street, Troy. 518-272-7520. www.oakwoodcemetery.org. National Register.* Samuel Wilson, the Troy meatpacker who came to be known as "Uncle Sam" to the American army during the War of 1812, and whose image as a personification of the United States later appeared on army recruitment posters, may be the most famous of the many local luminaries (also including Emma Willard and Russell Sage) buried in this large cemetery high above Troy. Small signs point the way to the Uncle Sam grave site. The view of the Hudson Valley from the cemetery's overlook is one of the best in the region. (Uncle Sam also figures elsewhere in the valley—see Catskill in Greene County.)

**Washington Park**. *Bounded by 2nd, 3rd, Washington, and Adams Streets, Troy. National Register.* Built in 1840, and one of the few private gated squares in an American city aside from Gramercy Park in Manhattan, this enclosed, tree-filled space in the residential section of Troy is

*Built in 1840, and surrounded by the elegant brownstones of Troy's one-time indus-trial magnates, Washington Park in Troy is one of the few private gated squares in an American city aside from Gramercy Park in Manhattan.*

surrounded by large, elegant brownstones that once belonged to the owners and managers of Troy's 19th-century industries. The annual Fence Show at the Arts Center of the Capital Region (see above) got its start in 1965 when artists began hanging their work on the iron fence around Washington Park. Walking tour guides to the park are available at the RiverSpark Visitor Center (see above).

## Festivals, Fairs, and Celebrations

**Annual Holiday Greens Show**. *518-272-7232. www.rchsonline.org*. The Rensselaer County Historical Society and the Van Rensselaer Garden Club coordinate this annual display of holiday greenery in the historic 1827 Hart-Cluett House in Troy. The show takes place the same weekend as the Troy Victorian Stroll (see below).

**Celebration of Celts**. *518-851-9670. www.celebrationofcelts.com*. This two-day spring festival honors the history, dance, and music of the eight Celtic nations.

**Music in the Park**. *518-273-0834. www.troyny.gov*. A series of evening concerts each summer in Riverfront Park in Troy.

**Powers Park Concert Series**. *Powers Park, 110th Street, Lansingburgh. 518-270-4624. www.troyny.gov*. In the gazebo in Powers Park in Lansing-burgh, concerts and events take place after 6 pm on summer weekends.

**Rensselaer County Apple Festival**. *1297 Brookview Station Road, Schodack. 518-732-7317. www.goold.com.* This Columbus Day weekend celebration of arts and agriculture takes place at Goold Orchards. It features crafters, dancers, and musicians.

**Schaghticoke Fair**. *69 Stillwater Bridge Road (at Routes 67 and 40), Schaghticoke. 518-753-4411. www.schaghticokefair.com.* Dating from 1819, the third oldest county fair in New York State begins on the Wednesday before Labor Day and continues through the weekend at the fairgrounds in Schaghticoke. The Rensselaer County Agricultural and Horticultural Society, which runs the fair, encourages hands-on participation at exhibits of horses, sheep, goats, cattle, and poultry. "Tasting, seeing, hearing, and literally feeling agriculture in action is one of the best experiences we can offer."

**Troy Flag Day Parade**. *Troy Flag Day Parade Committee, P.O. Box 56, Troy 12181. 518-272-7396 www.troyny.gov.* Taking place in early June on the weekend before the national observance of Flag Day on June 14, this well-attended local event dates from 1967 and is considered the largest parade of its kind in the country, with upwards of 40,000 spectators lining the two-mile route along 4th Street from 4th and Main in South Troy to 4th and Federal downtown. President Woodrow Wilson issued a proclamation calling for a nationwide observance of Flag Day on June 14, 1916, and the day of observance (not a holiday) was formally established by an act of Congress in 1949.

**Troy River Street Festival**. *518-273-0552. www.troyny.gov.* Downtown Troy comes alive each June with live music, antiques, arts and crafts, and food from local restaurants.

*River Street in downtown Troy has been transformed into a thriving art and antiques district.*

**Troy Victorian Stroll**. *518-274-7020. www.troyvictorianstroll.com*. Coordinated by the Rensselaer County Regional Chamber of Commerce, this extravaganza of shopping, music, and other entertainment takes place 10 days after Thanksgiving each year in downtown Troy.

## Also Nearby

Just within the border of Rensselaer County, 26 miles northeast of Troy along Route 7, is Hoosick Falls, where an icon almost as famous as Uncle Sam, the American primitive painter Grandma Moses, was first discovered, lived most of her life, and is buried. Her grave site can be visited at Maple Grove Cemetery on the south side of the village, and her farm—where her great-grandson Will Moses, also a painter, now lives and works (518-686-4334; www.willmoses.com)—is located six miles north of Hoosick Falls in Eagle Bridge.

About 35 miles east of Troy, on Route 2, just over the Massachusetts border in Williamstown, Massachusetts, is the Francine and Sterling Clark Museum (413-458-2303; www.clarkart.edu; fee), known throughout the world for its French Impressionist paintings and other European and American art from the Renaissance to the present, including its strong collection of Winslow Homer, John Singer Sargent, and other 19th-century American painters, and its silver. Every summer, the Williamstown Theatre Festival (413-597-3400; www.wtfestival.org) mounts new and classic plays and trains emerging actors in its theaters. Just three miles farther east, in North Adams, is MASS MoCA (413-662-2111; www.massmoca.org; fee), the large and daring contemporary art museum founded in 1999.

## Visitor Information

**Arts Center of the Capital Region**. *265 River Street, Troy 12180. 518-273-0552. www.artscenteronline.org*. Formerly the Rensselaer County Council on the Arts, this nonprofit arts organization provides grants, classes, and studio and exhibit spaces for artists and information for the general public on gallery openings, performances, and events throughout Rensselaer County and the region. See main listing under Troy, above.

**Capital District Community Gardens**. *40 River Street, Troy 12180. 518-274-8685. www.cdcg.org*. Established in 1975, this community service organization helps residents of Albany, Rensselaer, and Schenectady Counties create and maintain community gardens. The group also organizes street tree plantings and other urban greening programs.

**Center for Land Use Interpretation**. *53 Third Street, Troy. 310-839-5722. www.clui.org*. The Northeast Regional Office of the California-based nonprofit organization provides information, publishes books, and hosts exhibits in its storefront gallery to increase and diffuse knowledge about how land in the Hudson Valley and elsewhere is apportioned, used, and perceived.

**Hudson Mohawk Industrial Gateway**. *One East Industrial Parkway, Troy 12180. 518-274-5267. www.hudsonmohawkgateway.org*. The offices of this preservation organization devoted to the industrial heritage of Troy and its surroundings are in the former Burden Iron Works, an 1882 Romanesque industrial building in South Troy once owned by an inventor who made a fortune automating processes formerly done by hand. Henry Burden became especially famous during the Civil War for his horseshoe-making machine, which could produce one horseshoe per second.

**Rensselaer County Tourism**. *518-270-2959. www.rensco.com*. This Web site offers a calendar of upcoming cultural events throughout the county, maps, and information on restaurants, hotels, transportation, and things to see and places to go.

**RiverSpark Visitor Center**. *251 River Street, Troy 12180. 518-270-8667. www.troyvisitorcenter.org*. Part of the officially designated Hudson-Mohawk Heritage Area, which includes the communities of Cohoes, Colonie, Green Island, Troy, Waterford, and Watervliet, this tourist information center is a good place to start when planning a visit to Troy, or when first arriving. See listing under Troy, above.

# SARATOGA COUNTY

As visitors drive into Saratoga Springs, a sign welcomes them with the words "Health, History, Horses," but a fourth word might be added to round out the reputation of this famous resort town (though it would disturb the alliterative harmony): arts. Like Rensselaer County to the south, Saratoga has successfully parlayed its traditional reputation—in this case as a place of horse racing, mineral springs, and historical battlefields—into a 21st-century one as an important center of the arts and culture in New York State, with institutions great and small offering an array of ballet, symphonies, chamber music, opera, theater, and contemporary art.

Drawing audiences to Saratoga Springs from throughout the Hudson Valley and from as far away as Montreal, Boston, and Buffalo is of course the Saratoga Performing Arts Center, popularly known as SPAC—the outdoor stage in Saratoga Spa State Park that is the summer home of the New York City Ballet and the Philadelphia Orchestra. Antoine Predock's 2000 Francis Tang Museum, at Skidmore College, attracts visitors to provocative exhibits of contemporary and multidisciplinary art, and the Arts Center, run by the Saratoga County Arts Council at 320 Broadway in downtown Saratoga Springs (518-584-4132; www.saratoga-arts .org), hosts gallery shows, performances, classes, and a film series.

Located at the confluence of the Hudson and Mohawk Rivers, Saratoga has benefited from its position at the junction of north-south and east-west transportation routes. The abundantly interesting architecture to be found here, from the colonial to the contemporary (with an emphasis on the Victorian), attests to the ongoing financial strength of local citizens and institutions. The state legislature designated Saratoga a county separate from Albany County in 1791. Its name is a corruption of the Mohawk *sah-rah-ka*, said to mean "the side hill."

The county seat, Ballston Spa, once rivaled its neighbor five miles to the north as a health and commercial center and supplier of mineral water, but Saratoga Springs outstripped it in gambling and horse racing. Today the very useful Saratoga County Historical Society is located in Ballston Spa (6 Charlton Street;

*Accessed down the lovely Avenue of Pines, and home to the Saratoga Performing Arts Center, the National Museum of Dance, and the Spa Little Theatre, the 2,200-acre Saratoga Spa State Park is home to a working mineral springs, a golf course, a hotel, tennis courts, and miles of hiking and cross-country ski trails.*

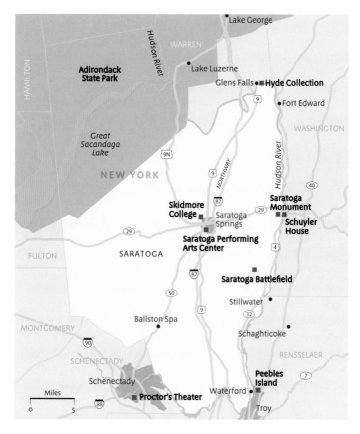

Within the map:

Lake George

WARREN

Hudson River

Adirondack
State Park

HAMILTON

Lake Luzerne

Glens Falls ● ■ **Hyde Collection**

● Fort Edward

(9)

WASHINGTON

Great
Sacandaga
Lake

NEW YORK

(9N)

(9)

NORTHWAY

Hudson River

(40)

**Skidmore
College** ■

(87)

Saratoga
Springs

(29)

**Saratoga
Monument**
■ ■

**Schuyler
House**

(29)

**Saratoga Performing
Arts Center**

(4)

FULTON

SARATOGA

(87)

■ **Saratoga Battlefield**

(50)

Stillwater ●

(9)

(32)

Ballston Spa ●

Schaghticoke

MONTGOMERY

(90)

RENSSELAER

SCHENECTADY

**Peebles
Island**

(7)

Schenectady

Waterford ● ■

Miles

■ **Proctor's Theater**

0    5

(88)

Troy

www.brooksidemuseum.org), while the Saratoga County Arts
Council (320 Broadway; www.saratoga-arts.org) and the Saratoga
Springs History Museum (Canfield Casino; www.saratogahistory
.org) are *in* Saratoga Springs. Visit all three, online or in person,
for up-to-the-minute listings of festivals, concerts, openings, and
other events throughout the county.

National and state parks of enormous interest can be found
in Saratoga County—a day touring the battlefield and historical
sites at Saratoga National Historic Park might be followed by an
evening performance of the Philadelphia Orchestra or the New
York City Ballet at SPAC in Saratoga Spa State Park. The National
Museum of Dance, the Racing Museum and Hall of Fame, the
New York State Military Museum, even a National Bottle Museum
offer unexpected pleasures and insights. And of course the
racecourse, still fused in many people's minds with the name
Saratoga, beckons horse lovers and the just plain curious every
day of the week but Monday from late July until late August.

## BALLSTON SPA

Named for Eliphalet Ball, one of its original settlers, this village with its well-preserved colonial and Victorian architecture is the seat of Saratoga County and the site of once-famous mineral springs. Free summer concerts in Wiswall Park downtown, a winter festival that includes sledding and candlelight skiing, and shops, restaurants, and antiques stores all reward a visit. The one remaining year-round spring, the Old Iron Spring at the corner of Front Street and Fairgrounds Road, with its historic eight-sided pavilion, has been supplying the local waters continuously since 1874.

**Brookside Museum/Saratoga County Historical Society**. *6 Charlton Street, Ballston Spa 12020. 518-885-4000. www.brooksidemuseum.org. National Register.* Home to the Saratoga County Historical Society's collection of local memorabilia, the museum offers three permanent exhibitions, including a display focusing on the long history of sports and culture in the area, and two galleries that host a variety of rotating exhibits. The museum also houses an extensive research library on local history and genealogy. *Open Tuesday through Friday, 10 am until 4 pm, and Saturday, 10 am until 4 pm. Fee.*

**National Bottle Museum**. *76 Milton Avenue, Ballston Spa 12020. 518-885-7589. www.nationalbottlemuseum.org.* Few people realize that until 1903, when the glass manufacturer Michael Owens patented his ideas for making glass bottles by machine, all of the bottles in the United States— whether for mineral water, whiskey, medicine, or milk—were made by hand. With constantly changing exhibits, this curatorial and collecting institution is a kind of information center for bottle enthusiasts. Constantly changing exhibits illuminate the colorful history of American commercial life, bringing to light, through the evidence of these colorful and often beautiful wrought glass containers, businesses that flourished and died without a trace except for the bottles in which their now-forgotten products were once encased. Glassblowing demonstrations and workshops take place throughout the year. *Open June 1 through September 30, 10 am until 4 pm daily; October 1 through May 31, Monday through Friday, 10 am until 4 pm. Fee.*

## SARATOGA SPRINGS

The races, the stately homes, the beautiful parks and gardens, and the quietly elegant life in summer have long drawn the wealthy to Saratoga Springs, and the city has fared better than most upstate towns over the years. The more recent strengthening of its cultural life and other amenities, such as excellent restaurants, have attracted a year-round population, some of whom work in the state capital, a 45-minute drive to the south.

*The Canfield Casino was built in 1871 as a gambling establishment and is now the home of the Saratoga Springs History Museum.*

**Arts Center of the Saratoga County Arts Council**. *320 Broadway (at Congress and Spring Streets), Saratoga Springs, 12866. 518-584-4132. www.saratoga-arts.org.* Mounting regular exhibits in its galleries and performances in its theater, this busy arts center on the edge of Congress Park offers classes, workshops, and services for artists and sponsors the annual Art in the Park and Art in Public Places programs as well as a wide range of live music from classical to new and experimental. Local and regional theater companies frequently take up residence for their productions. Also taking place here is the Saratoga Film Forum (518-584-3456; www.saratogafilmforum.org), which screens independent and foreign films three times a week. *The Arts Center is open Monday through Friday, 9 am until 5 pm, and Saturdays from 11 am until 5 pm; films are screened Thursdays and Fridays at 8 pm and Sundays at 3 pm.*

**Canfield Casino/Saratoga Springs History Museum**. *Congress Park, Saratoga Springs. 518-584-6920; www.saratogahistory.org. National Register.* Constructed as a gambling casino in 1871 by an unknown architect and renovated in the 1890s, this reddish brick Renaissance Revival building in Congress Park is currently the home of the Saratoga Springs History Museum. Tiffany glass windows, Italian gardens, and a large dining room with stained glass depicting signs of the zodiac provide a setting for permanent and changing exhibits on the history of Saratoga Springs. *Open Memorial Day through Labor Day, daily, 10 am until 4 pm, and from Labor Day through Memorial Day, Wednesday through Sunday, 10 am until 4 pm. Fee.*

**Children's Museum at Saratoga**. *69 Caroline Street, Saratoga Springs 12866. 518-584-5540. www.childrensmuseumatsaratoga.org.* Founded in 1990, and in its present location since 1994, this teaching museum dedicated to children ages 2 to 7 presents interactive exhibits, special events, and workshops in science, history, community living, and the arts. *Open during the winter, Tuesday through Saturday, 9:30 am until 4:30 pm, and Sunday, noon until 4:30 pm, and during the summer, Monday through Saturday, 9:30 am until 4 pm. Fee.*

**Congress Park**. *Saratoga Springs 12866. www.saratogaspringsvisitor center.org. National Register.* This 32-acre greenspace in downtown Saratoga Springs was created in 1822 and is the site of one of the most famous of the original springs of the town, called Congress Spring. With landscape changes by Frederick Law Olmsted in 1876, the park evolved over the decades into a lush park of paths winding through monuments, fountains, and more than 45 species of trees. A restored Marcus Charles Illions carousel—the only two-row Illions carousel still in working order—brings pleasure to people of all ages throughout the year (hours vary according to weather and season).

**Lester Park**. *Lester Park Road (also known as Petrified Gardens Road, 3 miles west of Saratoga Springs off Middle Grove Road), Saratoga Springs. 518-474-5877. www.nysm.nysed.gov/exhibits/longterm/lesterpark.* Run by the New York State Museum in Albany, this unusual natural history park is devoted to a series of strange and quite beautiful natural formations, called stromatolites, that were created by microscopic organisms about 490 million years ago when what is now Saratoga Springs was situated at the edge of a tropical reef south of the equator.

**National Museum of Dance**. *99 South Broadway, Saratoga Springs 12866. 518-584-2225. www.dancemuseum.org. National Register.* Occupying the former Washington Bath House, this museum on the edge of Saratoga Spa State Park features exhibits, performances, and educational programs that focus on the legends of dance in America. Among these are George Balanchine, who previewed many of his great ballets in Saratoga Springs during the New York City Ballet's annual season at the Saratoga Performing Arts Center. The museum was established in 1986 by Nancy Norman Lasalle, a patron of the City Ballet and its affiliate, the School of American Ballet. *Open Tuesday through Sunday, 10 am until 5 pm. Fee.*

**National Museum of Racing and Hall of Fame**. *191 Union Avenue, Saratoga Springs 12866. 518-584-0400. www.racingmuseum.org.* Located across Union Avenue from the racetrack, this museum dedicated to the sights, sounds, and history of Thoroughbred racing, one of America's oldest sports, presents both permanent and changing exhibits of racing memorabilia, trophies, silks, history, and examples of equine art. The museum also houses a library of Thoroughbred racing materials; the Hall of Fame, created in 1955 to recognize and honor deserving horses, jockeys, and trainers; and a gift shop. *Open September through June, Monday through Saturday, 10 am until 4 pm, and Sunday, noon until 4 pm; and with extended hours during the racing season in July and August, daily, 9 am until 5 pm. Fee.*

**New York State Military Museum/Veterans Research Center**. *61 Lake Avenue (Route 29, 3 blocks east of Route 9), Saratoga Springs 12866. 518-581-5100. www.dmna.state.ny.us/historic. National Register.* Located in the 1889 Saratoga Springs Armory designed by Isaac Perry, this important collection of New York State military artifacts contains more than 10,000 items dating from the American Revolution to the 2003 invasion of Iraq. Changing exhibits take place here on such subjects as New York State in the American Revolution. *Open Tuesday through Saturday, 10 am until 4 pm, and Sunday, 12 pm until 4 pm. Free.*

**Saratoga National Historical Park**. *648 Route 32, Stillwater 518-664-9821. www.nps.gov/sara. National Register.* About 15 miles southeast of Saratoga Springs, this 2,800-acre National Park incorporates the separate properties of the Saratoga Battlefield, the Saratoga Monument, and the Schuyler House.

- Saratoga Battlefield. Saratoga's location on the Champlain-Hudson corridor and at the junction with the Mohawk Valley ensured that it would eventually become a spot of military importance. When the Americans under Generals Gates and Benedict Arnold forcefully met the British troops marching down the Hudson in 1777, the British general John "Gentleman Johnny" Burgoyne, unable to advance farther toward his comrades in Manhattan yet cut off from the rear, his supply line stretched too thin and his troops being picked off one by one by the Americans, threw up his hands and surrendered. The story of what took place in the woods and fields here, with their wonderful views of the Hudson, is told in helpful signs. A 10-mile self-guided tour can be taken by car or bicycle and starts at the visitor center. Visitors receive a map and brochure at the toll gate (fee). The battlefield is open daily during daylight hours. *The tour road is open April 7 through September 30, 9 am until 7 pm; October 1 until daylight savings time begins, 9 am until 5 pm; and daylight savings day through November 30, 9 am until 4 pm. The visitor center is open 9 am until 5 pm daily. Fee.*

- Saratoga Monument. *Burgoyne Street, Victory 12871.* Commemorating the surrender of General John Burgoyne, commander of the British

*Completed in 1887, but commissioned ten years earlier, the Saratoga Monument commemorates the surrender of British general John Burgoyne to the American army on October 17, 1777—a turning point in the American Revolution.*

forces, to the American commander Horatio Gates on October 17, 1777, this 155-foot obelisk was commissioned by local citizens for the centennial of the Saratoga victory in 1877, though it was not completed until 1887. Niches in the four sides contain statues of three important generals from the Battle of Saratoga: Daniel Morgan, commander of the riflemen (facing west); Horatio Gates (facing north); and Philip Schuyler (facing east, toward his house). The niche on the south side would have contained a statue of Benedict Arnold, who also distinguished himself at Saratoga, but because of his later betrayal it is left empty. *Open Memorial Day weekend through Labor Day, Wednesday through Sunday, 9:30 am until 4:30 pm. Free.*

- Schuyler House. General Philip Schuyler was perhaps the most prominent local citizen at the time of the American Revolution. He led the American soldiers in the North Country during much of that time and was forced to give up his country house when General Burgoyne arrived and tried to break through the American defenses. Burgoyne eventually surrendered, but not before he had burned Schuyler's house to the ground. Promptly rebuilt after the war, it stands today as both a tribute to its owner and an example of a comfortable 18th-century Hudson Valley farmhouse. *Open Memorial Day weekend through Labor Day, Wednesday through Sunday, 9:30 am until 4:30 pm. Free.*

*The comfortable 18th-century farmhouse of General Philip Schuyler was burned to the ground by the British in 1777 and promptly rebuilt, and can be visited today under the auspices of the National Park Service.*

**Saratoga Performing Arts Center**. *Saratoga Spa State Park, Saratoga Springs 12866. 518-587-3330. www.spac.org.* This major regional performance facility, where the Grateful Dead once performed to a crowd of 40,000, is the summer home of the New York City Ballet and the Philadelphia Orchestra and the regular performing space of the Saratoga Chamber Music Festival, Freihofer's Jazz Festival, and the Lake George Opera. Major rock and pop stars perform and even record here. Opened in 1966, with design input from George Balanchine and Lincoln Kirstein of the New York City Ballet and Eugene Ormandy of the Philadelphia Orchestra, the open-air amphitheater ideally accommodates 5,200 people in its covered seats and as many as 20,000 on its lawn. *Fee.*

**Saratoga Race Course**. *267 Union Avenue, Saratoga Springs 12866. 518-584-6200 (racing season); 718-641-4700 (September through July). www.nyra.com.* Horses and horse racing are still a major part of the Saratoga heritage and culture. As they have since the track opened in 1863, horses continue to pound the track each summer at the oldest continuously operating thoroughbred track in America, and an average of 900,000 people continue to flock here from all over the country and world each year, filling local hotels and restaurants during racing season. Post time is 1 pm every day but Tuesday, when the horses are given a rest. A favorite treat is to eat breakfast at the track (7 am until 9:30 am) and watch the horses exercise. *Fee.*

**Saratoga Spa State Park**. *19 Roosevelt Drive, Saratoga Springs 12866. 518-584-2535. www.saratogaspastatepark.org. National Register.* Located on 2,200 acres on the south side of Saratoga Springs, this sprawling public park is the home of the Saratoga Performing Arts Center, the Spa Little Theater, and the National Museum of Dance (see separate listings). Besides working mineral springs, a golf course, a hotel, tennis courts, and playgrounds, the park also contains numerous trails for hiking and cross-country skiing. In 1912, in an attempt to protect the Saratoga mineral springs from commercial drillers who had begun lowering the water table in their attempts to extract carbon dioxide from the ground, the State of New York declared 800 acres around the springs as a state reservation. Over the years this protected land grew to its current size, with numerous buildings around the historic springs and roads, including the lovely Avenue of Pines, which is the main entryway to the park.

**Saratoga Springs Public Library**. *49 Henry Street (between Caroline and Philadelphia Streets), Saratoga Springs 12866. 518-584-7860. www.sspl.org.* Formed by public referendum in 1950 after merging with the Saratoga Athenaeum, a private subscription library begun in 1885, the Saratoga Springs Public Library is home to the Saratoga Room, a collection of local history, and regularly hosts the Poetry Zone open microphone night and the Writers on Reading series that brings well-known authors to town.

**Saratoga Springs Universal Preservation Hall**. *25 Washington Street, Saratoga Springs 12866. 518-584-2627. www.universalpreservationhall.org.* Built as a Methodist Episcopal church in 1841 and considerably enlarged in 1872, with a 3,125-pound broze bell founded in Troy, this splendid High Victorian Gothic building is under renovation to open as a nonprofit performance space and arts center.

**Skidmore College**. *815 North Broadway, Saratoga Springs 12866. 518-580-5000; http://cms.skidmore.edu.* An integral part of the culture of Saratoga

*Opened in 1966, the Saratoga Performing Arts Center is the summer home of the New York City Ballet and the Philadelphia Orchestra, and the major outdoor performing arts center of the Northern Hudson Valley.*

*Opened in 1863, and continuing to draw 900,000 people to Saratoga each summer, the Saratoga Race Course is the oldest continuously operating thoroughbred track in America.*

Springs, this liberal arts college of 2,400 students was founded for women in 1903 and began admitting men in 1971. The college hosts public concerts, readings, art exhibits, and dance and theater performances in various buildings on campus including:

- Francis Young Tang Teaching Museum and Art Gallery (518-580-8080; http://tang.skidmore.edu). Designed by the French architect Antoine Predock and opened in 2000, this stylish educational museum, with an audience from throughout the capital region and beyond, exhibits a broad range of contemporary art from the United States and abroad and addresses other disciplines as well, including the natural and social sciences, the performing arts, and the humanities. Open Tuesday through Friday, 10 am until 5 pm; Thursday, 10 am until 9 pm; and Saturday and Sunday, 12 pm until 5 pm. From June through August, the museum is open only until 5 pm on Thursdays but until 7 pm on Fridays. Fee.

- Arthur Zankel Music Center. Designed by EwingCole of Cleveland, Ohio, and including a 600-seat concert hall, a recording studio, and a 100-seat lecture and recital room, Skidmore's new 5,400-square-foot music building is scheduled to open in early 2010. The main concert hall will feature adjustable acoustics and a large stage intended to handle major orchestras as well as smaller chamber and jazz groups.

**Spa Little Theater**. *Saratoga Spa State Park, Saratoga Springs 12866. 518-584-2535. www.saratogaspastatepark.org.* Once used by the doctors at the Saratoga spa for lectures and entertainment, this 496-seat auditorium is now the permanent residence of several performing arts companies, including:

- The Home Made Theater (518-587-4427; www.homemadetheater.org), a professional community theater founded in 1985 that produces plays and offers classes and camps for young people.

- The Lake George Opera at Saratoga (518-584-6018. www.lakegeorge opera.org), an intimate opera theater started on the shores of Lake George in 1962 but resident in Saratoga since 1998; and

- The Saratoga Chamber Music Festival (www.spac.org/festivals.cfm), a salute each August to the power and excitement of this exacting art form, by some of the world's great musicians.

**Yaddo**. *Union Avenue, Saratoga Springs. 518-584-0746. www.yaddo.org/ garden*. Now one of the foremost artists' colonies in the United States, this mansion on the outskirts of Saratoga Springs was the home of financier Spencer Trask and his wife, Katrina. Although the 1893 house is not open to the public, guests may visit the splendid Italianate gardens to take in the bucolic environment of this 400-acre estate. *Open daily, sunrise to sunset.*

### Festivals, Fairs, and Celebrations

**Baroque Music Festival**. *165 Wilton Road, Greenfield Center 12833. 518-893-7527. www.baroquefestival.org*. Founded in 1959 to promote the genre of baroque chamber music, the Baroque Music Festival holds a five-performance concert series in its Saratoga Springs Festival Studio each July and offers other performances around the area at various times throughout the year. *Fee.*

*Built in 2000, and exhibiting a large range of contemporary art from the United States and abroad, the Francis Young Tang Teaching Museum at Skidmore College draws visitors from throughout the region.*

*Once used as a lecture hall by the doctors at the Saratoga Spa, the 496-seat Spa Little Theater is home to the Lake George Opera, the Saratoga Chamber Music Festival, and a community theater.*

**Black Crow Network**. *P.O. Box 5344, Clifton Park 12065. 518-383-3482.* Black Crow Network, based in Saratoga County, organizes events focused on the folk music and storytelling traditions of the Adirondacks and elsewhere in eastern New York. The organization combines displays of traditional cultural artifacts with these performances and collects stories and documents of rural life in the region.

**DanceFlurry Festival**. *P.O. Box 448, Latham, NY 12110. 518-384-3275. www.danceflurry.org.* Dedicated to "connecting and inspiring people through traditional music and dance," the DanceFlurry Organization (formerly Hudson-Mohawk Traditional Dance) presents contra, English, swing, family, and other types of traditional dance throughout the Capital-Saratoga region. Each February, the Dance Flurry Festival weekend in Saratoga Springs attracts more than 5,000 people of all ages to its diverse offering of dances, performances, workshops, jamming, and crafts. *Fee.*

**Saratoga ArtsFest**. *www.saratogaartsfest.org.* Taking place in mid-June each year, this three-day celebration of the arts features dance performances, readings, concerts, theatrical performances, and art exhibits by well-known and emerging artists at the great exhibit and performance spaces around Saratoga Springs.

**Saratoga County Fair**. *County Fairgrounds, 162 Prospect Street off Routes 50 and 67 (exit 12 from I-87), Ballston Spa 12020. 518-885-9701. www .saratogacountyfair.org.* Featuring everything from racing pigs to chain-saw art as well as the more traditional elements, this agricultural fair, founded in 1841, continues to draw as many as 80,000 people over five days in mid-July.

## Also Nearby

Located in the 1830 Greek Revival Hugh White Homestead, Waterford Historical Museum and Cultural Center (2 Museum Lane, behind Napa Plaza on Route 32, Waterford; 518-238-0809; www.waterfordmuseum .com.; National Register; free) features two period Victorian rooms from one of the home's later incarnations, a permanent exhibition on the history of Waterford, and changing exhibitions on local history and culture. The center is also home to the Annabel O'Connor Library for Local History, which provides access to genealogical and historical reference materials to the public for a nominal charge. In addition to its exhibition program, the society also offers an audio walking tour that highlights the architectural heritage of the village.

Twenty-five miles east of Saratoga Springs, across the Hudson River in Washington County, the old farming village of Cambridge is home to a busy arts center called Hubbard Hall (25 East Main Street; 518-677-2495; www.hubbardhall.org), which hosts numerous public workshops, a theater, a dance program, a store, and an art gallery in an 1878 rural opera house.

Eleven miles north of Cambridge, in the National Historic District in Salem, the Fort Salem Theater (11 East Broadway; 518-854-9200; www .fortsalemtheater.com; fee) has been presenting theater and cabaret in an 1840 Greek Revival brick church since 1972. Salem Art Works (19 Cary Lane; 518-854-7674; www.salemartworks.com) is a community of artists in a range of disciplines who offer exhibits, concerts, workshops, and a public sculpture garden.

## Visitor Information

**Saratoga County Arts Council**. *320 Broadway (at Congress and Spring Streets), Saratoga Springs 12866. 518-584-4132. www.saratoga-arts.org.* The source for the most complete information on arts and culture throughout the county. See complete listing under Saratoga Springs, above.

**Saratoga County Chamber of Commerce**. *28 Clinton Street, Saratoga Springs 12866. 518-584-3255. www.saratoga.org.* With information on shopping, hotels, and transportation, calendars of events, and listings of local attractions, this office and Web site are excellent places to visit when planning a trip to Saratoga Springs.

# WARREN AND ESSEX COUNTIES

Like the Catskill Mountains and the Shawangunks, the Adirondacks provided essential scenery for the grand landscape paintings of the Hudson River School, and one of the pleasures of a trip to Warren County and its northern neighbor Essex County is to immerse oneself in that still-wild landscape of rocky streams, immense stands of timber, lakes, and jagged peaks where snow lingers late into the spring—a landscape made eerily familiar and inviting, after all these years, by those paintings. New trails and canoe routes throughout the Adirondacks put this landscape within reasonable reach of most visitors, whether taking a day hike on the hills around Lake George or braving Mount Marcy, at 5,344 feet the tallest mountain in the state, for a glimpse of the Hudson's source.

These days, as elsewhere in the Hudson Valley, towns throughout the Adirondacks are experiencing a new surge of artistic activity, and not just among itinerant artists who take their sketches back to New York City to produce their final works, but by Adirondacks-based actors, sculptors, filmmakers, theater directors, writers, photographers, and painters who perform, exhibit, and publish locally as well as in the larger cities of Albany, New York, Boston, and elsewhere. Helping draw audiences for those works, new commercial and nonprofit galleries and a theater in a former Woolworth's store have opened in Glens Falls, which is also the home of annual art festivals and a Third Thursdays art walk. In the northern Warren County town of North Creek, a recently completed arts center has allowed a new theater group to flourish while providing a much-needed gallery for local artists.

The mill town and former trading post of Glens Falls has a history of involvement with the arts. Well worth a visit, the Hyde Collection, on Warren Street—a sort of Frick or Isabella Stewart Gardner Museum of the North Country—displays its substantial collection of old master and modern paintings in a Renaissance-style villa overlooking the Hudson and the paper mill once run by its owners. On Glen Street, the Chapman Historical Museum pos-

*Oils by Botticelli, Rubens, Renoir, and Rembrandt are among the treasures of the Hyde Collection, an art museum in a Florentine Renaissance–style house just above the Hudson River in Glens Falls.*

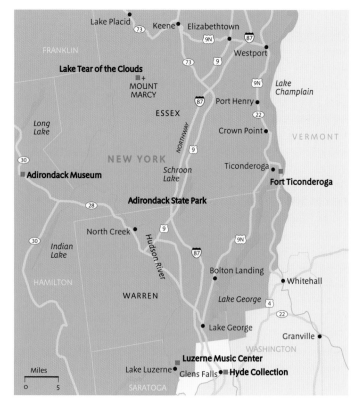

sesses a sizable collection of the works of Seneca Ray Stoddard, the prolific 19th-century photographer of the Adirondacks and Lake George who did much to publicize the woods, lakes, and hotels of the region to city dwellers hungry for the picturesque.

James Fenimore Cooper famously described the landscape of Warren County in his 1826 novel *The Last of the Mohicans*. His fictional account of the bloody battle at Fort William Henry, at the head of Lake George, in 1757, and its aftermath on Lake George and the hills around it, is still considered one of the best introductions to this region and its history. Travelers wishing to get a closer look at Cooper's sources can climb the many trails around Lake George (watch out for rattlesnakes), accessible from Hague, Bolton Landing, and Lake George Village; or visit Lake George Battlefield Park, at the head of Lake George, or Cooper's Cave, in Glens Falls, where legend puts Natty Bumppo and his friends as they tried to escape their pursuers.

West of Lake George, where the Hudson River bends down through Warren County from its source on Mount Marcy, Lake

Luzerne is the home of the Luzerne Music Center, a prestigious music camp whose student chamber and orchestra concerts, taking place in the open air or in a rustic lodge, draw large audiences. On Monday evenings in July and August, well-known performers join faculty for a long-standing concert series, the Luzerne Chamber Music Festival.

Formed from part of Washington County in 1813, Warren is named for General Joseph Warren, a Boston doctor who, though already appointed a major general, fought and died as a volunteer at the Battle of Bunker Hill in 1775. Soon after the American Revolution, Warren counties began to appear in his memory not only in New York but in Ohio, New Jersey, Virginia, Pennsylvania, North Carolina, and other states. The busy central avenue in Hudson (see Columbia County, above) is named for the general, as are streets in Manhattan and elsewhere.

The Lower Adirondack Regional Arts Council (www.larac.org), located in a renovated carriage house in Glens Falls, is a great source of information on cultural happenings throughout the county and region. The Adirondack Mountain Club (www.adk .org) in Lake George is an essential stop for information on the Adirondack outdoors and has maps, guidebooks, and advice not only on Mount Marcy and Lake Tear of the Clouds but on day and overnight hikes around Lake George and throughout the Adirondacks. Also in Lake George, the Lakes to Locks Passage organization (www.lakestolocks.org) provides information about water routes through the region.


## BOLTON LANDING

For 25 years, the American sculptor David Smith (1906–1965) lived and worked in this peaceful Lake George retreat that is still known more for its peregrine falcons and wild turkey than for the many artists who have made their homes here. Hiking trails reach the highlands of the Tongue Mountain Range and the Cat Thomas Reserve, while canoes provide best access to Northwest Bay Brook and other waterfront locations. Visit the state-sponsored Web site www.adkbirds.com for information on birding opportunities, and the Adirondack Mountain Club (www.adk.org) in Lake George for hikes.

**Marcella Sembrich Opera Museum**. *4800 Lake Shore Drive (Route 9N), Bolton Landing 12814. 518-644-2431 www.operamuseum.org. National Register.* The Polish soprano Marcella Sembrich (1858–1935) sang with the Metropolitan Opera during its first season (1883) and spent her

*Among the artists who have made lives on Lake George was the Polish opera singer Marcella Sembrich (1858–1935), whose waterside retreat in Bolton Landing has been a museum of personal and opera memorabilia since 1937.*

final 12 summers teaching and receiving friends at this pink cottage in Bolton Landing. Open as a museum since 1937 and full of personal and opera memorabilia, this waterside retreat is a memorial to a performing artist and to an earlier time on Lake George. The museum hosts a concert series each July and August. *Open mid-June through mid-September, daily, 10 am until 12:30 pm and 2 pm until 5:30 pm. Fee.*

**Up Yonda Farm Environmental Education Center**. *5239 Lake Shore Drive, Bolton Landing 12814. 518-644-9767. www.upyondafarm.com.* Under the jurisdiction of Warren County Parks and Recreation, this 73-acre onetime farm overlooking Lake George provides guided hikes for bird-watchers, animal tracking classes, nature programs, and trails through fields, woods, and wetlands. The view of Lake George from the summit of the property is one of the best available. The property is named after an expression by an early-20th-century owner, who referred to his farm as his place "up yonda."

## CROWN POINT
**Crown Point State Historic Site**. *739 Bridge Road, Crown Point 12928. 518-597-4666. www.nysparks.com/sites.* The strategic importance of Lake Champlain and the Champlain region during the 1700s becomes abundantly clear during a visit to the ruins of Fort St. Frederic at Crown Point. The 1734 French outpost was taken over by the English on their way to

*Located in the 1868 DeLong family mansion in Glens Falls, the Chapman Historical Museum is known for its period rooms and its substantial collection of the photographs of Seneca Ray Stoddard, the prolific 19th-century Adirondacks photographer.*

the conquest of Canada, and later by the Americans at the start of the American Revolution, and still stands at least ceremonial guard over the romantic, storied body of water that is the sixth-largest freshwater lake in the United States. Historical reenactments take place here regularly. *Open May until October, Wednesday through Monday, 9 am until 5 pm; the grounds are open until dusk through Columbus Day. Fee.*

## GLENS FALLS

The cultural hub of Warren County is home to numerous events throughout the year, including the Adirondack Theater Festival and the summer and fall art festivals of the Lower Adirondack Regional Arts Council (see Festivals, below). Restaurants, shops, and galleries abound on Glen and surrounding streets.

**Chapman Historical Museum**. *348 Glen Street, Glens Falls. 518-793-2826. www.chapmanmuseum.org. National Register.* Housed in a Victorian mansion built in 1868 by the DeLong family of Glens Falls, the museum of the Glens Falls–Queensbury Historical Association is devoted to Warren County and the southern Adirondacks. The museum is known particularly for its collection of the photographs of the prolific 19th-century Adirondacks photographer Seneca Ray Stoddard, which are shown in regularly changing temporary exhibits. The museum also offers a research archive and organizes the Glens Falls Collaborative Community History Project documenting the past of this important 19th-century trading hub. *Open Tuesday through Saturday, 10 am until 4 pm, and Sunday, 12 pm until 4 pm. Free.*

*Plaques at Cooper's Cave, on the Hudson River in Glens Falls, recount the industrial history of the northern stretch of the river and describe James Fenimore Cooper's use of the local landscape in* The Last of the Mohicans.

**Charles R. Wood Theater**. *207 Glen Street, Glens Falls. 12801. 518-798-9663. www.woodtheater.org*. Located in a former Woolworth's, this modern, 300-seat community performance space features dance performances, musicals, films, and live theater throughout the year—including the Adirondack Theatre Festival (see above). *Fee.*

**Crandall Public Library**. *251 Glen Street, Glens Falls 12801. 518-792-6508. www.crandalllibrary.org*. A central reference library that serves the residents of Saratoga, Washington, Warren, and Hamilton Counties, this public library in Glens Falls also houses the Folklife Center, a multi-disciplinary organization that collects and preserves stories, historical documents, and other local materials. The Folklife Center hosts readings, lectures, and other public programs. *Open Monday through Thursday, 9 am until 9 pm; Friday, 9 am until 6 pm; Saturday, 9 am until 5 pm; and Sunday, 1 pm until 5 pm.*

**Coopers' Cave**. *State Route 9, Glens Falls 12801. 518-761-3864. www.cityofglensfalls.com*. A viewing platform under the bridge between Glens Falls (Warren County) and South Glens Falls (Saratoga County) provides a look at a cave that is thought to have inspired James Fenimore Cooper during his visit to the area while preparing to write *The Last of the Mohicans*. Signs clarify and explore connections with the writer and his book, but the most interesting part may be the glimpse into the upper Hudson's industrial past. *Open Memorial Day through Columbus Day. Free.*

**Glens Falls Symphony Orchestra**. *7 Lapham Place, Glens Falls 12801. 518-793-1348. www.gfso.org.* Founded as a community ensemble in 1978, the Glens Falls Symphony Orchestra is now a professional orchestra, performing six concerts a year at the Glens Falls High School Auditorium. *Free.*

**Hyde Collection**. *161 Warren Street, Glens Falls. 518-792-1761. www .hydecollection.org. National Register.* In a Bigelow and Wadsworth–designed house built in the Florentine Renaissance style on a hillside above the Hudson, this serious art museum displays work from the 4th century BC to the 20th century in both permanent exhibits in the historic house and temporary ones in a modern addition, drawing on the museum's collection and works loaned by other institutions. Highlights of the collection include oils by Botticelli, Rubens, Renoir, and Rembrandt, early manuscripts, and French baroque furniture. *Open Tuesday through Saturday, 10 am until 5 pm, and Sunday, 12 pm until 5 pm. Suggested donation.*

**Lapham Gallery**. *7 Lapham Place, Glens Falls 12801. 518-798-1144. www .larac.org.* The public gallery of the Lower Adirondack Regional Arts Council (see Visitor Information, below) mounts four to six exhibits of contemporary art and crafts by Warren County and Hudson Valley artists annually. The gallery shop offers works of art and locally made crafts. *Open Monday through Saturday, 10 am until 3 pm.*

**The Park Theater**. *14 Park Street, Glens Falls. 518-798-1144.* Built in 1911, the former silent movie and vaudeville house reopened in 2005 as a performing arts center. *Fee.*

**World Awareness Children's Museum**. *89 Warren Street, Glens Falls 12801. 518-793-2773. www.worldchildrensmuseum.org.* With the aim of promoting cultural diversity and understanding, the museum exhibits artwork by children from around the world accompanied by folktales from those regions. Children are encouraged to carefully touch the objects on display so as to better understand the lives of their peers in all corners of the globe. *Open in the spring and fall, Tuesday through Friday, 10 am until 4:30 pm, and Saturday, 10 am until 2 pm; during the summer, Monday through Friday, 11 am until 3 pm.*

## LAKE GEORGE

The City of Lake George, which has been the county seat and political center of Warren County for nearly 200 years, is busy year-round with arts activities, outdoor recreation, and amusement parks. Shelving Rock and Prospect Mountain are two hikes that provide good views of the lake, which is famous for the purity of its water, the drama of the hills that surround it, and its many islands (the islands are mostly public and can be reserved for camping and picnicking—visit www.lakegeorge .com for more information). Nesting peregrine falcons are frequently observed on Prospect Mountain, whose summit is reached along the roadbed of an old cable railway. The state Web site www.adkbirds.com provides more complete information on birding in Lake George, and the Adirondack Mountain Club (see below) has maps and trailhead locations.

**Lake George Arts Project Gallery**. *Old County Courthouse, 290 Canada Street (at Route 9), downtown Lake George 12845. 518-668-2616. www .lakegeorgearts.org. National Register.* Formed in 1977, the Lake George Arts Project sponsors a summer concert series at Shepard Park, an annual jazz festival, and changing exhibits in its gallery in the old county courthouse building on Route 9. *The gallery is open Tuesday through Friday, 12 pm until 5 pm, and Saturday, 12 pm until 4 pm.*

**Lake George Battlefield Park**. *Fort George Road, Lake George 12845. 518-668-3352. www.dec.ny.gov/outdoor/9177.html.* Operated by the New York State Department of Environmental Conservation, this picnic area at the southern end of Lake George contains signs that tell about the important events and battles that took place here during the American Revolution and the earlier French and Indian War (1754–63).

**Lake George Historical Association Museum and Bookstore**. *518-668-5044. www.lakegeorgehistorical.org. National Register.* Created in 1969,

*Famous for its mountain shoreline, its history, and its association with artists from James Fenimore Cooper to David Smith, Lake George (seen here from the lookout at the Cat Thomas Preserve) still serves as a kind of doorway to the Adirondacks.*

*The art gallery of the Lake George Arts Project and the museum of the Lake George Historical Association share space in the restored 1845 Warren County Courthouse, a pleasant retreat in downtown Lake George.*

the museum is located in the restored 1845 Warren County Courthouse and features rooms (including an old jail cell) from early courthouse days as well as exhibits on Lake George hotels and mansions of the late 19th and early 20th centuries, the ice industry, and the incline railroad that once helped tourists reach the summit of Prospect Mountain. *Open late spring through early fall; check Web site or call for current hours.*

**Sacred Heart Church**. *50 Mohican Street, Lake George 12845. 518-668-2046. www.sacredheartcatholiccommunity.com.* Stained-glass windows depict the history of Lake George and its environs.

## LAKE LUZERNE

**Kinnear Museum of Local History**. *52 Main Street, Lake Luzerne 12846. 518-696-4520.* Victorian furnishings and Adirondack memorabilia are on display in this small museum in the famed resort community. *Open year-round; call for hours.*

**Luzerne Music Center**. *203 Lake Tour Road, Lake Luzerne. 518-696-2771. www.luzernemusic.org.* Bert Phillips and Toby Blumenthal started the Luzerne Music Center in 1980, and every summer since then this Adirondack music camp has hosted the Luzerne Chamber Music Festival each Monday night in the rustic lodge that is the center of musical activities at the camp. Guest artists of international stature perform works from the traditional to the experimental, from the Renaissance to the modern.

**Pulp Mill Museum**. *Mill Street, Lake Luzerne 12846. 518-696-2711.* Pulp and paper were once the biggest businesses in these parts, and they remain important. Some of the now unusual machines that powered this and other New York State industries in earlier times are displayed

*At the Luzerne Music Center in Lake Luzerne (page 273), chamber and orchestra concerts take place each summer in a rustic lodge.*

at this museum of industrial machinery. Among its features is the first American-made grinding machine, made by Bagley and Sewell of Watertown. *Open July 1 through Labor Day, Saturday and Sunday, 10 am until 2 pm.*

## LAKE PLACID

**Lake Tear of the Clouds/Mt. Marcy**. *Adirondack Loj Road, Lake Placid 12946. 518-523-3441. www.adk.org.* About 65 miles north of Lake George, between the towns of Keene and Lake Placid, is the trailhead for the Van Hoevenberg Trail, the most direct route to the summit of Mount Marcy, the tallest mountain in New York State, and Lake Tear of the Clouds, the source of the Hudson. The rigorous 16-mile round-trip takes a full day and requires proper gear and conditioning, but from the top of Marcy you can see all the way to Montreal, and you can throw a wood chip into Feldspar Brook below Lake Tear of the Clouds and imagine it ending up in New York Harbor. The Adirondack Mountain Club regularly updates its excellent map and guidebook to the High Peaks region.

## NORTH CREEK

**Our Town Theatre Group**. *P.O. Box 586, North Creek, NY 12853. 518-494-5280.* With performances in the Tannery Pond Community Center (see below), this community theater has been mounting plays, a film series, readings, and workshops throughout the year since 1997. *Fee.*

**Tannery Pond Community Center**. *228 Main Street, North Creek 12853. 518-251-2421. www.tpcca.org.* Completed in 2002, this busy arts center

*Lake Tear of the Clouds has excited the imaginations of New Yorkers since Verplanck Colvin discovered and named it in 1872. The rugged 16-mile round-trip hike takes a full day.*

in northern Warren County contains a theater and a gallery that mounts monthly exhibits of contemporary art by artists from Warren County and the Hudson Valley. *Open Monday through Saturday, 9 am until 4 pm, and some Sundays.*

## QUEENSBURY

**Visual Arts Gallery of Adirondack Community College**. *640 Bay Road, Queensbury 12804. 518-743-2328.* Exhibits in the gallery change regularly. *Call for information.*

**Warren County Historical Society**. *195 Sunnyside Road, Queensbury 12804. 518-743-0734. www.warrencountyhistoricalsociety.org.* Chartered in 1997 and located in the old Queensbury Fire Hall, the society has begun a multiyear project to collect and preserve historical artifacts, archival materials, and documents; locate and designate sites of unusual interest or importance; and provide support for researchers and historians. *Open year-round, Tuesday and Thursday, 9 am to 5 pm.*

## TICONDEROGA

**Fort Ticonderoga**. *Route 74 (1 mile east of Route 22), Ticonderoga 12883. 518-585-2821. www.fort-ticonderoga.org.* National Historic Landmark. Built in 1755–57 by the French and fought over for half a century by the armies of five nations, this major historic site rewards the visitor with a better understanding of the strategic importance of the bluff overlooking the connecting route between Lakes George and Champlain. The view of Lake Champlain from the ramparts is breathtaking, the cannon, guns, and other instruments of war arranged around the site are astonishing, and the shop has one of the best selections of books about Native Americans and 18th-century New York to be found anywhere in the state. *Fee.*

## Fairs, Festivals and Celebrations

**Adirondack Theatre Festival**. P.O. Box 3202, Glens Falls 12801. 518-798-7479. www.atfestival.org. Founded in 1995, the monthlong summer series presents new work by American playwrights at the Charles R. Wood Theater (see Glens Falls, above).

**Fall and Spring Art Festivals**. Lower Adirondack Regional Arts Council. 7 Lapham Place, Glens Falls 12801. 518-798-1144. www.larac.org. Each year for many years, the arts council has organized regional art festivals in the spring and fall featuring music, food, and crafts and centered around juried art shows. The two-day spring festival takes place in early June in City Park in downtown Glens Falls, while the Fall Festival, also two days, takes place in early November at Adirondack Community College in Queensbury.

**Luzerne Music Festival**. 203 Lake Tour Road, Lake Luzerne. 518-696-2771. www.luzernemusic.org. During July and August each year great performers join faculty at the Luzerne Music Center for concerts in a rustic lodge (see Lake Luzerne, above).

**Siege of Fort Henry Reenactment**. 518-668-5722. Each September in Lake George, dedicated history buffs reenact the siege of Fort William Henry (1757), a battle at the foot of Lake George during the French and Indian War in which the French general the Marquis de Montcalm defeated the English lieutenant colonel George Monro in a siege described by James Fenimore Cooper in *The Last of the Mohicans*.

*At 5,344 feet, Mount Marcy is the tallest mountain in New York State, and on a clear day the view from the top extends far south into the Hudson Valley and north to Montreal.*

**Washington County Fair**. Route 29, Greenwich, New York 12834. One of the great annual events of the North Country, this annual agricultural fair in late August in Greenwich (23 miles southeast of Glens Falls) features, aside from the traditional farm animals, food, rides, arts and crafts, and music, a farm museum displaying artifacts of rural life in Washington County from the 1800s to the 1940s.

## Also Nearby

Twenty-five miles east of Glens Falls, at Granville in Washington County, exhibits at the modern and fascinating Slate Valley Museum (www .slatevalleymuseum.org) tell the story of slate production in the region, while the Pember Museum of Natural History (www.pembermuseum .com) contains, in antique glass cases, a collection of what surely must be some of the most exotic animals ever to be shot and stuffed. Thirty miles northeast of Glens Falls, along the Champlain Canal at the headwaters of Lake Champlain, the former railroad hub and mill town of Whitehall earned a place in history as the "Birthplace of the American Navy" after Benedict Arnold launched his fleet there before the Battle of Valcour Island on October 11, 1776. A bridge over the canal has been turned into a popular local theater (http://bridgetheater-whitehall.com), and the Skenesborough Museum (518-499-1155) provides a rewarding overview of canal and railroad life and the early days of steamboats and sailing ships on Lake Champlain.

Fifty-four miles northwest of Lake George, at Blue Mountain Lake in Hamilton County, is the Adirondack Museum (518-352-7311; www .adkmuseum.org). Opened in 1957 in an 1876 Adirondack log hotel, this important museum of the North Country exhibits historic artifacts, photographs, archival material, and fine art documenting the storied and colorful past of the Adirondacks. Its historic photographs alone number more than 70,000 and include prints by Seneca Ray Stoddard, Alfred Stieglitz, and Eliot Porter. The museum has more than 2,500 oil and watercolor paintings, prints and artists' sketchbooks, and the largest collection of rustic furniture in the United States. The grounds feature not only a Pullman railroad car, a locomotive, carriages, and a complete blacksmith's shop, but one of the best collections of boats in New York State and maybe even the entire United States. Open mid-May through mid-October, daily, 10 am until 5 pm.

## Visitor Information

**Adirondack Mountain Club**. *814 Goggins Road (Route 9N South, just off I-87 at exit 21), Lake George 12845. 518-668-4447. www.adk.org*. This walk-in information center at the Lake George exit from the Northway is useful for anyone interested in gaining a direct experience of the Adirondacks. The center provides books, maps, and other information on trails and canoe and snowshoe routes in the Adirondack Forest Preserve and nearby parks and waterways. *Open year-round, Monday through Saturday, 8 am to 5 pm.*

**Arts Council for the Northern Adirondacks**. *645 Main Street, Westport 12993. 518-962-8778. www.artsnorth.org.* Located in the historic Westport Heritage House in the Lake Champlain community of Westport this art and community center is an excellent source of information on cultural organizations and events throughout the Adirondacks, and provides a performance space, a walk-in information center, grants for artists, and an arts directory with the latest openings and performances.

**Lake Placid/Essex County Convention and Visitors Bureau**. *49 Parkside Drive—Suite 2, Lake Placid 12946. 518-523-2445. www.lakeplacid.com.* The official Essex County tourist site provides extensive information on restaurants, hotels, and places to go and things to do in the county in all four seasons.

**Lakes to Locks Passage**. *1340 State Route 9, Lake George 12845. 518-597-9660. www.lakestolocks.com.* Located in the Lake George Municipal Center, the local office of this state service organization provides information on tourist routes connecting Lake George, the Champlain Canal, the Hudson River, and the Chambly Canal to the Richelieu and St. Lawrence Rivers in Canada.

**Lower Adirondack Regional Arts Council**. *7 Lapham Place, Glens Falls 12801. 518-798-1144. www.larac.org.* The arts service organization for the lower Adirondacks is a great source of information on cultural events and places of interest throughout Warren County and surrounding areas. The council exhibits regional art in its Lapham Gallery, organizes classes and workshops, presents theatrical performances, gives grants to artists, and offers works of art and locally made crafts at its shop. *Open Monday through Saturday, 10 am until 3 pm.*

**Warren County Tourism**. *1340 State Route 9, Municipal Center, Lake George 12845. 800-958-4748. www.visitlakegeorge.com.* This Lake George office provides travel itineraries; guides to fishing, museums, whitewater rafting, and canoeing; a calendar of events; and listings of restaurants and hotels.

# RESOURCE DIRECTORY

**Adirondack Mountain Club.** 518-668-4447. www.adk.org. Operating a Web site and several local information centers, this useful organization provides books, maps, and other practical information on trails and canoe and snowshoe routes in the Adirondack Forest Preserve, runs a popular lodge for hikers at the base of Mt. Marcy, and helps conserve the Adirondack wilderness.

**Art Along the Hudson.** www.artalongthehudson.com. Begun in 2004, this coordinated series of monthly arts festivals in cities along the Hudson River brings art and sculpture exhibits and free concerts and performances to the streets of Kingston, Hudson, Beacon, Catskill, Poughkeepsie, Rhinebeck and Newburgh. See listings under each city for local information.

**Half Moon/New Netherland Museum.** 518-443-1609. www.newnether land.org. A reproduction, built in 1989, of the 85-foot square-rigged yacht that Henry Hudson sailed into New York Harbor and up the Hudson River in 1609, the *Half Moon* serves as a traveling museum, docking at cities up and down the Hudson and providing tours below and above deck and classes on the history of New Netherlands.

**Historic Hudson Valley.** 914-631-8200. www.hudsonvalley.org. Founded by John D. Rockefeller Jr. in 1951, this preservation and education organization maintains and operates six significant historic sites along the river of which five are in Westchester County: Washington Irving's Sunnyside; Kykuit, the Rockefeller house in Tarrytown; Philipsburg Manor in Sleepy Hollow; the Union Church of Pocantico Hills; and Van Cortlandt Manor in Croton-on-Hudson. Historic Hudson Valley also operates Montgomery Place in Annandale near Bard College. Originally called Sleepy Hollow Restoration, the organization adopted its present name in 1987 as part of an expansion beyond the Tarrytown-Croton area.

**Hudson River Heritage.** 845-876-2474. http://hudsonriverheritage.org. This regional nonprofit organization acts as steward for the Hudson River National Historic Landmark District, a 32-square-mile area stretching from Staatsburg, in Dutchess County, to Clermont, in Columbia County. In addition to operating a useful Web site, the organization hosts tours of houses and landscapes in the district including a popular annual Country Seats Tour. Its symposia and lectures on such subjects as romantic-era landscapes and ice-boating on the Hudson are always well attended.

**Hudson River Lighthouse Coalition.** 518-828-4385 x105. www.hudson lights.com. This organization operates a useful Web site with practical and historical information on the seven remaining lighthouses on the river, the Little Red Lighthouse, the Sleepy Hollow Lighthouse, the Stony Point Lighthouse, the Esopus Lighthouse, the Rondout Lighthouse, the Saugerties Lighthouse, and the Hudson-Athens Lighthouse.

**Hudson River School Art Trail.** 518-943-7465. www.thomascole.org/trail. This multicounty project undertaken by Cedar Grove, the Thomas Cole National Historic Site, in partnership with Olana, the National Park Service, and Greene County Tourism, operates a Web site and publishes a brochure guiding visitors to the sites where many of the famous paintings of the Hudson River School were made, including Kaaterskill Falls, Sunset Rock, and the site of the Catskill Mountain House. The Web site and brochure contain maps, directions, and reproductions of images created at the different locations. Brochures are available at Cedar Grove, Olana, and by mail.

**Hudson River Valley Greenway.** 518-473-3835. www.hudsongreenway.state.ny.us. This state-sponsored planning group works with communities along the Hudson River to preserve scenic, natural, historic, cultural, and recreational resources while encouraging compatible economic development.

**Hudson River Valley Institute/Marist College.** 845-575-3052. www.hudsonrivervalley.org. Located at the Marist College in Poughkeepsie, the academic arm of the Hudson River Valley National Heritage Area (see Resource Directory) maintains a digital library and a useful and comprehensive Web site with detailed information on the valley.

**Hudson River Valley National Heritage Area.** 518-473-3835. www.hudsonrivervalley.com. Established by Congress in 1996, this federally sponsored program is one of 40 similar programs set up by the National Park Service and the Department of the Interior at historically important sites throughout the country. Its mission is "to recognize, preserve, protect and interpret the nationally significant cultural and natural resources of the Hudson River Valley for the benefit of the Nation." The Heritage Area operates a useful Web site that ranks and organizes listings of cultural organizations, publishes informative brochures on different themes, and organizes events.

**I Love New York.** 1-800-CALL-NYS. www.iloveny.com. The official New York State tourism office and Web site provide clear information on cultural events, interesting places to visit at different times of the year, and places to eat and stay in New York City, Albany, and up and down the Hudson Valley. Also visit the affiliated Web site, www.travelhudsonvalley.org, for hotels, restaurants, places to shop, and cultural events in the valley.

**Metropolitan Waterfront Alliance.** www.waterwire.net. This advocacy organization works to improve water quality, transportation, recreation, and waterfront accessibility in the harbor and waterways of New York City and New Jersey. The Web site provides information on waterfront events and symposia.

**New Jersey Department of Environmental Protection, Division of Parks and Forests.** www.state.nj.us/dep/parksandforests. The Web site provides useful information on historic sites and parks in the Hudson Valley and elsewhere in New Jersey.

**New York City Department of Cultural Affairs.** Dial 311, outside of NYC, call 212-NEW-YORK, www.nyc.gov/html.dcla. The agency provides financial support for cultural organizations throughout the city. Cultural programs and activities are listed on the agency's Web site. See also the Web site of NYC & Company, www.nycgo.com.

**New York City Department of Parks & Recreation.** Dial 311 for all Parks & Recreation information; outside of NYC, call 212-NEW-YORK. www .nycgovparks.org. The agency maintains New York City's 27,000 acres of parks. Numerous community and cultural events take place in these parks and are listed on the agency's Web site.

**New York–New Jersey Trail Conference.** 201-512-9348. www.nynjtc. org. An excellent source of hiking maps, this federation of hiking clubs, environmental organizations and individuals, with a membership of more than 100,000, is dedicated to building and maintaining marked hiking trails and protecting related open spaces in the two states.

**NY State Arts/NYC-arts.** www.nystatearts.org and www.nyc-arts.org. Designed to provide complete information on the arts in New York City and State, these Web sites offer in-depth profiles of every cultural organization and long-term information about programs. These and a companion site—www.nyckidsarts.org—are run by the Alliance for the Arts (www.allianceforarts.org).

**New York State Bridge Authority.** 845-691-7245. www.nysba.net. Created in 1933, this state agency maintains and operates the Rip Van Winkle Bridge, the Kingston-Rhinecliff Bridge, the Mid-Hudson Bridge, the Newburgh-Beacon Bridge and the Bear Mountain Bridge.

**New York State Canal Corporation.** 1-800-4CANAL4. www.nyscanals.gov. A subsidiary of the New York State Thruway Authority, this state agency is responsible for preserving and promoting New York's inland waterway, 524 miles of navigable canals and towpaths including the Erie, Oswego, Champlain and Cayuga-Seneca Canals.

**New York State Council on the Arts.** 212-627-4455. www.nysca.org. The principal organization supporting arts and culture in New York State makes more than 2,500 grants each year for artistic programs in every arts discipline throughout the state.

**New York State Department of Environmental Conservation.** www.dec.ny.gov. This state agency is charged with conserving, improving, and protecting New York's natural resources and environment.

**New York State Office of Parks, Recreation and Historic Preservation.** 518-474-0456. www.nysparks.state.ny.us. The state agency is responsible for parks and historic houses throughout the Hudson Valley, and its Web site is an excellent source of information.

**Palisades Interstate Park Commission.** 845-786-2701. www.palisades parksconservancy.org. Formed in 1900, the federally chartered bistate commission oversees 21 state parks and eight historic sites comprising 110,000 acres in New York and New Jersey. Contact the commission, online or at its headquarters in Bear Mountain State Park, for trail maps and guides.

**Parks & Trails New York.** 518-434-1583. www.ptny.org. An advocacy and promotion organization based in Albany, Parks & Trails New York provides information on over 90 multiuse trails across the state. The group organizes bike tours of the Erie Canalway and Hudson River Valley and provides detailed maps of the state's abundant greenway and park system.

**Port Authority of New York and New Jersey.** 212-435-7000. www.panynj.gov. Established in 1921, this bi-state agency oversees the Port of New York and the interstate bridges and tunnels including the George Washington Bridge, Outerbridge Crossing, the Goethals and Bayonne Bridges; the Holland and Lincoln Tunnels; Newark, LaGuardia, and Kennedy Airports; and the Port Authority Bus Terminal.

**Riverkeeper.** 800-21-RIVER. www.riverkeeper.org. Since its creation in 1966 as the Hudson River Fishermen's Association, this environmental watchdog group has monitored the ecology of the river and brought hundreds of successful court cases against polluters.

**Scenic Hudson.** 845-473-4440. www.scenichudson.org. The largest environmental group focused on the entire Hudson Valley, this advocacy and preservation organization was founded in 1963 to protect and restore the valley and its landscape. Among its many accomplishments have been the creation, improvement, and operation of 40 parks and preserves along the river, including Poets' Walk in Red Hook, Madam Brett Park and Long Dock Beacon Park in Beacon, and Stockport Flats in Greenport just north of Hudson.

# INDEX